THE AIMS OF EDUCATION

For many years, the aims of education have been informed by liberalism, with an emphasis on autonomy. The aim has been to equip students mentally to be autonomous individuals, able to live self-directed lives. In this volume, international philosophers of education explore and question diverse strains of the liberal tradition, discussing not only autonomy but also other key issues, such as:

- social justice
- national identity
- curriculum
- critical thinking
- social practices

The contributors write from a variety of standpoint, offering many interpretations of what liberalism might mean in educational terms. The result is a challenging collection of new research, which is sure to stimulate debate.

The Aims of Education will have wide appeal among philosophers, educationists, teachers, policy makers and those interested in the future of education.

Roger Marples is a Senior Lecturer in Education at the Roehampton Institute, London, where he has overall responsibility for the degree in Education. He has extensive teaching experience and served on the Associated Examining Board's Working Party on Philosophy, which successfully pioneered A Level Philosophy.

ROUTLEDGE INTERNATIONAL STUDIES
IN THE PHILOSOPHY OF EDUCATION

THE AIMS
OF EDUCATION

Edited by Roger Marples

London and New York

First published 1999
by Routledge
11 New Fetter Lane, London EC4P 4EE

Simultaneously published in the USA and Canada
by Routledge
29 West 35th Street, New York, NY 10001

Editorial material and selection © 1999 Roger Marples

Individual chapters © 1999 the individual contributors

Typeset in Garamond 3 by Stephen Wright-Bouvier of
The Rainwater Consultancy, Faringdon, Oxfordshire.
Printed and bound in Great Britain by
Biddles Ltd, Guildford and King's Lynn.

British Library Cataloguing in Publication Data
A catalogue record for this book is available
from the British Library

Library of Congress Cataloging in Publication Data
The aims of education / edited by Roger Marples.
p. cm.
Includes bibliographical references and index.
1. Education—Aims and objectives. 2. Education—Philosophy.
3. Autonomy (Psychology) 4. Educational change. I. Marples, Roger.
LB41.A36353 1999
370' . 1—dc21 98–42157
CIP

ISBN 0–415–15739–0

CONTENTS

CONTENTS

CONTRIBUTORS

Robin Barrow is Dean and Professor of Education at Simon Fraser University, Vancouver. A Fellow of the Royal Society of Canada, Professor Barrow is the author of numerous books and articles in the fields of classics, philosophy and education, including *The Philosophy of Schooling*, *Understanding Skills* and (with Geoffrey Milburn) *A Critical Dictionary of Educational Concepts*.

David Carr is reader at the Moray House Institute of Education, Edinburgh. He has published widely in philosophical and educational journals and is the author of *Educating the Virtues*. He is currently engaged in editing two educational philosophical collections of essays for Routledge, one in knowledge, truth and education, the other (with Jan Stewart) on virtue ethics and moral education.

Penny Enslin is Professor of Education at the University of Witwaterstrand, Johannesburg. Her research interests are in the areas of practical philosophy, feminist theory and education. Recent publications include: 'The family and the private in education for democratic citizenship', which is in David Bridges (ed.) *Education, Autonomy and Democratic Citizenship in a Changing World*, and 'Contemporary liberalism and civic education in South Africa'.

Peter Gilroy is Senior Lecturer in Education at the University of Sheffield, Director, CPD and deputy editor of the international *Journal of Education for Teaching*. His publications include *Meaning within Words* and *Philosophy, First Language Acquisition and International Analyses of Teacher Education*.

Morwenna Griffiths is Professor of Educational Research at Nottingham Trent University. Her current research interests focus on social justice, gender and educational research. She is the author of *Educational Research for Social Justice: Getting off the Fence*; *Feminisms and the Self: The Web of Identity*; *Self-identity, Self-esteem and Social Justice*; (with Carol Davies) *In Fairness to Children*; and *Working for Social Justice in the Primary School*, and she has edited (with Barry Troyna), *Anti-racism, Culture and Social Justice in Education*, and (with Margaret Whitford) *Women Review Philosophy: New*

Writing by Women in Philosophy, and (with Margaret Whitford) *Feminist Perspectives in Philosophy*.

William Hare is Professor at Mount St Vincent University, Halifax, Nova Scotia. He is the author of *Open-mindedness and Education*, *In Defence of Open-mindedness* and *What Makes a Good Teacher*. Professor Hare has published numerous articles in philosophy of education.

Kevin Harris is Professor of Education at Macquarie University, Australia. He has written many books on the politics and philosophy of education, including *Education and Knowledge* (Routledge) *Teachers and Classes* (Routledge), and *Teachers: Constructing the Future* (Falmer Press). He has contributed numerous chapters to edited books, and has consistently published articles in journals such as *The Journal of Philosophy of Education*, *Educational Philosophy and Theory* and *The Australian Journal of Education* over the past twenty years. Professor Harris is a Fellow of the Philosophy of Education Society of Australasia.

Paul H. Hirst is Emeritus Professor of Education at the University of Cambridge and Visiting Professorial Fellow at the University of London, Institute of Education. He has written extensively in philosophy of education, particularly in the area of curriculum theory, educational theory and practice, and moral, religious and aesthetic education. His major publications include *Knowledge and the Curriculum* (with R. S. Peters), and *The Logic of Education*. He has recently edited (with Patricia White) a four-volume international collection, *Philosophy of Education: Major Themes in the Analytic Tradition*.

Roger Marples is Senior Lecturer in Education and responsible for the Educational Studies Programme at the Roehampton Institute, London. He has contributed to philosophy of education journals in Britain and the USA and has written on cross-curriculum themes, and the curriculum and qualifications for post-16 students.

Richard Pring is Professor of Educational Studies and Director of the Department of Educational Studies at the University of Oxford. He is joint editor of the *British Journal of Educational Studies*. Recent books include *Closing the Gap: Liberal Education and Vocational Preparation* and (with G. Walford) *Affirming the Comprehensive Ideal*.

Ben Spiecker is Professor of Philosophy and History of Education at the Vrije Universiteit, Amsterdam. His publications and current interests lie in the areas of moral, civic and sexual education.

Paul Standish teaches philosophy of education at the University of Dundee. He is the author of *Beyond the Self: Wittgenstein, Heidegger and the Limits of Language* (1992). His recent publications include *Teaching Right and Wrong: Moral Education in the Balance*, edited with Richard Smith (1997) and with Nigel Blake, Paul Smeyers (and Richard Smith), *Thinking Again: Education after Post-modernism* (1998).

Jan Steutel is Reader in Philosophy of Education at the Vrije Universiteit, Amsterdam. His publications and work in progress focus on moral education with special reference to virtue theory.

Kenneth A. Strike is Professor of Education at Cornell University. He has been a Distinguished Visiting Professor at the University of Alberta, is a Past President of the US Philosophy of Education Society and is a member of the National Academy of Education. He is the author of several books and over 100 articles. Recent publications include *The Ethics of Teaching* (with Jonas Soltis), *The Ethics of Schools Administration* (with Jonas Soltis and Emil Haller), *Liberal Justice and the Marxist Critique of Schooling*. His current work is concerned with exploring the normative aspects of school restructuring.

James C. Walker is Professor of Education at the University of Western Sydney, Nepean. His publications are wide ranging, in philosophy, educational policy, curriculum and youth studies. In recent years he has been especially interested in professional organisational learning, particularly in relation to teacher education. He was leader of the research team which undertook the first comprehensive analysis of philosophy, content and change in Australian teacher education programmes.

John White is Professor of Philosophy of Education at the Institute of Education, University of London. His interests are in interrelationships among educational aims and applications to school curricula, especially in the arts and personal and social education. His books include *Towards a Compulsory Curriculum* (1973), *Philosophers as Educational Reformers* (1979) (with Peter Gordon), *The Aims of Education Restated* (1982), *Education and the Good Life: Beyond the National Curriculum* (1990), *The Arts 5–16: Changing the Agenda* (1992) and *Education and the End of Work: Philosophical Perspectives on Work and Learning* (1997). In addition he has written over 100 articles and chapters. He is Honorary Vice-President of the Philosophy of Education Society of Great Britain, a Fellow of the US Philosophy of Education Society, and an overseas member of the Russian Academy of Education.

Christopher Winch is Professor of Philosophy of Education at University College, Northampton. He is the Author of *Language, Ability and Educational Achievement* (1990), *Quality and Education* (1996) and *The Philosophy of Human Learning* (1998).

PREFACE

The Aims of Education is a new collection of essays written by some of the most distinguished philosophers of education in Britain, North America, Europe, Australia and South Africa. There is surprisingly little in book form specifically concerned with the aims of education and it is with the intention of filling this gap that the present collection has been produced. All of the essays are designed to promote wide-ranging discussion of what education should be concerned with as we enter the new millennium.

Only two contributors to this volume were privileged to read essays other than their own. Apart from the editor, John White had the brief of commenting freely on others' work. He is critical of most, before going on to develop what he considers to be a defensible version of liberalism with its associated value of personal autonomy. Many of the essays in this collection are within the so-called liberal tradition and are concerned with the promotion of autonomy as an educational aim. Sympathetic as White is with such a laudable goal, he remains dissatisfied with the ways in which it is cashed out in this volume.

If autonomy, in its different forms, is the central concern of several essays within this volume, it is not the exclusive preoccupation of all the contributors. Morwenna Griffiths is concerned with, among other things, social justice; Penny Enslin with national identity; David Carr with curriculum; William Hare with critical thinking; Paul Hirst is at pains to explicate what he refers to as social practices, which in many ways represents a repudiation of his earlier attachment to the centrality of forms of knowledge to discussions of educational aims. Kevin Harris asks questions about whose aims should be realised, while Paul Standish considers the possibility of education without aims. My own contribution is critical of White's earlier work on the aims of education.

The essays in this volume are lively, challenging and varied. It is hoped that they will stimulate debate among all those who, since Plato, have recognised the importance of the relationship between education and the kind of life worth living.

Roger Marples
24 July 1998

1

AIMS!

Whose aims?

Kevin Harris

There is a common belief, significantly shared by many beginning formal
tertiary studies in education, that 'education' has a fixed meaning, and distinct
aims, which can be unveiled either by turning up a dictionary or by consulting
a favoured authority. So, in the very first lecture of every course I give, I stress
that 'education' is a changing, contested and often highly personalised, historically and politically constructed concept. To illustrate this I read a few dictionary definitions of 'education', as well as a selected set of stated 'aims of education'. When students hear that D. H. Lawrence claimed education should aim
to 'lead out the individual nature in each man and woman to its true fullness',
that for Rousseau the aim of education was 'to come into accord with the
teaching of nature', that R. M. Hutchins saw the aim of education as 'cultiva-
tion of the intellect', that A. S. Neill believed the aim of education should be to
'make people happier, more secure, less neurotic, less prejudiced', and that
John Locke claimed 'education must aim at virtue and teach man to deny his
desires, inclinations and appetite, and follow as reason directs'; hopefully the
penny has dropped. Just in case it hasn't I add in that while Pope Pius XI was
declaring that the aim of education was to 'cooperate with divine grace in
forming the true and perfect Christian', Sergei Shapovalenko insisted that
education should aim 'to inculcate the materialist outlook and communist
mentality'. That usually does the trick.

What I have done in this exercise is to display a small selection of what
R. S. Peters called 'high level directives for education'. Providing such
directives, and arguing over their substance, was once a staple activity of
philosophers and philosophers of education; but much of that changed when
philosophy of education entered its analytic phase in the 1960s. At that

1

time Peters wrote (1966: 15) that 'Few professional philosophers would now think that it is their function to provide . . . high-level directives for education or for life; indeed one of their main preoccupations has been to lay bare such aristocratic pronouncements under the analytic guillotine'.

The preoccupation Peters spoke of is clearly evident in L. M. Brown's 1970 volume, *Aims of Education*, which Jonas Soltis prefaced and praised thus:

> it provides an organised way to intelligently examine the many types of aims which have been or yet may be advanced seriously as the proper ends for education. . . . No single answer to what we should aim at is advocated, but the basis for thinking intelligently about this central educational issue in today's complex world is put within the reach of the thoughtful reader.

Brown, in a manner largely characteristic of the philosophy of education dominant at the time, argues a Wittgensteinian preference for considering not 'aims' *per se* but rather 'members of the aim-family', and he devises the term 'ends-in-view' to include three members of the 'aim family' – namely, 'ideals', 'objectives' and 'goals', which are themselves subjected to further analysis and distinction.

Peters too had followed this analytic approach – both more often and more stringently. In the overall process substantive pronouncements and judgements tended to disappear from the scene as the meta-language was increasingly subjected to analysis. 'Aims' were differentiated from 'goals' and 'objectives', and even whether educators should have aims was debated long and seriously. Peters (1973: 11–28) fuelled this particular debate by raising the question as to whether education had, or could possibly have, aims extrinsic to itself.

Interestingly, this approach was also underpinned, originally, by the notion that 'education' had a fixed, or central meaning – which could be revealed by conceptual analysis. So, while 'aims' were differentiated from 'goals' and so on, many philosophers simultaneously also sought to reveal *the* necessary and sufficient conditions for *the* concept of 'education', and thus ostensibly display more clearly *the* aims of education. Thankfully, this practice itself was guillotined, and by 1970 even Hirst and Peters, who had been so instrumental in attempting to fix a concept of 'education', had come to recognise the 'fluid' and historical nature of their object of analysis (Hirst and Peters 1970: 25). Hirst and Peters insisted, however, that 'education' was always a normative concept, from which they concluded: 'That is why there is a lot of talk about the aims of education: for in formulating aims of education we are attempting to specify more precisely what qualities . . . we think it most desirable to develop' (1970: 16).

I suspect they might be right. But what they did not address is who was being referred to by the twice-used, encompassing 'we'. I shall argue in this chapter that concentrating on that question can provide philosophers of education with an alternative, and more profitable, approach to consideration of the aims of education.

Locating the aims of education

When analytic philosophers claimed that 'in formulating aims of education we are attempting to specify more precisely what qualities we think it most desirable to develop', 'we' tended to be either self-referential, possibly to include other acceptable wise, rational and disinterested people, or to suggest a public consensual mode. As was so often the case, reality went missing.

Just as 'education' is a changing and often personalised, historically and politically constructed concept (with no absolute correct meaning to retreat to), so too is it a historically and politically constructed changing social practice. This elementary recognition has far-reaching implications for considering the aims of education. It indicates, to begin with, that the aims of education, like both the concept and the process of education, are social, historical, ephemeral and changing. But such simplicity conceals an inner complexity.

At any time and place many people and many institutions proclaim different, often competing aims for education. Aims, like all matters of policy, are contextual, political, normative, dynamic and *contested*. But the dynamic contest is also continually resolved, or momentarily settled, in that policy does become manifested in distinct and definite practices. The trick is to recognise how such settlements come about. Thus there is point in investigating who has a voice in formulating aims of education, whose aims are legitimated, whose destination and ends are taken as desirable, and whose aims are pursued in the formulation of educational policy and practice – and why.

To begin to illustrate this I shall now recount an instance in which holders of conflicting aims of education engaged in a bitter ideological and political struggle for control of educational policy and practice – namely, the infamous case regarding two social science courses – Man: A Course of Study (MACOS) and Social Education Materials Project (SEMP) – in Queensland, Australia. I do not claim my account (which is necessarily selective) to be neutral, let alone theory-free. I also acknowledge that in telling the story I am drawing largely from primary data collected by John Freeland (1979a, 1979b), and Richard Smith and John Knight (1978).[1]

3

A case study: MACOS and SEMP in Queensland

In the late 1970s the Queensland government engaged in a number of significant interventions in education. In 1976 secondary punitive procedures were invoked when four teachers were sacked following convictions on minor drug offences. In 1977 a homosexual teacher was dismissed. In the same year an English resource book by the somewhat unconventional but generally well-respected educator, Henry Schoenheimer, was banned. And then, on 17 January 1978, the Queensland Cabinet banned the use of MACOS in schools, and followed this up by banning SEMP on 22 February.

MACOS is a social studies course for 11-year-old primary school pupils. It was conceived largely by Jerome Bruner, and first appeared in American schools in the early 1960s. Bruner was honoured by the American Education Research Association and the American Educational Publishers' Institute for his role in the MACOS project, which was referred to as '". . . one of the most important efforts of our time" to relate research and theory in educational psychology to instructional materials' (Smith and Knight 1978: 227). It was brought to Australia in 1973 for trialling in all six state education systems, with its trial in fifteen Queensland schools having the full support of the Queensland Department of Education.

The Queensland trial, however, was met by a small but well-organised network of Christian fundamentalist moral crusaders, who engaged in a concerted campaign of ideological challenge and political lobbying.

MACOS had faced a similar campaign a decade earlier in the USA, falling foul of the Moral Majority and other conservative and fundamentalist organisations. Much of the material used to attack MACOS in Australia came from the USA, having found its way into the hands of a momentarily influential Christian fundamentalist, Rona Joyner.

After a long period in the political wilderness, Joyner, known as a distributor of John Birch Society publications, had gradually built up credence in right-wing provincial organisations, and eventually she developed national and international connections. By 1977 she headed two organisations: the Society to Outlaw Pornography (STOP) and the Committee against Regressive Education (CARE). Joyner regarded the Bible as the single repository of truth and law. She thus held to the Biblical view of creation and to the notion of original sin, she stood as a champion for traditional Christian 'family values', and consequently she opposed the teaching of evolution and anything that bore a humanist trait. She did not regard herself and her followers as a minority, but rather proclaimed that she was 'one with God' and that 'one with God is a majority'.

Joyner opposed MACOS because it displayed alternatives to nuclear family life,[2] and to fundamental textual Christian knowledge. Labelling it as a threat to 'the light of Christianity', she organised mass STOP and CARE letter-writing campaigns to metropolitan and regional newspapers. In the course of these campaigns Queensland parliamentarians received carefully orchestrated propaganda about MACOS, as well as significant mail, particularly from country areas, opposing MACOS.

CARE and STOP, along with the larger and longer-established Festival of Light,[3] also invited Norma Gabler, a Texan who listed her occupation as 'text book watcher', and who had campaigned against MACOS in America, to visit Queensland in July 1977. She met Department of Education executives, professional educators and publishers, where she spoke out against MACOS. When criticised she walked out of one meeting and fell silent in the other (Smith and Knight 1978: 228). More significantly, however, she was guest speaker at a morning tea hosted by Flo Bjelke-Petersen, the Premier's wife.

Attacks on MACOS were also made by other conservative, religious and fundamentalist groups, such as the Queensland Conservative Club, the Festival of Light, the Community Standards Organisation, Parents of Tertiary Students, the Christian Mission to the Communist World, the Catholic Women's League, the League of Nations, the National Civic Council, the Committee on Morals and Education, Parents Campaigning for Responsible Education, and one organisation with a delicately contrived acronym – Ladies in Line against Communism. Queensland's ruling National Party took serious heed of the attacks, and on 17 January 1978 Cabinet banned the use of MACOS in Queensland schools.

Not surprisingly, many teachers, parents and academics protested; the Executive of the Queensland Teachers Union expressed concern at 'Government intervention based on vocal minority pressure'; and the media became heavily involved. The Premier, Joh Bjelke-Petersen, responded with public assurances that his 'Ministers are in 100 per cent agreement that MACOS goes', adding that 'Teachers will comply' (*Courier-Mail* 1–2–78); while Rona Joyner welcomed the ban with the hope that the decision would become a yardstick for the removal of other unsuitable material from school courses. STOP and CARE sent letters of congratulation to Cabinet ministers.

The banning was not, however, universally welcomed by the Christian church. Many church leaders, like the Anglican Church of Queensland's Director of Christian Education, the Reverend Father Riordan, castigated the government for giving in to a small minority despite what he termed the 'good advice' it had received from educators. The Uniting Church publicly rejected the inference that MACOS was 'anti-Christian'. And across the border in New South Wales, Catholic schools continued to teach MACOS with barely a hiccup.

Meanwhile, buoyed with success, Joyner turned her attack to the SEMP programme being developed for secondary school use by the Canberra-based Curriculum Development Centre with the full cooperation and participation of all six state education departments and the Church-dominated private schools' Head Masters' Conference of New South Wales. Although the programme was by no means complete, Joyner saw it as 'worse than MACOS because SEMP is dealing with things right here in our own society . . . we will try to have something done about this, but I hope it doesn't take as long as it did with MACOS' (*Courier-Mail* 2–2–78).

She put together small, decontextualised extracts from the SEMP Teachers Handbook. She then wrote a STOP and CARE newsletter linking SEMP with MACOS, which she distributed widely, encouraging recipients to write letters of outrage to newspapers, their local members, Cabinet ministers, the Minister for Education and the Premier. She sent her extracts from SEMP, along with copies of her propaganda material, to all Cabinet ministers.

In response, Cabinet, as it had done with MACOS, convened during the parliamentary recess. It then overruled the advice of national and state educational bodies and authorities, and banned the use of any part of SEMP products in Queensland state high schools. The Premier, unfazed by the bypassing of normal parliamentary procedures, or by the fact that the only SEMP material actually seen by Cabinet ministers was the selection of out-of-context samples forwarded to them by Rona Joyner, declared: 'If you could see some of the stuff in SEMP, I bet you would not want your kids to wade through it . . . it is the moral aspect of the course that we object to' (*Courier-Mail* 23–2–78).

At this point the tide turned swiftly. Even the *Courier-Mail*, Queensland's only state-wide daily paper, and at the time strongly supportive of the government, reported (on 24 February 1978) that pressure groups had won out over reputable educators regarding SEMP, and for the first time it questioned Rona Joyner's influence on Cabinet. It also published a reader's letter which played with the acronyms by urging Queenslanders to STOP CARE.

The story need be taken no further. Instead, we might backtrack through the drama and look more specifically at the diverse aims of education that were explicitly and implicitly propounded by the central players.

STOP and CARE insisted unequivocally that 'Government schools should uphold the laws of God'. Rona Joyner declared that 'Children don't go to school to learn to think. They go to learn to read and write and spell correctly' (*Gold Coast Bulletin* 9–3–78). And in an earlier tirade against 'communism, socialism and humanism' she added: 'Schools are there to teach the Christian ethic' (*The Australian* 24–2–78).

The Premier called on education to reinforce traditional values and serve the common good, managing simultaneously to invoke the threat of communism and Nazism:

> The philosophy of education in Queensland must be geared to the service of our society and people, and it must never become the plaything of educators who seek to overturn or pervert education for

their own narrow social objectives. . . . Both SEMP and MACOS presented a philosophy which was questionable in the light of our traditional values. . . . MACOS and SEMP contain much of the same underlying philosophy which sustains the secular humanism of both the socialist and national socialist ideologies.

(*Goondawindi Argus* 5–3–78)

But the Premier had other sights in view as well. He doggedly opposed the form of liberal education along with the liberal democratic aims propounded by Jerome Bruner. Thus, whereas Bruner had said of MACOS particularly, and 'democratic education' generally, that it should: 'make it possible for a growing mind to develop according to its own interests and values and to make it possible for people to find their own ways of contributing to the society' (Smith and Knight 1978: 227), the Premier claimed (now meshing his belief with a direct threat to teachers) that:

> The emphasis today must be on technical training. There are enough white collar workers today looking for jobs already. The notion that children should be allowed to do their own thing and be turned out as little liberal arts graduates must go . . . any teacher who wants to try a challenge need have no doubt the Government means what it says. They have been warned and already 700 of their colleagues are unemployed in Queensland.
>
> (*Sunday Mail* 26–2–78)

The Premier also appeared to be testing Cabinet's power against educators and the Department of Education with regard to pronouncing educational aims and implementing educational policy. Schools, he indicated, are to do the government's (namely, the Cabinet's) bidding:

> Educators will get the message that we will only allow wholesome, decent, practical material in schools. . . . And we want the Department . . . to get a clear understanding this is what the Government intends to happen. . . . We expect the Department to be alert to what the Government wants [taught in schools].
>
> (*Courier Mail* 23–2–78)

In contrast, and more in line with what Bruner sought, Malcolm Skilbeck, Director of the Curriculum Development Centre whose work on SEMP was temporarily intruded upon, stated that while

> The materials have been attacked for not promoting the values the Queensland Government and people wish to see enshrined in schools . . . The central thrust of SEMP [and one might presume the aim of education]

is that high school students should be enabled to become socially intelligent, knowledgeable and concerned citizens.

(*Canberra Times* 27–3–78)

The last word in this particular 'debate' on the aims of education might be left to a National Party minister and member of the colourful Catter family in Australian politics:

> To use the expression used in SEMP itself, it presents people with alternative life styles. Although much more so, that was the general idea in MACOS. . . . All I can say is that a generation of children grew up without having a look at these alternatives and, as far as I can see, they are reasonably happy and successful people. . . . I certainly do not think we should give people in schools a licence to go around putting these alternatives before children.[4]

(*Hansard* (QLD) 4–4–78)

Theorising the empirical: a role for philosophers

The above example, extreme though it may be, has shown the contextual, political, normative, dynamic and contested nature of educational policy; it has shown how a large number of contemporaneously stated aims of education can be caught up in the complexity of educational policy; and it has identified some of the players in one particular instance of contest.

However, it has to be recognised that in recounting instances such as the above, what is displayed and identified depends largely on what lenses are being looked through, or how the empirical matter is selected, organised and theorised (I indicated that my essay was neither neutral nor theory-free). Others (for instance, Rona Joyner) might give different accounts. In interpreting such situations, as Seddon (1990: 131) reminds us: 'The key issue is . . . the adequacy of perspectives and starting points which can illuminate . . . aspects of social life and the meanings one makes from the interplay of empirical data and theoretical categories.'

And here is a cue for philosophers of education; for surely matters relating to 'adequacy of perspectives' and 'illuminating meanings made from the interplay of the empirical and the theoretical' are firmly within their compass. For instance, with regard to the above example, it is surely legitimate for philosophers to investigate starting points or perspectives which can adequately tie a concern for 'traditional values', technical and vocational education, service to the community and a fear of revealing alternatives with anti-humanism, anti-socialism, anti-intellectualism, anti-liberalism, along with flexing political muscle at teachers individually and the Department of Education specifically.

Such investigation would readily reveal that it would be bordering on the facile to give too much of the 'credit' for determining educational policy to Rona Joyner. It is true that she appealed to the Premier, his wife and people close to them. She also keyed in to particular anxieties of rural Australia in the late 1970s brought about by recession, youth unemployment, changes in values, growing permissiveness, children drifting to the large cities, and general increased insecurity in a once stable environment. And she appealed particularly to the meek, the pious and the elderly by advocating the old (secure, right) ways, and by suggesting (in the manner of Goebbels) that the world was coming under the grip of an international conspiracy, whereby the rich (particularly the Jews, along with their academic acolytes) and simultaneously the communists, were seeking to take control and establish a single, dominant world order. But even given all of that, it is unlikely that her intervention alone could so strongly influence educational policy.

It would be similarly facile to see the whole affair as an aberration within the democratic process – notwithstanding the facts that in Queensland at the time the National Party, through an infamous gerrymander, had a large majority in Parliament, and little effective opposition, even though it drew less than 30 per cent of the overall vote; that National Party ministers and the Premier shared the agrarian fundamentalism of their constituents, who were, in general, rural, deeply religious, and not highly educated (Smith and Knight 1978: 241); that Queensland has no House of Review; and that Parliament at the time met infrequently, most policy decisions being made by a tightly controlled Cabinet – all of which created a situation ripe for legislation of minority views.

The above factors are all relevant; but are hardly sufficient to account adequately for a government legitimating the fundamentalist values of small groups such as STOP and CARE in a matter as encompassing as educational policy. A proper explanation requires that a wider perspective be taken; and I would suggest that a potentially useful starting point for this might lie in considering the major and common player in all instances of educational policy making: the state. Dale (1992: 388) puts this even more forcefully, claiming that 'A focus on the State is not only necessary, but the most important component of any adequate understanding of educational policy. Of that there can be no doubt.'

What there can be much doubt about, however, is how the state is theorised, and how the state 'works' with regard to forming and implementing educational aims and policy. Recent policy sociology has been of much value with regard to the latter issue, and I shall note some of its contribution in that area before turning to the related former issue and a possible role for philosophy.

There was a time in the not too distant past when much social theory, both idealist and materialist, shared the misconception that the state determined educational aims and related policy through official civil agencies, and everybody else more or less fell into line. More recent policy sociology, however, has revealed the error in regarding social policy and practice as top-down, neatly following linear processes, and it has also shown that within socio-historical contexts many players might have differing aims regarding the educational process. Numerous models have been proposed and developed in order to tease out the complexity of policy and practice, and all, in their own ways, find empirical support that educational practice does not simply embody and follow the aims and policy directives which the political and civil arms of the state decree. For instance, well into the debate, Bowe and Ball focused on the essentially contested nature of policy, and they located policy arenas containing facets of 'intended policy', 'actual policy' and 'policy-in-use'. Later (Bowe and Ball 1992: 6–14), they recognised policy-as-legislated, policy-as-interpreted and policy-as-implemented, with much variance and slippage both between and within and those stages. Following Codd (1988), they recognised further complexities, given that policy is always expressed as a text which is then open to a plurality of readers and readings (witness the readings of MACOS), and consequently to a plurality of practices.[5]

The same can be said about 'aims of education'. These too could be regarded not only as 'high-level directives' laid down before practitioners while being taken to an analytic guillotine by philosophers, but rather as competing statements of values and intent, contested in and between the arenas of formation and implementation, and eventually subject to a plurality of readings and a plurality of practices.

It is in this general area that philosophy of education might complement and supplement policy sociology; for policy sociology requires a conceptualisation and clarification of the very nature of the state in order to direct its empirical eye. There are thus many issues open to philosophy, and in this particular context I shall focus on three which I believe to be central to an understanding of the state and its relation to educational policy.

Firstly, there is a role for philosophy in theorising the state as an economic–political entity and thus clarifying its role in social conservation and capital accumulation. This is arguably the primary task because, notwithstanding whatever rich detail may be revealed in analysing the state, it remains the case that state power ultimately seeks to legitimate, secure, promote and conserve the conditions or relations of production which enable, maintain and secure capital accumulation. That might be viewed or described differently ('fostering economic growth', 'global positioning', 'gaining a competitive market edge' and so on) but without capital accumulation any society collapses – and it is the function, if not the *raison d'être* of the state to act as a relatively autonomous power structure primarily seeking to secure and maintain conditions conducive to the accumulation of capital so that economic, and then political and ideological, collapse does not occur.

This viewpoint exposes the Queensland affair in a particularly interesting light. Throughout the entire contest over curriculum and educational aims, the Queensland government talked of democracy and of having been elected democratically to represent the views of all the people. But it also talked of strength and power; of providing leadership and stability to Queensland at a time of social change and fiscal crisis in Australia. And it did provide stability – of a sort. Having supported favoured allies, and having represented favoured views in order to test its power with MACOS and SEMP, it was soon to further de-legitimate and even foreclose other forms of discourse and thought, and to control values further and exclude alternative ways of thinking and acting. There quickly followed things previously virtually unknown in modern Australia: a ban on strikes, legislation to sack striking employees, restrictions placed on materials used in schools and universities,[6] and a banning of street marches and public rallies. Under Bjelke-Petersen's Nationals, law, order and stability (many saw it as fascist repression) did come to reign in Queensland. And with that followed a massive inflow of investment capital, industry relocation and unprecedented capital growth. Thus it could be argued that the Nationals used the MACOS/SEMP affair, and the minority fundamentalist interests involved, as part of an overall strategy to establish and define power relations within the state and also to help set up broader conditions favourable to capital accumulation.

A second issue beckoning philosophers is the role of the state in legitimating and de-legitimating knowledge. This is not, as I have argued repeatedly elsewhere, a neutral exercise (and it is certainly not the conservation and promotion of some 'historically established' essential worthwhile content). Rather, a central and necessary part of the instantiation and exercise of state power is to seek to conserve, reproduce and further particular knowledge and value systems considered well-placed to ensure capital accumulation and social reproduction.[7] This might require ignoring or silencing some voices, de-legitimating and/or foreclosing forms of critical thought regarded as potentially disruptive to the process of accumulation and reproduction, and possibly promoting knowledge better suited to the production of compliant citizens. The MACOS/SEMP affair can clearly be recognised in this light – especially given that Cabinet ministers openly declared their desire to exclude alternative knowledge which they regarded as a threat to stability.[8]

A third issue of particular pertinence to philosophers of education is the place of education, and especially universal compulsory schooling, within the state. The state is a historically changing entity, and consequently education is always being structured and positioned, and restructured and repositioned, to the state's general and strategic needs of conservation and capital accumulation. So, what particularly requires clarification is how, in the messy contest of educational policy, the state might attain and maintain privileged control of the knowledge and values promulgated through formal and informal education systems. Philosophy of education could serve in clarifying if, how and in what ways schooling transmits and legitimates knowledge and values thought best able to secure conditions for capital accumulation and social reproduction. It could also valuably examine how schooling, while operating within the ambit of democracy, autonomy and education might, on occasions, simultaneously seek to deny to future citizens the critical faculty, level of autonomy and other elements of liberal democratic living which could endanger the process of producing the relations and conditions through which the state defines itself, and in terms of which it seeks to conserve itself (Harris 1995: 227). Again, the tangles in the Queensland affair illuminate this level of struggle for and in schooling.[9]

Conclusion

I have indicated in this chapter that philosophy of education might have more to do with the aims of education than make 'aristocratic pronounce-ments' or subject such pronouncements to an 'analytic guillotine'.[10] By moving towards both social philosophy and epistemology – that is, by theorising the role of the state, and especially its relation to power and knowledge – philosophy might clarify the dynamics of social contest and, drawing on policy sociology's engagement with the empirical, help us understand whose aims get translated into educational practice, and why.

Notes

1 I am using, with their kind agreement, their location of media statements, published letters and *Parliamentary Proceedings (Hansard)*, and also their examination of STOP and CARE activities, publications and correspondence.
2 For example, extended families. There is no discussion of homosexuality in either MACOS or SEMP, yet Joyner managed to intimate that the programmes actually endorsed the practice.
3 This particular organisation is an effective political lobbyist, and currently has two repre-sentatives in the Upper House of the NSW Parliament.
4 Catter may be referring to the people who, reasonably happy in their ignorance of alterna-tives, voted for him and the Nationals.
5 There are now commentators who see Bowe and Ball's analysis as too simplistic. For an overview of recent literature, see Hatcher and Troyna (1994).
6 My own book, *Teachers and Classes*, was the object of Queensland government attention in the early 1980s. Academics and students were placed under some pressure not to use it.
7 Currently institutions of higher education are witnessing particularly dramatic curricular revaluations. The humanities and the arts seem to be losing status while Graduate Schools of Management flourish. This may have something to do with matters of accumulation within current global economic conditions.
8 The works of Michael Apple and Jean Anyon provide a useful insight into the politics of 'official knowledge' and the politics of schooling.

12

9 National Party Minister Colin Lamont, in a lovely touch illustrating policy sociology's recognition of tension between legislation and practice, between the aims a government decrees and the aims teachers, principals or directors follow, confessed in Parliament that 'the Director of Primary Education said to me, "No matter what you people in parliament do, you won't change the way I want to run my schools"' (*Hansard* 13–9–77).

10 I am not advocating that either practice be abandoned. Both have considerable value; notwithstanding the fact that philosophers of education, whether of a substantive or an analytic bent, have rarely been included, sought or attended to by the state's civil agencies regarding educational policy or aims.

Bibliography

Bowe, R. and Ball, S. with Gold, A. (1992) *Reforming Education and Changing Schools*, London: Routledge.

Brown, L. M. (1970) *Aims of Education*, New York: Teachers College Press.

Codd, J. (1988) 'The construction and deconstruction of educational policy documents', *Journal of Educational Policy* 3(3): 235–48.

Dale, R. (1992) 'Whither the state and educational policy: recent work in Australia and New Zealand', *British Journal of Sociology of Education* 13(3): 387–95.

Freeland, J. (1979a) 'Class struggle in schooling: *MACOS* and *SEMP* in Queensland', *Intervention* 12: 29–62.

——(1979b) 'STOP! CARE to COME and PROBE the right-wing PIE', *Radical Education Dossier* 8: 4–7.

Harris, K. (1995) 'Education for citizenship', in W. Kohli (ed.) *Critical Conversations in Philosophy of Education*, New York: Routledge.

Hatcher, R. and Troyna, B. (1994) 'The "policy cycle": a ball by ball account', *Journal of Educational Policy* 9(2): 155–70.

Hirst, P. H. and Peters, R. S. (1970) *The Logic of Education*, London: Routledge.

Peters, R. S. (1966) *Ethics and Education*, London: George Allen & Unwin.

——(1973) 'Aims of education – a conceptual enquiry', in R. S. Peters (ed.) *The Philosophy of Education*, London: Oxford University Press.

Seddon, T. (1990) 'On education and context', *Australian Journal of Education* 34(2): 131–6.

Smith, R. and Knight, J. (1978) '*MACOS* in Queensland: the politics of educational knowledge', *Australian Journal of Education* 22(3): 225–48.

2

'OR WHAT'S A HEAVEN FOR?'

The importance of aims in education

Robin Barrow

> Ah, but a man's reach should exceed his grasp,
> Or what's a heaven for?
> *Robert Browning*

A note on the idea of truth

Richard Tarnas has suggested that on the eve of the postmodern era 'modern man was a divided animal, inexplicably self-aware in an indifferent universe' (Tarnass 1993). Many scholars today would have us believe that the postmodern condition has human beings nursing an even more acute alienation and anomie. The Western tradition, in its long-drawn-out argument between faith and reason and between nominalism and realism, and in its scientific and philosophical revolutions, has left us with a commitment to rationality and a powerful conception of the autonomous human mind, while at the same time suggesting that certain knowledge will always be beyond our grasp, and increasingly emphasising the relativity of our judgements and pronouncements to time, place, and our way of looking at the world, particularly as determined by our language. In extreme cases, the implication is taken to be that there is no reality, there are no facts, there is no truth; there are only fluctuating and conflicting structures imposed on the world by individual minds.

In this debate, while there is undoubtedly much of great subtlety and significance, there is also all too often a failure to observe some fairly basic distinctions. In particular, it is important to distinguish between the idea of truth (and related ideas such as reality and fact) on the one hand, and the idea of knowledge on the other. There is, for example, a very important difference between maintaining that there is no reality (no world out there, no facts, nothing given), and maintaining only that we can never truly know that reality or be certain that we understand it correctly. Similarly, there is a significant difference between the questions of what knowledge

14

means, whether knowledge is attainable (that is, whether we can ever know or be sure that we know something), and how we may come by knowledge (for example, whether a Kantian view of mental structures coinciding with the material world is to be preferred to a Platonic view of forms or a Lockean view of sense impressions).

As a premiss for this chapter, I would suggest that while there are many plausible arguments to suggest (1) that much of what we might be inclined to take as knowledge of a given reality is in fact no such thing, and (2) that we can seldom, if ever, know that we know something, it is not at all plausible to suggest that there is nothing to be known or that the very idea of knowledge is confused and incoherent. The idea of truth, the idea of various contingent facts about the physical world and logical constraints on our reasoning seem to me to be inescapable both logically and psychologically. I do not, for example, believe that there ever have been or could be individuals who could in sincerity profess that they do not believe in the idea of truth, since as a matter of fact in all sorts of trivial ways every day they live their lives on the assumptions that some things are true and others false. Furthermore, there must be a truth of some sort, even if it is only that everything is purely a matter of appearances. So, while we may argue about whether we can ever ascertain the truth, and, more specifically, about what contingent and logical truths we should believe in, we have no reason to conclude and no psychological possibility of concluding that the idea of truth is meaningless.

A related point that I need to make at the outset is that conceptual analysis, whatever one's particular view of the nature of the exercise, is necessarily idealistic. I do not by this mean to refer to or endorse 'idealism' as a philosophical position. I mean something simpler and more mundane, though I believe it to be of considerable importance: when we attempt to articulate what we understand by an educated person, by justice, by evil, or by any other complex and abstract concept, we are necessarily trying (however imperfectly) to articulate an idea of the perfectly educated person, perfect justice, perfect evil.

What is the essence of education?

The relevance of the above to what I now wish to argue is that I see the question of what our educational aims should be as being of critical importance, yet widely disparaged. It tends to be superficially dismissed as a hangover from a past in which it was believed that an objective truth about reality could be discerned from an abstract contemplation of something like Platonic forms. In fact, however, it is a necessary and crucial step in making sense of our world. No matter how much our view of life will in fact be inescapably governed by time and place, and no matter what the difficulties in establishing ultimate value claims, we can do no other (short of reverting to complete nihilism) than assume that there are more and less plausible conceptions of education and seek to ground our practice in the most plausible account of the ideal.

Some years ago work on aims in education tended to focus on two points: (1) the distinction between aims and objectives, and (2) the claim that the aims of education are intrinsic to the concept.

The former concern has always struck me as rather sterile and questionable. Certainly, in terms of clearing the ground and tidying up our thoughts, it would be useful if we all distinguished clearly between aims and objectives, and there may be some warrant in usage for the view that 'aims' are more general than 'objectives' – for example, 'The derivation of educational aims from values, educational objectives from aims' (Goodlad and Richter 1966); 'As a rule [the aim] is too general to guide specific instructional decisions. That is the function of objectives' (Pratt 1980). But the fact of the matter is that people generally do not make such a distinction, using the words rather as interchangeable, and it is noticeable that authors who make the distinction, such as Pratt, go on to qualify the word 'objectives' with the adjective 'specific'. More troubling was a particular tendency to equate 'specific objectives' with 'behavioural objectives', since an objective or aim can quite well be specific without being behavioural (for instance, my specific aim in this lesson is to bring students to appreciate this poem). The consequent attempts to design curriculum exclusively in terms of behavioural objectives involved a gross distortion of the educational enterprise, which surely involves much, such as the fostering of appreciation, which is not well caught in behavioural terms. In any event, there does not seem to be any warrant for insisting that aims are necessarily more general than objectives, and the attempt to do so involved the kind of procedure that helped to give 'ordinary language' philosophy a bad name.

By contrast, Peters' succinct recognition that the aims of education are intrinsic to it remains extremely important (Peters 1966). While we might have extrinsic reasons for educating people (such as to serve the economy), the fact remains that the normative force of the word is the consequence of its inherent valued objectives or aims. To argue about the aims of education is to argue about what it is to be educated. It is, therefore, worrying that today there is relatively little discussion of the aims (or the concept) of education. This I relate to three main considerations, although I do not venture to go deeply into what was cause and what effect: a general decline of interest in philosophy of education; the influence of so-called 'postmodern' ideas on truth and knowledge generally, and value judgements in particular; and the widespread enthusiasm (oddly at a variance with the postmodern *Zeitgeist*) for focusing on means rather than ends, and technical solutions to problems of all kinds.

What this means in practice is that, since the ends of education are largely ignored or treated as unproblematic, but in either event not emphasised and argued for, what actually goes on in school is increasingly driven by the extrinsic aims of, for example, industry, ideology, and the implicit assumptions of research methodology. In other words, because there is not widespread contemplation of what we take education to be, what we are necessarily aiming at if we are sincerely concerned to educate people rather than train them, socialise or indoctrinate them, there is correspondingly no widespread ability to argue against the assumption that the success of the educational system is to be judged in terms of such things as whether school leavers are well placed to find employment or whether they are politically correct, ecologically sensitive, caring individuals.

The reference to research methodology should perhaps be briefly explained. Any particular methodology itself carries with it certain implications about the nature of education or what constitutes educational success, although, sadly, such implications often seem to be not only implicit rather than explicit, but actually unrecognised. The consequence is that when we base our practice in, say, teaching reading or developing intelligence on the research in the field, we inevitably buy into the researchers' assumptions about what constitutes successful reading or being intelligent. Thus, in the absence of serious reflection on what kind of intelligence we expect an educated person to possess, in North America at least educational success is still to some extent judged in terms of measuring people's IQ. Technical argument about IQ testing abounds, but there is very little argument addressed to the point that intelligence as defined by such testing has no obvious educational value or even interest.

Many would perhaps accept that schools should have a responsibility for developing the physical health and the mental health (encompassing such things as confidence) of individuals as well as socialising them. But such concerns seem distinct from the business of educating them. The Western tradition to which I and most of those reading this are heirs, whether we like it or not, in fact provides us with a very consistent concept of education defined in terms of understanding. Shifts in views of education over the centuries arise not from any rejection of this fundamental criterion, but from shifts in views about the nature of knowledge and understanding. It therefore seems not unreasonable to argue that the essence of education today is the provision of understanding of the dominant traditions of thought and inquiry in the Western tradition, including of course, recognition of the limits of the appropriateness of a given type of understanding in respect of what kinds of issue it can deal with, and recognition of what is taken to be problematic within the field. Thus, an educated person would be expected to understand the nature of scientific inquiry, and that would include understanding that it is appropriate for examining questions in the physical realm but not the aesthetic, and understanding such things as Popperian theories of falsifiability, Kuhnian theories of paradigm shifts, and, more generally, contemporary concerns about the possibilities of science. By the same token, an educated person would be expected to understand something of the nature of the aesthetic domain, not necessarily in order to appreciate art or to be a creative artist, but in order to understand an undeniable aspect of human experience. Without striving for completeness, I would add the moral and the religious as further types of understanding central to our way of looking at the world, mathematical understanding as a unique network of ideas, and history and literature as species of inquiry that speak most directly to attempting to understand what it is to be human.

This conception of education is outlined on the grounds that it is a variant, designed to take account of contemporary thought, of a conception that has remained constant since the time of Plato. It carries with it a commitment to the ideal of autonomy, for the point of providing understanding is to give the individual the opportunity to see things for themselves, to make their own sense of the world. That remained true even when, for example, the Catholic Church was intellectually and politically in the ascendant. For while the Church argued that the way to truth was through the teachings of the Church, and believed as against, say, a Lutheran view, that the Church hierarchy were best able to see the truth, the interest was none the less to pass on understanding of the truth to all.

Now, it has been argued that postmodernism has brought about the death of autonomy as an ideal, since if everything is necessarily how you see it, everyone is necessarily autonomous. (Alternatively, if everything is the product of the individual's time and place, no one is autonomous.) But this kind of reasoning, even when fully explicated rather than summarised all too briefly as here, seems a classic example of scholastic hair-splitting. There is a very straightforward difference, in any age and whatever the prevailing epistemological views, between giving people received answers to specific questions (or giving them nothing), and giving people access to understanding the ways in which we have heretofore tried to make sense of our world. It is the latter that I maintain as a matter of historical fact has always been the essence of the Western view of education: development of an understanding of how we try to make sense of our world. Not only is this what education has meant, it is also an ideal to strive for regardless of what we call it.

The importance of the question

And so I come to my main concern in this chapter, which is not to argue for this conception of education, but to argue for the vital importance of considering the nature of education – of articulating and arguing for specifically educational aims. Despite what I have tried to argue, it will still be maintained by some that any such account of what it is to be educated is an idle exercise. It may be said that it represents no more than a view that arises out of the author's limited background and experience; that it is rivalled by quite other conceptions, which have nothing more, but nothing less to recommend them; that the mere articulation of a concept cannot and will not outweigh political and other pragmatic realities; and, in sum, that this kind of philosophical activity is an idle, abstract exercise, issuing forth in unrealistic and unattainable ideals.

In response to such a view, I suggest that the claim that the analysis of a concept such as education is no more than the articulation of an arbitrary perception which, while it may be explicable in sociological or autobiographical terms, is not in principle justifiable, is plainly inadequate. First, the concept belongs to a historical tradition of considerable sophistication and longevity. Second, such a conception is arrived at by reasoning according to certain rules, and by reference, where appropriate, to facts that are themselves defined as facts in accordance with certain rules of evidence and reasoning. In other words, conceptions can be compared in respect of their clarity, completeness, coherence and compatibility with other ideas. They are subject to restraints of logic and physical fact. That line of reasoning could be swept away, if we accepted an extreme view to the effect that all the rules of reasoning and all the presumed facts that we accept were themselves matters that can be rejected or ignored. But there is absolutely no reason to accept such a contention, and it flies in the face of what we actually believe. The assumption that ideal accounts, such as conceptualisations necessarily are, are by the nature of their ideal quality also vague, unreal and impractical is facile. Clearly there need be nothing vague about them. They are unreal in the limited sense that in reality we do not encounter the perfectly educated person, the perfectly just society and so on but that does not make them unreal in the sense of unrealistic or impractical. Their practical value resides in how we treat them. An analysis of the concept of education or an attempt to articulate its intrinsic aims serves, or should serve, as a statement of the criteria against which to judge our relative success or lack of it in seeking to educate people in practice.

It really does not matter that analysing the concept or articulating the aims of education is in some sense an idealistic and even subjective matter. For the sense in which it is subjective is the sense in which it may be readily agreed all human knowledge claims are subjective – namely, uncertain and to some extent influenced by one's other beliefs, which may themselves be to a greater or lesser extent the product of one's time and place. But that is quite distinct from subjective in the sense of arbitrary and without rational foundation. Analysis is governed by rules to which we are as a matter of fact committed and which we neither have reason to reject nor can intelligibly do so. In arguing that education is essentially about the development of mind and proceeding to articulate that conception in such a way that we expand on what is meant, in clear terms, coherently and consistently with other beliefs that we have about, for example, what humans are capable of and what matters to us, we increase our understanding of the nature of the enterprise we are concerned with. One may play with the hypothesis that a view of education that took no account of the history of the idea, that was presented in unclear and incoherent terms, and that ignored other beliefs we actually have, might be equally valid, useful, worthy of respect, rational and so on; but nobody actually does believe the hypothesis, and it is far from clear what 'valid', 'useful', 'worthy of respect' and 'rational' could mean on such a hypothesis.

The unattainability of the ideal is not only no objection, it is part of what makes analysis so important. For in attempting to explicate the inherent aims of education we are not simply asserting a set of random values; we are trying to understand more fully a particular phenomenon or practice. We are trying to articulate the values that are presupposed. Those who wish to are free to argue that they do not value education in this sense, but at least they and we will know precisely what it is they are rejecting.

For those of us who do not reject it, an account of the aims of education in ideal terms serves as a set of criteria against which to determine and judge our practice. The extraordinary idea that it is in some way idle or pointless for our reach (our aims) to go beyond our grasp (what we can successfully achieve), leads directly to the practical corollary that we will aim no further than our grasp. This of course ensures that our world, our reality, will be defined in terms of where we are now rather than in terms of where we might be; it also leaves us with no criteria against which to judge success: we grasp what we grasp. The vacuum that is left by an abandonment of inquiry into the aims of education is all too readily filled by the imposition of extraneous ends by various interested parties. Thus it is that the nature of education is increasingly dictated by the demands of industry, government, religious pressure groups and the like. The various demands of such interest groups might conceivably be reasonable and possibly should be a concern of the schooling system. But even when the demands are reasonable they are not a substitute for specifically educational demands. Without an educational ideal, we have no argument to support those specifically educational demands.

The most important point to emphasise is the distinction between the question of whether we can hope to ascertain the truth and the question of whether there is a truth to be ascertained (in some, if not all, spheres). There is certainly a sufficient accumulation of data and theory to make it plausible to suggest both that claims to knowledge are relative (to time, place, culture, individual perception and so on) and that we can never know that we know. An obvious example is provided by the rejection of Newtonian physics (notwithstanding its explanatory power for a long period of time and its apparent pragmatic justification) in the light of such things as Einstein's theory of relativity. Nor have we any particular reason to think that contemporary physics will not be superseded. Such considerations may well be sufficient to establish that any claim to knowledge should at best be regarded as tentative. But 'tentative' is not the same as 'relative'. A given claim may in fact be relative in the sense of based on nothing other than some aspects of culturally contingent factors. And very possibly all claims are to some extent influenced by some such factors. But these considerations do not in themselves establish that all claims are necessarily no more than relative to contingent conditions in some way. And no amount of such evidence and epistemological theorising is sufficient to show that there is no truth to be ascertained.

As to the question of whether there is any truth to be ascertained, this, it would seem to me, must be answered in the affirmative both psychologically and logically. How, psychologically, could individuals, who even when in the extreme of what we term mental disorder, still organise their lives around some distinction between what is the case and what is not, totally and sincerely embrace the idea that there is in principle no such thing as truth? Logically, how could one present such a claim, since the claim itself would be presented as a truth?

As to the more specific question of whether there can be such a thing as conceptual truth, it will be noted that I do not claim that there is. Rather, as I have argued elsewhere, the question of conceptual correctness, in the sense of the question of whether a given account of, say, education can be regarded as the truth, is meaningless (Barrow 1984, 1990). But this does not mean that education can be defined in any way one chooses. There are logical and (physical) factual constraints on what one can intelligibly say. An account of education, if it is really an account of what loosely we refer to as education, as opposed to an account of what we refer to as marriage or beauty, must be an account of something to do with the business of acquiring knowledge. Because it is a fact that that is broadly what the term means in the English language. Beyond that, in trying to articulate and explicate this rough idea, we are further constrained by the need to be clear, coherent, detailed and consistent with our other beliefs. And some of those other beliefs will pertain to empirical facts (such as what the human brain is in fact capable of). As we have seen, it is possible to question the certainty of our other empirical beliefs, and it is possible in principle to question our rules of logic. (Perhaps, for example, there is no merit in consistency.) But in fact we cannot psychologically or logically mount a successful argument for rejecting either our commitment to the conventional rules of logic or the idea that there are some facts to be taken account of, albeit our view of what they are should be recognised as tentative.

The importance of emphasising the need for inquiry into the aims of education, which I take to be another way of referring to the need to examine the concept of education, cannot therefore be dismissed as an inherently subjective or relativistic activity. Once that is conceded, its practical importance becomes self-evident. In the world as we understand it, constituted as we are, we have to determine our educational practice, and judge our degree of success in that practice, primarily by reference to our understanding of the nature of the enterprise (of the concept). When we do not do this, we are simply abandoning education as such, and leaving the way open for other forces to determine some species of upbringing that may have nothing to do with education at all.

References

Barrow, Robin (1984) *Giving Teaching Back to Teachers*, Brighton, Sussex: Wheatsheaf.

——(1990) *A Critical Dictionary of Educational Concepts*, 2nd edn, London: Harvester, Wheatsheaf.

Goodlad, J. I. and Richter, M. N. (1966) *The Development of a Conceptual System for Dealing with Problems of Curriculum and Instruction*, Los Angeles: Institute for Development of Educational Activities, University of California.

Peters, R. S. (1966) *Ethics and Education*, London: George Allen & Unwin.

Pratt, David 1980) *Curriculum: Design and Development*, New York: Harcourt Brace Jovanovich.

Tarnas, Richard (1993) *The Passion of the Western Mind: Understanding the Ideas That Have Shaped Our World View*, New York: Ballantine.

3

THE AIMS OF EDUCATION AND THE PHILOSOPHY OF EDUCATION

The pathology of an argument

Peter Gilroy

> That was a way of putting it – not very satisfactory:
> A periphrastic study in a worn-out poetical fashion,
> Leaving one still with the intolerable wrestle
> With words and meanings.
>
> T. S. Eliot, *East Coker*, ii

It almost goes without saying that a general approach to educational issues as typified by the Great Educators or Whitehead's *The Aims of Education*, and which was dismissed by Peters as 'undifferentiated mush' (Peters 1966a: 7), is of little help in understanding quite how one might come to some grasp of the aims of education. However, the important point I intend arguing for is that their work was rejected by Hardie, Peters and others not simply because much of the material was poorly argued, but also because it could not withstand the assault of a particular approach to the philosophy of education, conceptual analysis. I wish to argue that a consideration of much that has been written about the aims of education, from Peters in the early 1960s to Winch in 1996, reveals a discipline that seems unable fully to accept that there are serious flaws in a purely analytical approach to educational issues.

However, some approaches to examining the aims of education do indeed make use of an alternative approach to the philosophy of education, without fully identifying it for what it is. I will therefore begin by examining briefly the conceptual approach to understanding the aims of education and show how this is founded on a terminally flawed approach to philosophy. I will continue by identifying another approach to philosophy of education and show how some philosophers of education have made use of its insights. In this way the chapter can be seen as an examination of the usefulness of an alternative to conceptual analysis using the particular example of 'aims of education' as a case study. For reasons that will become clear I will say rather less about aims and rather more about the way in which aims are examined.

The traditional approach

Attempts to pigeon-hole thinkers into neat categories tend to be somewhat artificial, but the 1960's and 1970's dominance of the Peters' conceptual approach to philosophical thinking is well documented. It is this way of dealing with philosophy of education that I am identifying as the Traditional Approach and its methodology is well illustrated in Peters' treatment of aims.

Peters begins by establishing that although an inquiry into the aims of education deals with two questions ('What do you mean?' and 'How do you know?'), he will focus on the first question (Peters *et al.* 1965: 12). He continues by analysing the concept of education in order to understand the nature of education's aims. In so doing he produces his well-known conclusion that education is a normative concept that identifies what is intrinsically worthwhile by 'laying down criteria to which a family of activities must conform' in order that such activities can properly be identified as *educational* activities (ibid.: 15). Given this conclusion about the concept 'education' it follows that in attempting to understand what is meant by the aims of education one has to accept that it is the normative aspect of 'education' that 'aims' are picking out: that is, the aims of education are identified by means of the norms that are part and parcel of 'education'.

Peters then has, to his satisfaction at least, answered the question he began with, namely, 'What is meant by the aims of education?' Understanding the meaning of 'education' involves understanding the different criteria that are involved in elucidating the concept and so coming to see that any aim of education must be related to the intrinsically worthwhile as identified by his analysis of the concept of education. Furthermore, his logically tight connection between the two concepts reveals that there is no meaningful way of producing some sort of over-arching aim statement, as such a statement would simply be 'drawing attention to what it means to educate . . . someone' (ibid.: 21) and so would be a mere tautology (ibid.: 27).

One way of criticising this approach is to concentrate on the analysis of education and show how this might be problematic, which would then, given the tight connection asserted between education and its aims, serve as a critique of his understanding of the aims of the education. Thus Woods offers counter-examples to Peters' analysis of education which purport to show that Peters is prescribing one use of the term over another (ibid.: 33), as does Dray (ibid., pp. 36–7). It would follow that Peters' understanding of the aims of education is equally prescriptive and would require a justification that goes beyond conceptual analysis (see also Earwaker 1973: 246). Peters' response is to dismiss the counter-examples as 'derivative', 'quaint', or not 'the primary use of the concept' (Peters *et al.* 1965: 48) and to reiterate his view that his analysis is substantially sound.

The point to notice here is that the defence is, on one level, watertight because the criteria for identifying what is derivative, quaint or primary are the very criteria being criticised. The vicious circularity is thus both a strength (in that it allows for a rebuttal of any criticism couched in terms of counter-examples) and a weakness (in that it is ultimately logically unsound). It is the logical weakness that indicates a more fundamental form of criticism, based upon the kind of philosophy Peters sees himself as using and the meaning theory attached to it.

Critique

It will be recalled that Peters began by claiming that within his view of philosophy there were two questions that had to be answered, one of meaning and one of justification, and that he makes it clear that in examining the aims of education he is interested only in the first of these questions. Now even on his terms it should be noted that what is interesting about Peters' way of treating the topic is that in an important sense the question of what meaning can be attached to 'aims' which Peters takes as central has not in fact been answered. We are informed about the way in which the concept of *education* is to be understood, but nothing directly on the concept of *aims*, except *en passant*.

In response it could be argued that as the two concepts are supposed to be inextricably intertwined, then in providing an understanding of the meaning of education Peters has also provided an understanding of the meaning of 'aims'. However, the way in which aims and education are supposed to be linked is not well established. Peters himself seems unsure, in that he accepts that the connection cannot be as tight as his talk of tautologies seemed to suggest, but at the same time does not want the connection to be nothing more than a contingent *de facto* one (Peters *et al.* 1965: 49): that is, the connection is neither purely analytic nor synthetic. Unfortunately, quite what the connection might be is left unclear, especially as in a later publication he reverts to talk about the link being some sort of 'conceptual truth' (Hirst and Peters 1970: 28).

I could develop this line of attack,[1] but want instead to argue that Peters' explication of the aims of education as well as the problems it causes him are an inevitable result of his conception of philosophy. There are two elements to his understanding of the nature of philosophy. The first is, echoing Locke, that Peters sees himself *qua* philosopher as an under-labourer involved in a second-order inquiry the prime task of which in 'the uncultivated field of the philosophy of education' is 'to clear away some of the rubble which has prevented many clear-cut furrows being driven through this field in the past' (Peters 1966b: 88). The second concerns the creation of these 'furrows', in that they will be produced by means of a form of conceptual analysis which will primarily be a search for criteria of meaning. This last is for Peters paramount, in that 'the search for such criteria is the kernel of philosophical inquiry' (Peters 1966a: 16). Moreover, these criteria are essential for grasping the meaning of a concept like education in that they represent an 'explication of its essence' (ibid.: 90).

This criterial approach to philosophy of education also leads Peters to claim that the evaluative aspects of social concepts like education are 'a matter of logical necessity' (ibid.: 91). This is because, although the principles which his criterial approach identify as giving meaning to concepts like education are indeed social, certain principles, identified by a transcendental argument, are presupposed in any rational discourse, so at this point their justification ends, as he claims that they are logically necessary for rational discourse (ibid.: 165).

Given this approach to philosophy of education it is inevitable that Peters should examine the aims of education in the way that he does. It is similarly inevitable that he focuses on the meaning question, rather than the justification question, if only because he has no way of answering questions about ultimate justifications without appealing to his version of a transcendental argument. Furthermore, his approach to understanding meaning has to be based on a search for normative criteria that will explain the essence of a concept, thus leaving little or no substantive content with which to answer his question, 'What do we mean when we talk of the aims of education?' Consequently, at the end of this process, and as a direct result of his conception of philosophy of education, we are no nearer (and for Peters cannot, *qua* philosopher of education, be any nearer) a substantive answer to the question posed. What has occurred is that ground has been cleared (the under-labourer conception) and essentialist criteria for education have been identified (an essentialist form of conceptual analysis), with the claim made that aims and education are necessarily juxtaposed (Peters *et al.* 1965: 28). Armed with this version of conceptual analysis that is all that can be said about the aims of education.

Criticism that is levelled at him for not giving a clear account of what the objective, intrinsic aims of education actually might be (White 1982: 4), or for linking the understanding of aims to a particular analysis of education (Wringe 1988: 24) misfires. The lack of a substantive account of aims, as White himself makes clear, is a result of Peters' approach to conceptual analysis (Peters *et al.* 1965: 6), and if this style of philosophy of education is what he is using, then, unless it is used in some contradictory way, the lack of any substantive argument is to be perceived as a necessary result of using this methodology. The linking of aims to education is in part at least a result of wanting to clear ground and remain at the formal level of conceptual analysis, so again, given the methodology that Peters identifies, this follows naturally from the approach he takes as read to the philosophy of education.

Clearly, what is required is another approach to philosophy of education, which could possibly generate a different approach to understanding the aims of education. It is to this which I now turn.

An alternative philosophy of education

Following Peters' approach I now wish to turn to questions of meaning – in particular, the way in which a philosopher might identify the meaning of a term like 'aims'. As I have just shown, Peters' approach is to search for essential and normative criteria that will identify central, essential meanings of the term under consideration, even if that term appears on the surface at least to be closely tied to particular social contexts.

Such an approach to meaning bears significant similarities to that which Wittgenstein criticised and which, in a somewhat different form, he once held. During the early period of his life Wittgenstein argued for a rigorous form of essentialism, Formal Semantics (see Gilroy 1996: 100ff.). Briefly, he can be seen as developing Frege's movement away from traditional Ideational theories of meaning towards one that properly takes account of the way in which he believed language to be 'governed by logical grammar – by logical syntax' (Wittgenstein 1921, section 3.325). His theory of meaning was dualistic at this time, in that the meanings of ordinary language were the result of a truth-functional analysis of a logically pure 'language' which was composed of 'elementary propositions' (ibid.: section 5.3). In this way an infinite regress of analysis of analysis, comparable to the problems that Plato identified in his Third Man argument with his theory of Forms (see Gilroy 1996: 21), is avoided, in that analysis of ordinary language actually ends when it hits the bedrock of elementary propositions. In this way the results of such an analysis produce conclusions about meaning which benefit from the purity of formal logic, although at considerable cost, in that, although meaning is thus located in the formal area of elementary propositions, Wittgenstein recognises that he is unable to give a single example of such a proposition, as to do so would introduce the substantive and messy realm of actual language use.

Peters, of course, is not directly involved with the modern empiricist, metaphysical underpinnings of such a theory, nor for that matter with Formal Semantics *per se*. However, Peters' meaning theory is clearly part of a general attempt to analyse actual use in order to identify criteria which can then act as formal reference points to support claims about the essential meaning of the terms analysed. It is in this sense that I would argue that such a conception of meaning is dualistic, in that on the one hand it accepts that there exists ordinary use and on the other claims the need for formal criteria which are supposed to govern such use so as to give language its 'correct' meaning. Similarly, the regress of analysis identified earlier is supposedly halted by means of the transcendental argument, where analysis in effect meets the bedrock of rationality.

Given this similarity, then it should come as no surprise that the arguments that Wittgenstein came to use against his account of meaning based on Formal Semantics should apply with equal force to Peters' account of meaning. The most important point of change is the recognition that attempts to analyse meaning so as to reach some sort of essence of meaning is radically to misunderstand both the nature of philosophy in general and meaning theory in particular. The approach to philosophy that Wittgenstein came to develop 'undercuts a very long philosophical tradition . . . accepted . . . by those analytical philosophers who aim only at stating precisely the necessary and sufficient conditions for the application of some linguistic expression' (Pitcher 1964: 163) and is in effect a natural development of the approach first identified by Frege.

Frege, among other advances, recognised that meaning was not located in individual words, arguing that philosophers should instead consider the 'entire declarative sentence' (Frege 1892: 214). This holism of meaning is then taken further by Wittgenstein, who first located meaning within a system of propositions (Wittgenstein 1921: section 2.0123), as outlined above, then broadened his approach so as to locate meaning within the use of language in social situations. This extreme holistic approach to meaning has a number of significant results, in particular the recognition that philosophy should proceed by accepting that the phenomenon of language is not one where essences of meaning usually exist, but is instead a functional tool for communication where the absence of 'strict meaning . . . is not a defect', but rather just the way things happen to be (Wittgenstein 1933: 27). It follows that a search for essences of meaning, however that search proceeds, is usually inappropriate in that meaning is rarely based upon such essences.

What replaces his earlier logical, analytical search for meaning is instead a more sociological conception of meaning. With such a conception of philosophy comes a description of the multifarious ways in which language is in fact used and an acceptance of meaning's 'indefiniteness' (Wittgenstein 1953: 227e). Such an approach to meaning also requires that the notion of criteria for meaning be recognised, not as providing some form of logical necessity for the meaning of a term to be recognised, but rather as what might be termed a social necessity. What is meant by such necessity is that meanings are understood and their certainty is 'comfortable . . . not still struggling' (Wittgenstein 1949: 46e, section 357). Another way of putting this important point is that the infinite regress of analysis is halted, not by an appeal to some sort of logical bedrock, nor by means of the logical imperatives buried in a conception of rationality identified through some sort of transcendental deduction, but instead by the simple claim that meaning can be identified by recognising that the 'use of a word *in practice* is its meaning' (Wittgenstein 1933: 69). That is, understanding meaning ends at a point when one just points to the way the term under consideration functions in practice. For this reason such an account of meaning is best typified as a Functional one.

This all too brief account of meaning and its accompanying approach to philosophy[2] has an important impact upon Peters' account of aims. In the light of what has been presented here Peters can be seen as attempting to identify the essence of the meaning of 'aims of education' by identifying criteria for 'education'. In doing so he is doubly at fault. First, he is using a particular conception of philosophy which is flawed, in that it does not recognise that linguistic or conceptual analysis has serious difficulties which relate to its dualistic conception of meaning. Second, the analysis itself produces an artificial conception, in that apparently only one use of 'aims' is to be accepted as 'central', even though at the same time the existence of a variety of uses is accepted. As Peters himself once wrote: 'The meaning of a word is inseparable from the variety of contexts in which it is used. To treat one property as "essential" . . . would be to make one context a standard for all contexts' (Benn and Peters 1959: 58).

It follows that philosophical inquiry into meaning is now to be seen as a substantive, functional inquiry into language use in appropriate and varied social contexts, not a formal, conceptual analysis of individual concepts. This change in the nature of philosophical inquiry is of particular relevance to a subject like philosophy of education, which by its very nature deals with a social phenomenon, education.

If we now return to the two questions which Peters claims need to be answered when dealing with the aims of education, it should be seen that in passing over the functional approach to philosophy he is doubly at fault in his treatment of them. First, by concentrating exclusively on the first question ('What do you mean by the aims of education?'), he has assumed that his understanding of meaning is sound, whereas, as I have argued above, that is an aspect of his work which is seriously flawed. Second, in ignoring the second question ('How do you know?'), he leaves unanswered the ambiguity inherent in his phrasing of the question. If he is asking, 'How do we know what we mean by the aims of education?' then he is plunged deep into meaning theory, an area that he avoids. If he means 'How do we know what are the aims of education?' then his work can in fact be seen as providing an answer to that question, even though he says that he will not answer it, in that he claims that an analysis of education provides an answer to the question of its aims.

This is to say no more than Peters' conception of the philosophy of education is seriously flawed. How then would the alternative Functional philosophy of education treat the topic of the aims of education?

A functional approach to the aims of education

As has already been shown, such an approach centres upon the view that the meanings of terms are in most cases dependent upon the social contexts within which they function. In a sense then it would be possible to extend Gallie's arguments to show that all concepts would then be contestable. However, as education is by definition a social activity, the concepts that cluster around our use of educational terms are inherently and inevitably social, and so a philosophy of education should be expected to concentrate on understanding the social context within which education operates. It is this movement away from conceptual analysis towards functional analysis which should therefore typify this new approach to understanding the aims of education.

To call it 'new' is to ignore the fact that others have for some time made use of its insights and approach to the philosophy of education. For example, I have already remarked that Peters initially seemed to accept that a functional approach to philosophy was an acceptable one, when he warned that 'it is idle . . . to insist that one way of using . . . words alone is correct' (Benn and Peters 1959: 14), although by the time he gave his inaugural lecture he appears to have rejected this approach, insisting instead upon the need to search for essential criteria of meaning which represent 'impersonal standards' against which use can be judged (Peters 1963: 104). Another example of this early use of Functionalism in the philosophy of education would be Sockett, who argues that understanding our educational aims and objectives requires a 'fuller specification of the possible contexts in which these notions are used' (Sockett 1972: 31). Furthermore, because language is inevitably imprecise, then 'statements of aim will certainly be imprecise and indeterminate' (ibid.: 47), linked as they are to the particular rule-governed contexts within which aims operate: that is, provided teachers are in fact autonomous, 'particular teachers in particular schools' (ibid.: 49).

In a similar vein Wringe has argued that arguments about educational aims 'must necessarily involve more fundamental value judgements' (Wringe 1988: 17) and, by implication at least, this would appear to support a Functionalist approach to the topic. Indeed, his book proceeds by examining a whole series of different approaches which depend upon various evaluative assumptions, with the acceptance that because there can be no one universally accepted value system then any conclusion about the specific aim of education is 'necessarily contentious' (ibid.: 21). In the same way, Kelly's acceptance of the value-driven nature of discussion of the aims of education (Kelly 1989: 8) leads him to argue for what he identifies as a process account of the curriculum which is consistent with the Functionalist approach to the philosophy of aims elaborated above.

At this point I am merely indicating that others have made use of aspects of a Functionalist philosophy of education, based upon a Wittgensteinian account of meaning, to inform their approach to explicating what is to be understood by the aims of education. A more substantial account is that provided by White, and it is to this I will now turn.

White explicitly rejects the conceptual analysist's approach to the topic in favour of a 'practical' one (White 1982: 6). The important point to note in his early work is that he does not make use of the then dominant form of philosophy of education's transcendental deduction to support his conclusion that the main aim of education is to create morally autonomous persons, but rather accepts that he is appealing to 'fundamental attitudes about human life' which he believes are shared by all (ibid.: 129). This is both a strength and weakness in his argument, in that he avoids the crippling deficiencies of transcendental approaches to philosophy, but replaces them with the possibility that there could be counter-examples to his notion about what constitute fundamental attitudes to personhood. My own experience of an Asian society would therefore be relevant here in showing that for some members of that society a fundamental attitude to human life would place individual autonomy a distant third, as suggested by Singapore's popular slogan, 'Nation, then Family, then Self', founded as it is upon a Confucian value system.

Presumably it is this problem that led him to alter significantly the account in his subsequent publication. Here he appears to accept that not all societies necessarily support the kind of autonomy he argues for, qualifying his argument for autonomy with the phrase 'in an autonomy-supporting society' (White 1990: 105). In this way he allows for the functional approach to the social concept of aims: in recognising that different societies have a different value system from his own he is accepting the point that some societies do not see autonomy to be an aim whose achievement would necessarily produce well-being. His conclusions are therefore culture specific, as they must be if they are based on a Functionalist approach to the philosophy of education.

Conclusion

It would be a mistake to see the Functionalist approach to understanding the aims of education as sweeping all before it in the field of philosophy of education. Nor should one expect this to be the case, given Kuhn's explanation of paradigm shifts, conversions and the ways in which dominant and revolutionary communities of thinkers compete with one another. This said, it is still something of a surprise to find what appears to be a throwback to the Peters approach to the topic in Kazepides' discussion of educational aims.

Kazepides begins with what appears to be a straightforwardly Functional view of philosophy of education. He accepts that meaning questions are paramount and that 'the meaning of many words varies with different contexts' (Kazepides 1989: 51), but then continues by accepting a Peters-style approach to understanding education based on identifying criteria which, presumably, will capture the 'principles . . . immanent' in the subjects we teach (ibid.: 56). This traditional view of philosophy of education is especially well caught in a footnote where he criticises White's approach to the topic as, among other things, producing a 'programmatic definition of education' (ibid.: footnote 1, p. 58) which is, of course, for a Functionalist a strength of White's approach, not a weakness. Thus, when Kazepides castigates White for abandoning analyses, he has quite failed to see that White is no longer concerned with using what he perceives as an irrelevant approach to the philosophy of education, the traditional practitioners of which he politely dismisses as being 'of a more purely theoretical and specifically of a more lexicographical, turn of mind' (White 1982: 6).

It is a pity that White does not more directly address the nature of the form of philosophy of education of which he is making use. A more recent treatment of the subject, Winch's, also does not explicitly identify the Functionalist approach to the philosophy of education which appears to inform his arguments. However, talk of the way in which educational aims are dependent upon those values which a society takes as important (Winch 1996a: 35) is clearly within the Functionalist approach to philosophy of education, as is his view that 'the choice of aims is a political matter to be determined in accordance with a society's priorities' (Winch 1996b: 55).

Thus a Functionalist approach to the philosophy of education, based upon a Wittgensteinian approach to understanding meaning, leads to a quite different account of how to understand the aims of education. There is a soft determinism in inquiry, as the mode of investigation dictates what is to be investigated, how it is to be investigated and what is to count as a satisfactory investigation. The way in which philosophical discussion about the aims of education has proceeded represents an exemplar of this determinism. In this way the pathology of the arguments concerning the aims of education have been located firmly in the traditionalist's approach to the philosophy of education, and in particular in their meaning theory. In proposing a Functionalist cure to the problems which infect the traditional approach to philosophy of education, then, my argument has been that similar problems which infect the traditionalist's approach to understanding the aims of education might also be resolved, not least the apparent vacuity of a formal, asocial, analysis to a substantive, socially bound practice.

Notes

1 And have – see Gilroy 1982.
2 I have developed it at length elsewhere – see Gilroy 1996; ch. 8, *passim*.

References

Benn, S. I. and Peters, R. S. (1959) *Social Principles and the Democratic State*, London: Allen & Unwin.

Earwaker, J. (1973) 'R. S. Peters – the concept of education', *Proceedings of the Philosophy of Education Society of Great Britain* 4: 21–44.

Frege, G. (1892) 'Sense and reference', *Vierteljahrschrift fur wissenschaftliche Philosophie* 41; reprinted in *The Philosophical Review* 62(3) (May 1948): 207–30, M. Black (trans.).

Gallie, W. B. (1956) 'Essentially contested concepts', *Proceedings of the Aristotelian Society* 61: 167–98.

Gilroy, D. P. (1982) 'The revolutions in English philosophy and philosophy of education', *Educational Analysis* 4(1): 75–91.

——(1996) *Meaning without Words: Philosophy and Non-verbal Communication*, Aldershot: Avebury.

Hirst, P. H. and Peters, R. S. (1970) *The Logic of Education*, London: Routledge & Kegan Paul.

Kazepides, T. (1989) 'On educational aims, curriculum objectives and the preparation of teachers', *Journal of Philosophy of Education* 23(1): 51–5.

Kelly, A. V. (1989) *The Curriculum: Theory and Practice*, London: Chapman.

Peters, R. S. (1963) *Education as Initiation*, London: Harrap; reprinted in R. D. Archambault (ed.) *Philosophical Analysis and Education*, London: Routledge & Kegan Paul, 1965, pp. 87–111.

——(1966a) 'The philosophy of education', in J. W. Tibble (ed.) *The Study of Education*, London: Routledge & Kegan Paul, pp.1–23.

——(1966b) *Ethics and Education*, London: Allen & Unwin.

Peters, R. S., Woods, J. and Dray, W. H. (1965) 'Aims of education – a conceptual inquiry', in B. Crittenden (ed.) *Philosophy and Education*, pp.1–32; reprinted in R. S. Peters (ed.) *The Philosophy of Education*, Oxford: Oxford University Press, 1973, pp.11–29.

Pitcher, G. (1964) *The Philosophy of Wittgenstein*, Englewood Cliffs, NJ: Prentice-Hall.

Sockett, H. (1972) 'Curriculum aims and objectives: taking a means to an end', *Proceedings of the Philosophy of Education Society of Great Britain*, 6(1): 30–61.

White, J. (1982) *The Aims of Education Restated*, London: Routledge & Kegan Paul.

——(1990) *Education and the Good Life: Beyond the National Curriculum*, London: Kegan Paul.

Whitehead, A. N. (1932) *The Aims of Education and Other Essays*, London: Benn.

Winch, C. (1996a) 'The aims of education revisited', *Journal of Philosophy of Education* 30(1): 33–44.

——(1996b) 'Constructing worthwhile curricula', *Journal of Philosophy of Education* 30(1): 45–6.

Wittgenstein, L. (1921) *Tractatus Logico-Philosophicus*, London: Routledge & Kegan Paul; D. F. Pears and B. F. McGuines (trans).

——(1933) *The Blue and Brown Books*, Oxford: Blackwell, 1958.

——(1949) *On Certainty,* G. E. M. Anscombe and G. H. von Wright (eds), D. Paul and G.

E. M. Anscombe (trans.), 1969, Oxford: Blackwell, 1974.
——(1953) *Philosophical Investigations*, Oxford: Blackwell; G. E. M. Anscombe (trans.).
Wringe, C. (1988) *Understanding Educational Aims*, London: Unwin.

4

EDUCATION WITHOUT AIMS?

Paul Standish

I

A standard analysis of the aims of education might proceed by offering three possible areas for their location: first, to serve the needs of society; second, to pass on and develop those ways of knowing and understanding which are the common heritage; third, to help individual learners to develop, either through a process of unfolding from within or through an authentic creation of themselves.

Within these parameters, though not entirely co-extensive with these categories, ideas of progressivism (child-centred education) and liberal education can be differentiated. Most obviously progressivism is concerned with the third aim, with the development of the learner. The liberal position seems to align itself with the second aim, of the passing on of ways of knowing and understanding. These are slippery terms, however. The second and third aims, and thus the progressivist position, are liberal in that they are concerned in some sense with the freeing of the learner; both reject an education which is primarily instrumental. While in America John Dewey is thought of as a liberal,[1] in the UK he has been seen as a key figure in the growth of progressivism which the liberal education of R. S. Peters, P. H. Hirst and R. F. Dearden sought to criticise and oppose. It is in this latter sense of liberal education that the term is used in the present discussion. Thus the conception of freedom and how it is achieved are crucial points of difference between these positions.

If the first aim – of serving the needs of society – is not concerned with freedom in the same way, who might support it? The short answer is perhaps most people, including many employed in education. It is likely to

35

be favoured by those who call for a rejection of progressivism and a return to traditional education. This is commonly characterised in terms of formal methods of instruction and an authoritarian and didactic pedagogy, with the belief that education is primarily concerned with the passing on of facts and skills. When pressed about the substance of what is to be learned, advocates of this 'traditional' education may well be in favour of such subjects as business studies, information technology, enterprise skills, and whatever else is imagined to be conducive to the strengthening of industrial competitiveness. This may be traditional insofar as it points to certain instructional *methods*; the irony of the term in other respects hardly needs pointing up.

In contrast, liberal education is not primarily concerned with method, its quarrel with progressivism being concerned rather with questions of *content*, and with progressivism's failure adequately to address these questions. The fact that the modern restatement of liberal education in the 1960s is a renewal of an ancient idea underlines the strength of the traditions on which it draws. It is unfortunate that this has led to a tendency to call liberal education 'traditional education', leading to inevitable confusion with the more common employment of this phrase sketched above. It scarcely needs pointing out, of course, that there are robust traditions of progressivism as well.

A liberal education is primarily concerned with initiation into those ways of knowing and understanding which are the common heritage. It is not clear, however, that this aim is at odds with the third aim, the idea that the purpose of education is the development of the learner. For it might be held that the individual is indeed best developed precisely by being initiated into that common heritage, and, more strongly, that not to be so initiated is a kind of privation. Such thinking is particularly relevant to P. H. Hirst's forms of knowledge thesis: there are a number of distinct forms of knowledge, and a liberal education should encompass an introduction to each one of these; a person who has not been introduced to any one of these forms will be deprived of the ability to look at and to understand the world in that way, ultimately with effects on that person's practical reason. Such a limitation is a partial denial of freedom. What is rejected is the idea that a person can come upon such forms of knowledge by chance or by themselves: such possibilities of understanding are not matters of unfolding or development *from within* nor are they effected through a process of discovery in a kind of raw confrontation with the world.

At this point it is appropriate to register an important divergence between the ancient conception of liberal education and its restatement in the 1960s. In the classical ideal the learner is led towards the contemplation of truth. The metaphor of sight, of true vision, itself illuminates the kind of intimation of reality with which Plato is concerned. In the modern conception, in contrast, the emphasis is rather on the powers of reasoning which each of the forms of knowledge introduces to the learner. If the classical liberal education frees the learner by dispelling illusion and enabling the contemplation of objects of truth and goodness, the modern version empowers the learner by providing the ability to reason effectively across that range of modes of thought which have been passed down to us, and which can inform our rational agency. That this is the case is brought out especially by the preoccupation within the modern version with rational autonomy. In some respects this development was in keeping with formalistic tendencies in postwar British philosophy which shaped the approach of Peters, Hirst and Dearden, though in other respects it derives more obviously from Immanuel Kant. In his celebrated essay 'Autonomy and education', Dearden attributes the philosophical currency of the concept to Kant and succinctly expresses what is central to it: 'A man was autonomous, on Kant's view, if in his actions he bound himself by moral laws legislated by his own reason, as opposed to being governed by his inclinations' (Dearden *et al.* 1972: 58). The formalism of this reasoning contrasts with the substantive nature of the contemplation required by Plato's theory of the Forms. Not surprisingly, the metaphysical realism of this did not seem to be available or desirable to the modern philosopher of education, and so rational autonomy, which in principle leaves matters of substance as open questions, came very much to the fore.

A significant influence in this development is perhaps Peters' account of worthwhile activities (Peters 1966: 144–66). Peters rightly challenges instrumental conceptions of education on the grounds of their deferral of the question of justification. The absurdity of the merry-go-round of instru-mentalism suggests that at some point there must be a stop, a point at which something will be of value in itself. In other words, at some point we must be able to identify what is worthwhile in itself. Peters considers various possibilities, taking as relatively uncontroversial the notion of pleasure. He goes through a series of stages beginning with the pleasures of the flesh – of eating, drinking and sex. These, it is to be emphasised, are not mere animal satisfactions but possible occasions for the exercise of consider-able skill and style. They are, however, limited by the natural capacities and appetites of the body. Greater potential for enjoyment may perhaps be found in sports, games and similar pastimes. There the artificial object of the game enables the exercise and display of considerable know-how and the possibility for this to be developed and refined. Such pleasures extend to a delight in knowing about the game and in the appreciation of the prowess of others. They are nevertheless limited in terms of the range of their signif-icance, in terms of the bearing they have on the rest of a person's life and how far they enhance understanding of the world.

In the case of theoretical activities – the disinterested study of academic subjects – the limitations of these other sources of pleasure are not found. Theoretical activities do not depend on cyclical appetites but offer unlimited scope for the pursuit of interests, satisfaction being the greater the more one progresses; they are not competitive – noone has to lose and there is no shortage of the thing which is pursued; they have a rich bearing on one's life as a whole and illuminate the fields of one's action. At a slightly different level they help to answer the question which Peters introduced at the start: 'Why do *this* rather than *that?*' They give a clearer grasp of the different alternatives which are available, some of which would not be intelligible outside the frames of reference which they themselves provide, and, developing the ability to reason, they assist in the weighing up of those different alternatives. Behind this there is also the classical argument to the effect that human beings should develop that capacity which distinguishes them from other animals, which is reason. Socrates' remark that the unexamined life is not worth living stresses that human beings must ask questions about their own lives; not to do this is to fail to be fully human. Asking the question, of course, 'Why do *this* rather than *that?*' already shows some commitment to rationality.

The direction of the argument here is towards the view that rational autonomy is valuable as an end and not just as a means: it is central to the good life. The position of Peters, Hirst and Dearden on this point builds on the so-called transcendental or self-referential argument advanced above. But it is filled out in various ways. One will opt for the kinds of work and leisure pursuits which are rich in opportunities for the exercise of one's judgement. One could not rationally opt for a life in which it did not play a major part. One could not opt to give up one's freedom and to be a happy slave. It is perhaps here that we reach the apotheosis of the formalistic tendencies of modern liberal education, and here that we should begin to acknowledge some of the points of divergence and criticism.

Anyone surveying the literature on liberal education over the last two decades will be struck by the prominence which autonomy has acquired. The argument has been developed and complicated. Thus, rational autonomy may be highly valued but ultimately seen as a means rather than an end: having become rationally autonomous, one can then (rationally) give this up to become the happy slave. It may be seen in weak and strong guises, as requiring the exercise of autonomy within established practices, on the one hand, and as requiring the questioning of those practices themselves, on the other. Greater sensitivity to cultural difference has led to the claim that personal autonomy is not universally valuable, as there are societies in which there are valuable social institutions which are not autonomy-supporting. Numerous aspects of autonomy have been discussed since the time of Dearden's essay.

A move away from the formalism of the principle of rational autonomy is made where the possibility of its qualified subordination to a regime of ends is entertained. An important contribution to the development of this aspect of liberal education has been made by John White's writings on well-being, the outcome of a concern to give some substance to the idea of the good. This is found in the idea of informed desire-satisfaction, based on 'empirical features of our make-up, namely our desires and their satisfaction. It sees human beings as animals of a certain sort, endowed with certain innate desires, and their well-being as constituted by the fulfilment of desires based on these' (White 1990: 32). There is a clear resonance here with prevalent attitudes in favour of a naturalistic ethics.

In his recent inaugural lecture White has supplemented this with a humanistic concern for some kind of cosmic framework. Here it is acknowledged that '[a]s well as providing the ultimate framework, nature, globally or in its particular manifestations, can also be the object of many of our values' (White 1995: 9). These include: pleasures of the senses deriving from the natural world; attachment to the world as our dwelling place, in which the continuity of natural and social frameworks is realised; aesthetic delight in natural beauty; the sense of sublimity caused by nature in its more grand and terrifying aspects; wonder, which stops short of answers, at the very existence of the world; finally, respect for the world and concern with its conservation. Even for the non-religious person, White suggests, awe at natural phenomena has something of the quality of religious emotion. Nevertheless, the values identified here remain within the ambit of desire-dependent conceptions of the good and avoid what White finds to be the implausible underpinning of the Platonic and Christian metaphysics.

White ends his lecture with a plea for philosophy of education to take on the role of illuminating a non-religious cosmic framework in the education 'of *all* our children'. The concern with well-being and with the cosmic framework has taken us away from the centrality of rational autonomy, but it is worth registering the way that that aim may not be fully sensitive to the needs of *all* our children. It seems less convincing for those who are of lesser intelligence, in that the scope for its exercise in their lives is likely to be duly restricted. This does not, of course, necessarily undermine it as a principle. It does, however, perhaps remind us that those who advocate it, who are likely to be intelligent and rationally autonomous people, may lose sight of the fact that it is a peculiarly attractive principle *from their point of view*, one which they are particularly well disposed to enjoy and to value. Conversely, they may fail to see types of the good life which are not characterised by the principle. In this respect White's more substantive conception of human flourishing has rather more in its favour.

This attractiveness also helps to explain the way rational autonomy has come to be central to the *tacit* assumptions of educated people about the point of education. Such assumptions are in certain respects characteristic of the modern age – at least, it might be added, of what such people imagine their lives to be like, and at least, it might be further added, where such people are in work. Because it relates to these tacit assumptions and because most people who write about education are educated people, argument tends to be skewed in its favour. There is also, of course, the self-referential point: if one is discussing this issue one must value rational autonomy. Taking part (seriously and sincerely) in the argument demonstrates precisely this.

A challenge to the kind of self-perpetuating language which supports autonomy, and to the conception of the good life which seems to inform it, has been made under the banner of authenticity. This is, no doubt, an overworked term, but it is worth distinguishing divergent viewpoints which are associated with it. In its more crude versions authenticity can involve a direction towards the discovery of one's real nature; it can, alternatively, be shaped by a principle of self-creation. Such accounts align most obviously with the third aim above – of personal development. What is of most interest here, however, is the extent to which arguments from authenticity invite a re-appraisal of the terms in which the aims are expressed. They call into question the nature of the relation to the cultural heritage and also the epistemological presuppositions upon which an initiation into the forms of knowledge is based. Some accounts of authenticity then begin directly to question the way of reasoning behind the valuing of autonomy, pointing to its lack of sensitiv-ity to context and its failure adequately to recognise the nature of freedom and responsibility. As David Cooper puts it, 'When yoked to critical rational-ity, the concept has no place for those concerns where the giving and criticiz-ing of reasons is only modestly engaged, or for the importance, in the case of some individual convictions, of not being bowled over by judgements on the weight of evidence' (Cooper 1983: 25).

The liberal aims which have been entertained here have given voice to that critical rationality. It has worked its way through hierarchies of worth in a process of refinement and progressive clarity and precision. As Cooper's arguments may suggest, there is an internal relation between the discursive form in which the arguments are expressed and the values which are espoused – between clarity and enlightenment, it might be supposed. Peters' argument concerning self-referentiality recognises something impor-tant in recognising something of this. That relation, nevertheless, may be a limitation.

II

But must there be aims? The assumption that there must be accords with the principles of rational planning which in many respects characterise the modern world. The assumption that there must be invests in advance in that discursive form. Thus there are indeed difficulties in arguing against this, in that in argument one is almost bound to rely on those same princi-ples of rationality which inform the practice in question. When education is undertaken on a large, systematic scale – which is, of course, likely to be the case in the late twentieth century – scepticism about the giving of aims may seem like a kind of political irresponsibility. Surely there must be aims. And should these not be explicit?

Yet that large systematic scale makes it reasonable to question how far the presumption in favour of rational planning has been influenced by a sort of scientism or technicism. Scientism is familiar enough in the tendency to treat all manner of things as if they were the appropriate objects of empirical and systematic investigation. The optimism which was generated about making curriculum planning into a science has been an example of this; research into school effectiveness may be a more recent manifestation of this, symptomatic as this is of the more pervasive preoccupation with performativity. Technicism is similarly evident in the common assumption that all difficulties are in principle to be overcome by a technical solution. The vogue for skills and competences in education, and the tendency to reduce all learning to these terms, has borne witness to this.

At a more grammatical level, furthermore, it is worth instancing examples of valued practice where the aims are inexplicit or where there are no aims – or perhaps where talk of aims seems inappropriate. Indeed some of the most important aspects of people's lives – their intimate relationships, for example – seem to be characterised in this way. Within such practices there may be a great many smaller-scale practices in which aims can more or less be identified. But these are likely to be understood in the light of something which cannot be formulated in any tidy way and which would be inappropriately thought of in terms of aims. To ask for the aims of education may be like asking for the aims of a town. What, for example, are the aims of Aberdeen? The grammatical oddness here suggests that there may not be much sense in the question. The critic will respond that there are indeed aims of Aberdeen and these have been made quite explicitly by the members of the town's council, who have worked earnestly to devise their mission statement. A mission statement of this sort may or may not be desirable but it is clear that, although this may be an appropriate expression of the political intentions of a dominant faction, this hardly warrants their attribution to the town! While a town incorporates a diverse range of purposeful practices, it is not clear that aims of an over-arching kind can be given. The multiple smaller-scale projects which go to make up the life of the town will include in their number those where things do need to be planned out, sometimes systematically. But these will have their sense in the light of that larger purposiveness. Taking the aims of the town councillors as an expression of the aims of the town will be a kind of inappropriate metonymy prejudiced in favour of a particular group. The statement of aims may purport to be a description derived from a kind of analysis, apparently revealing the essence of the town or its foundations. It may be an expression of attitude or intent, designed to provide a steady orientation for policy. In both cases it seems to offer a security. But if such statements of aims are indeed ungrammatical or prejudicial, this may be an unwarranted security, one which is apt to distort our practices. It is not difficult to imagine a dystopia in which everything about the town *is* determined by the aims (and the surveillance) laid down by its governing body. This would be an Orwellian distortion of what we commonly think of and value as the town.

By analogy, the suspicion which emerges is that stating the aims of education may lead to a kind of stifling. A seemingly logical progression leads towards systems of aims and objectives and to a preoccupation with performativity which dominates the curriculum. It is not difficult to imagine the dystopia which this suggests. But surely this is to be too quick and too dismissive. It may be edifying to consider John Dewey's more balanced comments here. Over-arching or supposedly ultimate aims are to be viewed with caution, as these may exert a limitation on the 'freeing activity' which education should incorporate. He warns against the imposition of aims from outside, where the existing conditions are not taken as the starting point from which the aim is conceived:

> The vice of externally imposed ends has deep roots. Teachers receive them from superior authorities; these authorities accept them from what is current in the community. The teachers impose them upon children. As a first consequence, the intelligence of the children is not free; it is confined to receiving the aims laid down from above. Too rarely is the individual teacher so free from the dictation of authoritative supervisor, textbook on methods, prescribed course of study, etc., that he can let his mind come to close quarters with the pupil's mind and the subject matter. This distrust of the teacher's experience is then reflected in lack of confidence in the responses of pupils. The latter receive their aims through a double or treble external imposition, and are constantly confused by conflict between the aims which are natural to their own experience at the time and those in which they are taught to acquiesce.
>
> (Dewey 1916: 108–9)

Persons, parents and teachers have aims, Dewey reminds us, not an abstract idea like education. In contrast to the above, aims are to be understood first in terms of the purposiveness of human activity, as internally related to particular activities. Truly general aims, if such there are to be, should broaden the outlook, enabling a wider and more flexible observation of means and exposing the endless connections of particular activities: teaching and learning should lead indefinitely into other things. As a particular action will be compatible with a number of general ends, it may be that the more general ends we have the better. Just as a scene can profitably be surveyed from different mountain tops, so these will provide varied perspectives on our field of activity.

Dewey's emphasis on the need for sensitivity to context, to variety and to individual potential is established in part through a contrast with the rigidity of the kind of education Plato envisages in *The Republic*:

> Plato's starting point is that the organization of society depends ultimately upon knowledge of the end of existence. If we do not know its end, we shall be at the mercy of accident and caprice. Unless we know the end, the good, we shall have no criterion for rationally deciding what the possibilities are which should be promoted, nor how social arrangements are to be ordered.
>
> (Ibid.: 88)

Dewey criticises Plato's 'lumping together of individuals and their original powers into a few sharply marked-off classes' because the progress of knowledge has taught us that these are indefinitely varied and numerous (ibid.: 90). One way to put this, which maintains the down-to-earth tone, might be that Dewey is opposing this kind of top-down setting of aims in favour of a bottom-up approach arising from the learner's activities themselves.

Dewey is speaking of *The Republic* above all, and it is clear that this kind of interpretation is well enough established. If we attend to details of this work and to some of the dialogues, however, it is a different picture which emerges. As a first step in appreciating this we might consider the kind of voice and form in which Plato's ideas are expressed. Consider, first, the following words from *The Symposium*. These concern the way a man's love for beautiful things can be sublimated into a love of beauty and of goodness in itself:

> The man who has been guided thus far in the mysteries of love, and who has directed his thoughts towards examples of beauty in due and orderly succession, will suddenly have revealed to him as he approaches the end of his initiation a beauty whose nature is marvellous indeed, the final goal, Socrates, of all his previous efforts. This beauty is first of all eternal; it neither comes into being nor passes away, neither waxes nor wanes; next, it is not beautiful in part and ugly in part, nor beautiful at one time and ugly at another, nor beautiful in this relation and ugly in that, nor beautiful here and ugly there, as varying according to its beholders; nor again will this beauty appear to him like the beauty of a face or hands or anything else corporeal, or like the beauty of a thought or a science, or like beauty which has its seat in something other than itself, be it a living thing or the earth or the sky or anything else whatever; he will see it as absolute, existing alone with itself, unique,

eternal, and all other beautiful things as partaking of it, yet in such a manner that, while they come into being and pass away, it neither undergoes any increase or diminution nor suffers any change.

(Plato 1951: 93–4)

This then is the good which Dewey sees Plato as identifying as the starting point for the organisation of society. Of course, goals are spoken of here, and are these not of the order of aims and objectives, approached by way of a path of learning with 'due and orderly succession'? Yet it is clear that the tone of these words is different from that of Dewey's remarks on Plato and the nature of this warrants some examination. Imagine the trite absurdity of setting this erotic development down in terms of aims and objectives!

The idea of the good here is approached not by explicit statement or straightforward exposition but through a kind of lyrical intimation. The starting point of the passage finds the learner already partially initiated into the mysteries of love and that towards which attention is gradually to be directed is marvellous indeed. The nature of this marvel is pursued, in the long second sentence, through a cumulative series of negatives. The enigmatic and climactic 'absolute, existing alone with itself, unique, eternal', the most direct description of the good, then yields again to the negatives of the final phrases. The good is unstatable other than in these opaque terms; it is not to be approached directly. It requires this kind of difficult ascent; any premature or over-hasty identification would prove illusory. And the discursive form bears this out. This is not an essay by Plato. The speaker is Socrates but he is reporting the words of Diotima, the woman from Mantinea with whom he has previously discussed these matters. These might well be taken to be thoughts which Socrates would espouse, and Socrates himself might but be taken to epitomise one who has undertaken this type of ascent. But his position is subtly effaced: here, as elsewhere when love and the fate of the soul are being considered, Plato adopts the device of reported speech. This indirectness complicates the relation of the reader and of Socrates to what is being said, and indicates that what is to be understood here requires subtle intimation. Overt expression, it seems to be implied, would miss the point; it would distort the good which is the object of this erotic perfectionist longing, and perhaps dull the energy with which that longing is alive.

It is to be noted also that Diotima, unlike the other characters in the dialogue, is thought to have been Plato's invention. This intrusion of the fictional at a stage where the dialogue builds to its most serious point further suggests the need for an evocative indirectness, a recourse to the literary where the limitations of a more straightforward discursive are most acutely evident. Of course, Plato's thoughts are almost always hidden in the form of dialogue. It might be objected that *The Republic* is nevertheless far more clearly didactic; certainly it does not have the humour and vitality found here. But there also the deepest and most important thoughts seem to take a literary turn. Consider Iris Murdoch's words on the myth of the Cave:

> In the Cave myth the Theory of the Forms is presented as a pilgrimage where different realities or thought-objects exist for individual thinkers at different levels, appearing at lower levels as shadows cast by objects at the next higher level: an endlessly instructive image. The pilgrimage is inspired by intimations of realities which lie just beyond what can be easily seen.
>
> (Murdoch 1992: 399)

This 'endlessly instructive image' makes possible a thinking of what is not present, not overtly statable and not immediately available: these features are, it would seem, not just contingently related to the highest objects but essential to their reality; necessary also if learning is to avoid bedazzlement. This is an appeal to experience which points to the ways in which '[we] learn of perfection and imperfection through our ability to understand what we see as an image or shadow of something better which we cannot yet see' (ibid.: 405). In contrast to the binary opposition of the true and the false, this image and the kind of erotic progression which radiates through *The Symposium* admit the possibility of degrees of reality. Our understanding of the world is partial and veiled, our experience can lead us towards a clearer view – in a sense which, outside philosophy, is familiar enough: 'When she said that to me, suddenly I began to see the way things really were.'

Writing about the good in this way Plato writes about what an education might be; he presents, if you like, the aims of education. But the attention is turned increasingly away from the ineffable and fixed end and towards the movement of Eros, itself intimated by the literary movement in the text. Murdoch sees Eros, understood in the sense of this energy described and shown in *The Symposium*, as picturing 'probably a greater part of what we think of as "the moral life"; that is, most of our moral problems involve an orientation of our energy and our appetites' (ibid.: 497). Our practical lives, our relations with others, our work and leisure, what we do in school, provide daily experience of possibilities of good where the immediate incorporates a glimpse of something beyond.

Sometimes, in spite of his protests that he knows nothing, Socrates can appear as the teacher who has everything taped. But sometimes he is himself like Eros, poor and needy and (hence) desirous of the good. And then he can be seen as a terrible magician, in Diotima's words, and elsewhere a gad-fly, a sting-ray and a purveyor of drugs. Will these powers be goads to action, effective stimulants, or will they anaesthetise, deaden and distract? Ambiguity here, the risk of the situation, connects internally with the arousal and direction of passionate energy, with the kind of quest with which the learner must be engaged. There cannot be a mechanical effectivity in the teaching Socrates gives, for this would dissipate that energy. Nor is the matter which Socrates has to impart so much content to be packaged and passed on: he himself remains held in its thrall.

The good is not a particular, not a thing among others. Beyond the verbal formulas – 'the final goal', 'absolute beauty' – the good is to be understood in terms of what it is not, through the manner in which one's energies can be progressively directed towards it. The evocation of this energy blends into a literary and rhetorical intimation of what cannot directly be expressed. Murdoch's thoughts are never far from the *via negativa* here and the mystical tendencies in these reflections can be traced through the rest of the discussion from which these comments are drawn, its subject the Ontological Proof of St Anselm.

Frequently in her writings Murdoch has been concerned with the kinds of thinking about the religious which might be available but which have been suppressed by the tendencies of modern reason. Thus, the Ontological Proof – that God, conceived of as supreme perfection, cannot be thought not to exist (for this would be a lack of perfection), and so if we can conceive of him, as we surely can, he must exist – is apt to be thought of as 'a charming joke', in Schopenhauer's phrase (ibid.: 392–3). If we approach this with our usual critical capacities, we are likely to be frustrated, seeing nothing more than a bad argument. To what deeper truth might such reasoning appeal? The Proof offers the possibility of a thinking of God of a different kind from our accustomed images of the Creator. Above all, God is then not to be found in the order of contingent things; his existence is necessary. God is not an object, a strange body with remarkable (supreme) attributes. Again it is by negative expressions that the matter is addressed. The sense here is elusive and this, it would seem, is part of the point. The Proof is not an argument in any conventional sense; indeed it seems defiantly unconcerned with the obvious objections. It is rather an expression of a religious conviction, a kind of a priori to the possibility of any argument, the unconditional within which things come to be seen. One might think, perhaps, that the world is already meaningful is a condition for understanding it; that unconditional good is necessary for our finding value in the world, as the sun is necessary for our seeing shadows in the Cave.

We are offered stronger words drawn from Simone Weil's *Notebooks*:

'an orientation of the soul towards something which one does not know, but whose reality one does know', and 'an effort of attention empty of all content' which then 'catches' what is certainly its object, as when we try to remember a word. Also: 'Ontological Proof is mysterious because it does not address itself to intelligence but to love.'

(Ibid., p. 401)

Anselm does not seek understanding as a basis for belief but believes in order to understand. The danger without this unconditional element in the structure of reason and reality, in Paul Tillich's view, is that a certain approach to the possibility of the question of God is closed off, that God becomes a 'strange body' which once required heteronomous subjection and which the modern judgement autonomously rejects (ibid.: 391–2).

The loss which Tillich fears is to be understood as related to the overriding of that oblique and tentative approach to the question of the good which the imagery of Eros conveys. What is the consequence of this? To identify the good as having particular features (other than through negation) entails locating it within the range of predicates attributable to objects in the world. It amounts to reducing the good to an object. The direct statement of the good, its representation, must be avoided. For in the statement one can only produce a false version of the good, and this will be a false God. It is no surprise, then, that Murdoch connects this force of the Ontological Proof with the Second Commandment: 'Thou shalt not make unto thee any graven image' (Exodus 20).

The latter part of this chapter has found that the attempt to name the good is an attempt to identify something mysterious and marvellous. This has proved unsayable, other than in opaque, negative and oblique ways. The opening expository discourse has gradually given way to a language mobilised by rhetorical devices and the tropes of literature. This is not a matter merely of style. Something like this distinction is found in Michel Despland's contrast between didactic (or scholastic) theology and literarily crafted theology, as found, for example, in Kierkegaard's writings. What the latter singularly takes away, he seems to suggest,

> is the pretence of directly communicating true opinion, such truths as may be assimilated by the acquisition and interiorization of language. In ensuring the absence of such a lesson to be learned, in disrupting the expectations of the docile reader, the writer achieves something more important than the formulation of memorable sentences; he or she prevents the establishment of the wrong relationship between writer and reader, and facilitates the sort of relationship genuine spiritual discipline requires.

(Coward and Foshay 1992: 154–5)

It is perhaps not straining the meaning of these words too much to see figured in them teaching and learning. The dogmatic and didactic teacher who supposes that they are in possession of a set of truths which are to be communicated in the neutral medium of their words is challenged by the first sentence, as, at the opening of the second, is the docile student in complicity with this. Disrupting expectations prevents the kind of tranquillised acceptance which stands in the way of deeper engagement and at the same time animates the teacher's own text. That this is a discipline says something about the development of the mind but something also about what a subject involves. The spiritual nature of the discipline here is not remote from that Platonic perfectionist progression, nor from a liberal eduction understood in those terms.

How do these words help us to see the efforts of the liberal educators to answer the question of the aims of education? In the *via negativa* and the negative theology of which Despland writes, the kind of reality which God and the good are conceived to have is an open question. These religious approaches are designed to avoid bogus metaphysical constructions and the kind of objectification where false gods thrive. The oblique and indirect literary approach is necessary. Such a literarily crafted theology does not simply debunk its positive counterpart, though it does undo the claims of outright dogmatism. It is apparent here, and in the works of Jacques Derrida to which Despland is responding, that this way of thinking serves us best when it is held not to overthrow and replace but to complicate and destabilise, to test the limits of, more affirmative expression.

A literarily crafted philosophy of education would open the possibility of a way of thinking which would unsteady the discourse of liberal education. It would do this not to jettison liberal education but to resist the limitations to which its monologism makes it subject. In doing so it would keep liberal education open to that ancient sense of the good which modern formalistic and naturalistic tendencies have subdued or obscured. Sceptical of the direct representation of the good it would locate itself in a recollection of what has been said before, in a response to texts going beyond anything which could be made fully present. Its withholding and humility, sometimes its renunciation of the claim to know, would themselves be characteristics of that intimation of the good which defies clear statement in a set of aims. This is the kind of thing in which teacher and learner might well be enthralled.

We have come a long way from the scepticism expressed by Dewey concerning aims of education. If an aim is an external end to which the means is related only instrumentally, then education in liberal terms is indeed aimless; in *The Sovereignty of Good* Murdoch speaks of virtue as pointless. But clearly this is not the only possibility and it should not stop argument. Modern philosophies of liberal education have recognised correctly that the aims of education must be seen in terms of the good. Attempts to state these have been worthy forms of resistance against limited and debased practices of education, though themselves ultimately forms of limitation. If we look beyond these enlightened statements and survey the contemporary scene, we find the kind of inflexibility against which Dewey warned. The concern with accountability, quality assurance, objectives, performativity . . . the picture is familiar enough. If the good is ineffable, the statement of aims runs the risk of opening up a metaphysical perspective which reifies the good. The debased form which objective characterisations can then take becomes clear. Such rigid specifications promise the security of control, management information systems, lists. They have a glossy presentational allure which seduces many and for some becomes an obsession. The rational nature of their modes of organisation is hard to argue against. The metaphysical picture behind this is hard to escape.

The archaic and alien language of 'graven images' is not easily – not comfortably – related to our contemporary world. In the reifications of the language of objectives, however, do we not see false goods? Are there not dangers here of idolatry?[2]

Notes

1 Of course, the term 'liberal' has a range of (connected) senses, among which are (a) a political one, (b) a more technical one related to free market economics, and (c) the idea of a liberal education, which needs to be used stipulatively to avoid the broader connotations of (a).

2 This chapter is loosely based on talks given at the universities of Aberdeen and Utrecht in 1995. I am grateful to those present on those occasions for their comments.

References

Cooper, D. E. (1983) *Authenticity and Learning*, London: Routledge & Kegan Paul.

Coward, H. and Foshay, T. (1992) *Derrida and Negative Theology*, Albany, NY: State University of New York Press.

Dearden, R. F., Hirst, P. H. and Peters, R. S. (1972) *Education and Reason*, London: Routledge & Kegan Paul.

Dewey, J. (1916) *Democracy and Education*, New York: The Free Press.

Murdoch, I. (1970) *The Sovereignty of Good*, London: Routledge & Kegan Paul.

——(1992) *Metaphysics as a Guide to Morals*, London: Chatto & Windus.

Peters, R. S. (1966) *Ethics and Education*, London: George Allen & Unwin.

Plato (1951) *The Symposium*, London: Penguin.

White, J. P. (1990) *Education and the Good Life: Beyond the National Curriculum*, London: Kogan Page (in association with the Institute of Education, University of London).

——(1995) *Education and Personal Well-being in a Secular Universe*, London: Institute of Education, University of London.

5

LIBERALISM, CITIZENSHIP AND THE PRIVATE INTEREST IN SCHOOLING

Kenneth A. Strike

As the Platte River flows through the Great Plains of North America it spreads out into a broad, shallow and silt-laden stream that has been described as too thin to plough and too thick to drink. Sometimes liberal conceptions of education seem like the Platte. They provide too thin a soil to plant a robust conception of education, but they are too thick to avoid the complaint that liberal schooling imposes a substantive view of life.

Liberal soil is thin because liberals often demand that schools be impartial between competing religions, views of the good life or comprehensive doctrines. One 'thickening agent' of liberal schooling is citizenship. There is a growing literature that discusses citizenship in liberal democratic societies and argues for a substantial role for schools in promoting it.[1] While I have no doubt that schools in liberal democratic societies should promote citizenship, this project may create a view of schooling that is too thick. A view of liberalism in which the socialisation requirements of citizenship were so substantial as to preclude an adequate range of views of the good life would fail to do what liberalism chiefly intends to do: that is, to make it possible for people to live according to their own views of the good. Sometimes authors argue as though other interests must simply give way before the requirements of democratic social reproduction. In *Democratic Education*,[2] Amy Gutmann argues that the central goal of schooling is to produce democratic character. Her description of democratic character assumes a society in which a variety of good lives should flourish. However, since tolerance and the capacity for democratic deliberation are central to democratic character, schools must promote them. Part of this promotion is initiation into a shared secular and scientific language of public deliberation.[3]

Gutmann regards these requirements as inconsistent with the exemption from public education[4] granted to the Amish by the US Supreme Court under the free exercise clause of the First Amendment to the US Constitution.[5] Here democratic citizenship trumps the free exercise of religion and freedom of conscience.

Another illustration is the kind of debate about citizenship that has developed following the publication of Rawls's *Political Liberalism.*[6] There Rawls attempts to construct an understanding of liberalism in which justice as fairness is a political, but not a comprehensive, ethical doctrine. He argues that political liberalism is a free-standing doctrine which is consistent with a society characterised by reasonable pluralism and which is consistent with and can be constructed from a variety of comprehensive doctrines. Rawls also distinguishes between political liberalism and ethical liberalism. Ethical liberalism, the central value of which is autonomy, is itself a comprehensive doctrine and, as such, cannot be the normative basis of a liberal society characterised by reasonable pluralism.

This view suggests a less expansive picture of citizenship than Gutmann's.[7] However, this may be illusory. Eamonn Callan,[8] for example, persuasively argues that Rawls's commitment to the fallibility of human reasoning, a doctrine Rawls refers to as the burdens of judgement, has implications for citizenship that are corrosive of religion and would, if acted on educationally, develop capacities that are the equivalent of autonomy. So far as the requirements of citizenship are concerned, the implications of political liberalism turn out to be quite robust and are difficult to distinguish from those of ethical liberalism.

I assume that education for citizenship is an obligation of liberal democratic societies. However, I reject any assumption that the requirements of citizenship simply trump other interests. I claim instead that the requirements of citizenship must be *balanced against* other kinds of interests, such as the interest in freedom of conscience.[9] And if this is true then a consideration of the character of these interests is essential. For example, neither Gutmann nor Callan clearly identify freedom of conscience as a cost of their views and explain why freedom of conscience is trumped by the requirements of citizenship. Thus they are open to arguments[10] that agree with their characterisations of liberal citizenship, but claim that citizenship must be balanced against freedom of conscience in such a way as to produce different educational practices than those they advance. To complete the argument, we need a better characterisation of the interests to be balanced.

The character of these interests can be approached through a consideration of some points in *Political Liberalism.* The argument of *Political Liberalism* assumes that most people have and need what Rawls calls a comprehensive doctrine or a partially comprehensive doctrine. *Ex hypothesi*, political liberalism is too thin to sustain a vision of the good life. One role of comprehensive doctrines is to enable their adherents to conceive and reflect on the character of good lives – in Rawls's terms to exercise the second of their two moral powers.[11] Since political liberalism must be free-standing from and impartial between reasonable comprehensive doctrines, the concepts of political liberalism will not be sufficient to sustain an adequate level of reflection about good lives. If so, apart from some comprehensive or partially comprehensive doctrine people will not be able adequately to exercise one of the two moral powers that Rawls claims constitute people's moral personhood. People thus have a compelling interest in possessing a reasonable and coherent comprehensive doctrine.[12]

We should note Rawls's ambivalence towards comprehensive doctrines. While people need a comprehensive doctrine if they are to exercise their moral power of reflecting on a good life, nevertheless, *Political Liberalism* often regards comprehensive doctrines as 'the problem'. It is the plurality of comprehensive doctrines that prevents the state from being a thick moral community. It is comprehensive doctrines as well as people that can be unreasonable, and unreasonable comprehensive doctrines seem to contribute significantly to the creation of unreasonable people. Most interestingly, Rawls claims that 'a certain looseness' in comprehensive doctrines is a virtue in that it makes the process of reconciliation with justice as fairness easier.[13]

Looseness seems to mean that people have a comprehensive doctrine that is not well thought through or articulated in detail. Thus, for example, Rawls claims that people may not, initially, notice much connection between their comprehensive doctrines and justice as fairness, and may come to accept justice as fairness for reasons that are independent of their comprehensive doctrines. Having accepted it and discovered its value, they are then likely, should they notice a conflict between justice as fairness and their comprehensive doctrine, to adjust the latter to the requirements of the former.

This 'looseness thesis' seems entirely understandable. However, it is a problematic thesis. One reason concerns the burdens of judgement. Rawls argues that an acceptance of the burdens of judgement – that is, a recognition of the fallibility of human judgement – is essential to tolerance and reciprocity. Only if we recognise the burdens of judgement will we be able to see those who disagree with our comprehensive doctrines as reasonable and conscientious persons like ourselves, instead of people who are too stupid or pernicious to see the truth.[14] However, it may be that the looseness of comprehensive doctrines is a contributory factor to the failure of their adherents to recognise the burdens of judgement. After all, there is little better than the reflection required to produce a tighter version of one's comprehensive doctrine to also help one to understand the reasons people might have for disagreeing with it. Reflection on one's comprehensive doctrine may contribute to developing those habits of reflectiveness, reasonableness and discursiveness that are important to liberal societies. Conversely, having a loose comprehensive doctrine may be associated with holding it in the manner of a prejudice. These points may be especially true of religious comprehensive doctrines. Those who are well educated in their faith may be more rather than less likely to combine commitment with a decent respect for the burdens of judgement. Of course, the plausibility of this hypothesis has much to do with the content of a given religion and the character of religious education. It is not a point to be over-generalised.

A second and the principle reason to wonder at the looseness doctrine is that it seems to devalue the exercise of the second of Rawls's two moral powers in comparison with the first. What Rawls's thesis comes down to is that, for the sake of achieving an overlapping consensus, it is a good thing if people do the theoretical and practical reasoning associated with their comprehensive doctrine ineptly or unenthusiastically enough that potential conflicts with justice as fairness are minimised. There is thus a curious pecking order between justice as fairness and comprehensive doctrines and between the two moral powers such that justice as fairness is preferred to comprehensive doctrines and the first moral power to the second – at least when they might conflict. But political liberalism seems committed to the idea that the good of people's lives is constructed and lived largely in the private sphere and conceived by means of their comprehensive doctrines, and is not conceived, lived or constructed primarily within the domain of the political.[15] Thus this pecking order is in tension with the project of political liberalism.

Rawls describes a comprehensive doctrine as having the following features.[16] First, it is an exercise in theoretical reason that covers the religious, philosophical and moral aspect of life in a more or less consistent and coherent manner. Second, it is an exercise in practical reasoning in that it attaches significance to values and informs us as to how to order them. Third, comprehensive doctrines generally draw on evolving traditions of thought and doctrine.

This description suggests that comprehensive doctrines might be usefully viewed, not as conceptions of a good life, but as shared means by which individual conceptions of good lives are developed and reflected upon. That our comprehensive doctrines attach significance to and allow us to order values also suggests this distinction. So does the suggestion that comprehensive doctrines include religions and philosophies and that they are exercises in theoretical as well as practical reasoning. Religions and philosophies may inform views of good lives, but they exceed them in scope.

This, together with the suggestion that comprehensive doctrines draw on evolving traditions, suggests that comprehensive doctrines are more communal matters than are views of a good life.[17] Consider why. Traditions are sustained by certain kinds of associations, by dialogical forums. Groups of the like-minded must find institutions that allow them to talk or interact in order that their ideas can be developed, discussed, refined, modified and applied to matters of concern. Depending on the nature of comprehensive doctrines, the form of these associations may vary widely from churches, to professional associations, to chat groups on the Internet. These serve such functions as the refinement and elaboration of the comprehensive doctrine, its defence against competitors, the initiation and education of new members, and the application of the doctrine to matters of concern.

Views of the good life are more individual affairs. In order to have a view of a good life, one will need to decide such things as an occupation, a spouse, the kind of education desired and the nature of recreational pursuits. That one is a Christian, for example, may mean that one is inclined to see one's job as a vocation or that one is committed to the pursuit of an education that permits one to interpret scripture. Some values or practices may be required (love of God or prayer, perhaps) and others forbidden (worship of idols). The answers to many of the questions that must be answered in order to have a conception of a good life are influenced by, but not determined by, one's comprehensive doctrine. Some believers may be plumbers, some professors. Each individual is likely to have a quite unique concatenation of views of these various goods which, in total, constitutes that person's view of a good life. Thus views of the good are more individualistic than are comprehensive doctrines. Comprehensive doctrines are among the principal resources for reflecting on good lives, but, as the example suggests, there are others. Reflection on opportunities, talents and tastes presumably will count as well. Comprehensive doctrines help us to understand how these are relevant to life choices.

This view of the role of comprehensive doctrines in practical reasoning can help us understand the idea of a child's freedom to choose in education. It is plausible to believe that schools are places in which the decisions that go into the construction of a good life are thought about. Occupations may be explored, tastes acquired, patterns of relationship considered, a view of the point of one's education developed. Few comprehensive doctrines will resist the idea that such choices are appropriately made or reflected on in schools.

However, there is something wrong with the idea that comprehensive doctrines can be chosen in the same way. After all, a comprehensive doctrine is a tradition of practical and theoretical *reasoning*. If so, on what basis will a choice of a comprehensive doctrine be made by someone who does not currently possess at least a rudimentary one? Comprehensive doctrines are not the kinds of things that can be chosen by children. They are the kinds of things into which children are initiated. It is of course true that people may refine, reject or change their comprehensive doctrines for what seem to them to be good reasons. It is less clear that they can somehow choose an initial comprehensive doctrine for good reasons. What counts as a good reason will be internal to some comprehensive doctrine.

Thus the picture of schools in which children deliberate about a good life for themselves makes good sense. Moreover, such schools are unlikely to be rejected by many comprehensive doctrines since good lives are under-determined by comprehensive doctrines. However, schools in which comprehensive doctrines are themselves chosen (as opposed to criticised, modified or abandoned) make little sense. They assume a view from nowhere – a transcendent rationality that can be wielded by children.

The discussion suggests a fuller picture of the interests people have in comprehensive doctrines. This interest is the interest in the competent exercise of the second moral power and in constructing a coherent vision of a good life. The capacity to do so is a requirement of a life that makes sense. It is a precondition of a reasonable view of the good. This interest implies three further interests that are educationally relevant.

First, there is an interest in the conversational or dialogical development of one's comprehensive doctrine. Competence in one's comprehensive doctrine requires educational resources, people to talk with, and, especially, institutions devoted to the task of reflection within and about the comprehensive doctrine. It may require, at some point, associations that have some degree of insulation from the conversational forums of other comprehensive doctrines. Such conversational forums may be more important to comprehensive doctrines that have few adherents or that are further from the centre of the cultural mainstream. It is one thing for a comprehensive doctrine to lose out in the marketplace of ideas. Liberal societies have no compelling interest in securing for comprehensive doctrines freedom from criticism or in guaranteeing them members. But losing out in the marketplace of ideas needs to be distinguished from being unable to make the case for one's view because one's voice is overwhelmed by the din of the marketplace.

Second, there is an interest in being initiated into some comprehensive doctrine. Children need a starting place. Liberal societies have an interest in diminishing the educational capacity of illiberal comprehensive doctrines. But, *ex hypothesi* for political liberalism, they have no legitimate interest in selecting among otherwise reasonable, comprehensive doctrines.

Third, the interest in a coherent and reasonable, comprehensive doctrine may well require some form of criticism of comprehensive doctrines. Recall that Mill's defence of intellectual freedom involves not only the view that truth is achieved as the result of a process of free and open argument, but also that ideas that are unchallenged degenerate into clichés.[18] They lose their meaning even to their adherents. Thus, insofar as people have an interest in the truth, reasonableness or meaningfulness of their comprehensive doctrines, they have an interest (even if they resist it) in forums in which their comprehensive doctrines are challenged.

Let me summarise. I began with the suggestion that we need to find a principled way to balance the public and private interests in education. I then suggested that in order to think about this balance we needed a better account of the nature of private interests in education. I have resisted the suggestion that when the public interest in education conflicts with the private, we must simply prefer the public. The balance to be struck depends on the character of the interests involved. And I criticised Rawls for his own unique way of privileging the public over the private. I then used *Political Liberalism* to try to formulate a deeper understanding of the private interests in education. I argued that political liberalism has a strong interest in people having coherent and reasonable comprehensive doctrines. And I argued that this interest requires at least three things: (1) opportunity for initiation of children into some initial comprehensive doctrine; (2) closed forums in which the like-minded can perform the functions required for the maintenance, elaboration and application of the tradition; and (3) open forums in which comprehensive doctrines can be tested.

If so, political liberalism leads to a more robust private interest in comprehensive doctrines than is, perhaps, the case for other forms of liberalism and to a more robust interest in comprehensive doctrines than Rawls himself may recognise. However, I believe that these interests are not yet adequately characterised. This is a theme which I cannot here develop in any detail. Its elaboration requires the development of a line of criticism of political liberalism and exploration of its consequences. I will merely sketch a direction of inquiry.

Political liberalism does not give a very adequate characterisation of the forms of significant pluralism that exist in our society. Its pluralism is a pluralism of comprehensive doctrines. But little has been said of other forms of pluralism, such as race, ethnicity, culture or gender.

The essential point to be made about the forms of pluralism associated with race, ethnicity, culture or gender is that they may be viewed as involving forms of practical rationality that are distinguishable from the kind of practical rationality associated with comprehensive doctrines. In saying that cultures are forms of practical rationality, I mean that cultures, like comprehensive doctrines, contain standards for appraising and ordering values. Appiah, for example, describes culturally rooted collective identities as scripts, 'narratives that people can use in shaping their life plans and in telling their life stories'.[19]

The forms of practical rationality associated with culture have in common with comprehensive doctrines their historical character. Cultures involve tradition or traditions. And cultures, like comprehensive doctrines, allow people to order values, make choices, and achieve a conception of their good. However, while cultures may sometimes be associated with comprehensive doctrines in the way in which Catholicism is associated with being

Irish, they are not simply the expression of comprehensive doctrines. Nor do they stand or fall with the acceptance or rejection of associated comprehensive doctrines. Irish do not cease to be Irish if they become agnostics. Cultures involve practices, customs, a language and other elements that may order or influence thought about lives, but do not raise questions of truth or falsity in the way in which religions or philosophies do.

Reflection that is culturally rooted may be structured differently than reflection rooted in a comprehensive doctrine. It is more likely to have a narrative structure. It may appeal implicitly or explicitly to custom, tradition, solidarity or identity. Thus, within a tradition of practical reasoning that devolves from a comprehensive doctrine one is likely to provide arguments that claim, 'I do/choose this, because I have certain warranted beliefs from which the reasonableness of this action/choice follows.' But reasoning from the stance of a culture may say instead, 'I do/choose this because I am a member of culture C and this is how we Cs act/choose in this context.' Identification with a culture can constitute reasons. Acting authentically can be understood as expressing who one is, as action rooted in one's culturally acquired identity.

The distinction between practical reasoning that depends on a comprehensive doctrine and practical reasoning that depends on culture is, of course, an analytic abstraction, one that I do not claim to have characterised fully or adequately. Obviously cultures and comprehensive doctrines are tangled together in numerous and complex ways and most people will employ both forms of reasoning. It is, for example, misleading to suggest that religions are merely comprehensive doctrines as though they were nothing more than sets of metaphysical claims, lacked any narrative components, or did not function as part of the sense of identity of individuals or peoples. It is not my purpose here to assert that there are two sharply distinguishable forms of practical reasoning. Rather, the point is that Rawls's characterisation of pluralism as a pluralism of doctrines is too cognitive and too narrow. It misses those kinds of pluralism that are linked more to differences of language, custom and history than to disagreements about the truth of things. And it misses ways of thinking about lives that emphasise narrative, solidarity and identity. People are significantly different in ways other than that they disagree about their fundamental convictions.

We cannot rid ourselves of the significance of these forms of pluralism. We cannot reduce cultural pluralism to a plurality of voluntary associations. Cultures are things into which we are born. They form who we are and whose we are. They serve an orientating function. Thus, they are not the moral equivalent of bowling teams or volunteer fire companies. They go deeper. They are forms of practical rationality.

The following importantly follow: liberals must recognise that cultural differences produce tensions that are analogous to the conflicts between different comprehensive doctrines. This is the case because both comprehensive doctrines and cultures ground forms of practical reasoning about the nature of good lives. People disagree on how to act and how to live depending on their culture in a way that cannot be reduced to differences of comprehensive doctrines. Nor can cultural diversity be reduced to a pluralism of mere associations. Cultural diversity poses problems for politics that require something like an overlapping consensus to overcome. Thus liberalism cannot be uncritically dismissive or reductive about cultural diversity, or assume that culture-based differences need not be considered in describing pluralism or in trying to understand the character of an overlapping consensus. Unhappily, the emphasis placed by political liberalism on a pluralism of comprehensive doctrines may ignore or minimise some forms of private interests that are educationally important. It may, for example, recognise freedom of conscience as a significant interest to protect while missing the analogous interest in respecting people's identities.

A modest list of such culture-based educational interests might include the need for community and solidarity, the need for initiation into a culture, the need for a non-alienating and culturally appropriate educational environment, the need for a coherent and respected identity, freedom from cultural oppression and domination, and the opportunity for cultural reproduction. These interests, like freedom of conscience and the interest in a coherent and reasonable comprehensive doctrine, may require that we pay closer attention to the forms of association that we view as of educational significance and that we recognise the educational importance of forms of association rooted in particular cultures.

It would be premature to draw any detailed conclusions about institutional arrangements from these arguments. Perhaps the most obvious conclusion is that the three principal sets of private interest discussed – freedom of conscience, the need for an adequate comprehensive doctrine, and the need for rootedness in a culture – each suggest that we should pay more attention to the role of particularistic associations in education. It does not follow from this, however, that we should immediately dissolve public (state) schools and conduct schooling largely in groupings reflective of our comprehensive doctrines and cultures. This does not follow for several reasons. First, it may be that the educational functions best performed by particularistic associations can be adequately or best accomplished outside of public (state) schools in places such as churches. Second, I have argued that criticism is important to the integrity of traditions. By inhibiting criticism, closed educational forums may have costs as well as benefits for comprehensive doctrines and cultures. Third, different comprehensive doctrines and cultures may have different educational requirements depending on their character. Finally, of course, these private interests must be balanced against the needs of citizenship and the other public interests in schooling.

We should always be cautious about reading off institutional arrangements from philosophical arguments. The claim that private interests are best served in private associations and public ones in public institutions is not a priori true. It may well be that many private associations develop the skills and commitments of citizenship quite well. It may be that many private interests are well served in public places. If my arguments suggest anything immediately, it is not about institutional arrangements. It is about the kind of inquiry that needs to be conducted. That inquiry cannot ignore the interest in the private. Nor can it ignore the extent to which private interests do sometimes require private associations that serve educational purposes. Liberals who have been devotees of the private sphere cannot neglect its importance or character in thinking through educational arrangements. Nor can they proceed as though public interests function as trumps.

Notes

1 Some worthy examples are Eamonn Callan, 'Political liberalism and political education', *Review of Politics* 58(1) (1996): 1–33; Amy Gutmann, 'Civic education and social diversity', *Ethics* 105(3) (April 1995): 557–79; Stephen Macedo, 'Liberal civic education and religious fundamentalism: the case of God *v.* John Rawls' *Ethics* 105(3) (April 1995): 468–97; Terence H. McLaughlin, 'Liberalism, education, and the common school', *Journal of Philosophy of Education* 29(2) (1995): 239–55.

2 Amy Gutmann, *Democratic Education*, Princeton: Princeton University Press, 1987.

3 Gutmann, *Democratic Education*, p. 103.

4 Here the idea of public education or of public schooling is to be understood as it is in the United States. Public schools are government-operated common schools.

5 Gutmann, *Democratic Education*, p. 123.

6 John Rawls, *Political Liberalism*, New York: Columbia University Press, 1993.

7 This seems to be Rawls's view. See his discussion at pp. 199, 200.

8 Eamonn Callan, 'Political liberalism and political education', *Review of Politics* 58(1) (1996): 1–33.

9 I think it likely that Gutmann and Callan would agree with this. If I have a quarrel with them, it is that the need to strike a balance is not always apparent in their argument.

10 Kenneth A. Strike, 'Must liberal citizens be reasonable?' *Review of Politics* 58(1) (1996): 41–8.

11 Rawls, *Political Liberalism* (p. 19) characterises the two moral powers as a capacity for a sense of justice and a capacity for a conception of the good, together with the capacities for judgement, thought and inference connected with the exercise of these powers.

12 Here I use 'reasonable' roughly as Rawls does. A doctrine is reasonable when it enables its adherents to respect one another as free and equal citizens and to respect reciprocity. I will use the term 'coherent' to refer to those features of comprehensive doctrines that render them plausible (minimally worthy of belief) and functional in people's lives.

13 Rawls, pp. 159, 160.

14 Rawls, pp. 54–8.

15 See Rawls's discussion of civic humanism, p. 206.

16 Rawls, p. 58.

17 Thus, for me, the notion of a vision of a good life is closer to Rawls's notion of an individual's rational life plan. See John Rawls, *A Theory of Justice*, Cambridge, MA: Harvard

University Press, 1971. I do not believe that there is a disagreement here, only that my vocabulary is clearer for my purposes.

18 John Stuart Mill, *On Liberty*, New York: The Bobbs-Merrill Company, Inc., 1956, p.64.

19 K. Anthony Appiah, 'Identity, authenticity, survival: multicultural societies and social reproduction', in *Multiculturalism: Examining the Politics of Recognition*, edited by Amy Gutmann, Princeton, NJ: Princeton University Press, 1994, p. 160.

6

LIBERALISM AND
CRITICAL THINKING

On the relation between a
political ideal and an aim of education

Jan Steutel and Ben Spiecker

Presentation of the problem

Is modern liberalism, as a *political* ideal, intrinsically related to critical thinking, as an *educational* ideal? That is the central question of this chapter. It is not our intention to give a complete and well-considered answer to this question. Our main aim is to do some preliminary work, in particular by making relevant distinctions and by localising the real differences of opinion. First, however, we shall briefly clarify the core concepts of our question so that at least it will be clear what the issue is that we want to discuss.

The first central concept of our research question is *modern liberalism*. This concept refers to a political ideal; that is, to a normative conception concerning the basic structure of society. Following John Rawls (1993: 11–12, 257–8), such a structure can be regarded as the main political, social and economic institutions of a society, and how these institutions cohere into one system of social cooperation. A political ideal, including modern liberalism, actually functions as an aim that is considered to be directive for arranging such a framework of basic institutions.

Not only the subject but also the content of the political ideal of modern liberalism can be clarified by appealing to Rawls, in this case to the first and most important principle of justice that he has articulated and defended. This principle, the so-called principle of greatest equal liberty, is summarised by Rawls in the following way: 'Each person has an equal claim to a fully adequate scheme of equal basic rights and liberties, which scheme is compatible with the same scheme for all' (1993: 5). The main tenor of this principle is to protect the freedom of all citizens as much as possible by

61

assigning every adult member of society an optimal package of the same basic rights. The central components of this package are the well-known civic liberties (like freedom of thought and liberty of conscience), the political basic rights (like the right to vote and the right to run for public office), and also the fundamental rights that are covered by the so-called 'rule of law' (like the right not to be arrested at will or the right to impartial treatment in court). Because modern liberalism, as a political ideal, consists in the principle of greatest equal liberty, it exhorts us to arrange the basic structure of our society according to this package of basic rights and liberties (cf. Buchanan 1989: 854).

A second concept of our research question that needs some clarification is *critical thinking*. Critical thinking can be regarded as an educational ideal; that is, as a normative conception concerning the abilities and dispositions of the well-educated person. In agreement with Harvey Siegel (1988: 32–42), we want to defend the view that the content of this ideal is composed of two basic aspects: namely, the reason assessment component and the critical spirit component. The former component roughly consists in the ability to assess reasons according to appropriate principles; that is, the ability to determine to what extent the reasons offered do actually justify certain beliefs, claims or decisions. However, the critical thinker is not only able to assess reasons properly, but also has a well-developed disposition or willingness to engage in reason assessment, in particular because they fully recognise the value of critical thinking.

Elsewhere (Steutel and Spiecker 1997), we argued that this second component of critical thinking, the critical attitude, can be explained in terms of intellectual virtues. Well-known examples of such virtues are openmindedness, a love of truth, intellectual honesty, clarity, respect for evidence and the willingness to participate in rational discussions. Characteristic of intellectual virtues is that practising these traits will increase the chance that our opinion-forming practices result in beliefs that are true, valid or at least well-justified. In other words, when critical thinking is appraised as an educational ideal, the development of intellectual virtue is considered an important aim of education.

Finally, what is meant by an *intrinsic relation* between these two ideals? We could define such a connection in a very strict way – namely, in terms of a logical-deductive relationship. Then the relevant relation would obtain only if the ideal of critical thinking is logically implied by the ideal of modern liberalism. However, we prefer a less stringent definition, which refers only to good reasons. According to this somewhat broader definition, the two ideals would be intrinsically related if a person who endorses modern liberalism as a political ideal has *good reasons* to embrace critical thinking as an aim of education. If it is true that the ideal of modern liberalism logically implies the ideal of critical thinking, such a good reason could obviously be offered. But as we will demonstrate later, one can also provide good reasons that do not refer to such a deductive connection.

This characterisation of the intrinsic relation we are looking for indicates that in this context we are not interested in the reverse connection; that is, in the question whether a person who accepts critical thinking as an educational ideal has good reasons to subscribe to modern liberalism as a political ideal. Such a relationship can easily be defended and is not seriously contested by any philosopher. For example, in the works of Kant and Mill critical thinking is understood as a central component of individual autonomy. And they both regard the ideal of the autonomous person as a final justifying reason for arranging society in a liberal way.

In the formulation of our central research question we explicitly refer to a person. We could, however, also refer to a *body* or an *agency*, in particular to public bodies or government agencies. In the constitution of a democratic society the liberal package of rights and liberties is assigned to all citizens, regardless of their religion, view of life, political persuasion, race, gender or sexual inclination. The government in such a society is expected to uphold and to honour this constitution, which implies that it will regard the political ideal of modern liberalism as the final basis and touchstone for its policy. And our question is: has such a government good reasons for supporting, enabling or stimulating the development of its citizens in the direction of the ideal of critical thinking?

Irrespective of the answer to this question, it is obvious that the practical consequences can hardly be underestimated. Therefore, the search for an answer must be a careful and well-considered one. This chapter is intended as a contribution to such a search.

Critical thinking: three subjects

Critical thinking, in the active sense of the word, is always about some particular thing or subject. Though this may seem a trivial observation, realising that critical thinking always relates to something is of the utmost importance for a clear understanding of our question. It may be assumed that modern liberalism has no intrinsic relation to critical thinking about any topic whatsoever but, if at all, only to critical thinking about particular (types of) subjects. Which subjects could these be?

Political policy and legislation

Publications on the relation between modern liberalism and critical thinking induce us to make a distinction between at least three relevant subjects. A first and often mentioned subject of critical thinking consists in political policy and legislation, including the justifications offered. Political authorities, in the broad sense of that term, make decisions, take measures and introduce laws. And the question whether such political and legislative activities are right or just is often regarded as an important subject of critical reflection.

There is hardly any difference of opinion between liberal philosophers concerning this particular subject. The *communis opinio* is that if we are advocates of the ideal of modern liberalism, we have good reasons to make sure that our children will grow into citizens who are able and disposed to assess critically the main lines of government interference and legislation, in particular by participating in the public debate about the way a just society should be organised. What are those reasons?

The most important reason that is put forward is the fact that a properly functioning democracy needs critical citizens in at least two ways. First, covered by the principle of greatest equal liberty is the political right of citizens to elect representatives who govern in their name. Realising this ideal of representative democracy requires citizens who are able and disposed to evaluate critically the performance of those officials. Second, a striking feature of a liberal democracy is the so-called ideal of public justification. Political policy and legislation should be based on public discussions; that means, on the exchange of reasons that are openly accessible and widely acceptable to reasonable citizens, even though these citizens may disagree fundamentally among themselves about what sorts of life are choiceworthy. This ideal, which functions as a criterion of political legitimacy in a liberal state, is crystallised in a number of institutions, like organised critical opposition, recurrent open discussions, freedom of the press and the free collection and dissemination of information. Such institutions would wither and perhaps even perish were they not sustained by citizens who are willing and able to participate in public discussions on political policy. In short, a flourishing democracy needs citizens who are characterised by *political* autonomy – that is, by 'a critical, questioning attitude toward official decisions, and self-critical participation in public debate' (Macedo 1992: 217; cf. Scheffler 1973: 136–45; Siegel 1988: 60–1; Kymlicka and Norman 1994: 365–6).

Conceptions of the good and the liberal-political framework

A second subject of critical thinking that is mentioned in relevant publications concerns the relation between the liberal-political framework of rights and duties on the one hand, and determinate conceptions of the good life on the other. The former component of this relation, the liberal-political framework, comprises the basic rights and liberties that are covered by Rawls's first principle of justice. Furthermore, such a framework encompasses corresponding duties. Citizens of a liberal society do not only have civil and political rights, they also have the moral duty to respect the exercising of these rights by their fellow citizens. The latter component of the indicated relation, a determinate conception of the good, can roughly be defined as a more or less explicit and coherent complex of beliefs about what is valuable in human life, about the things that make our lives worthwhile or satisfying. In any case, an ideal of the good life comprises a certain scheme of our final ends; that is, of the things that we regard as choiceworthy for their own sake and that guide our long-term projects. But also the values that are involved in our attachments to others and in our loyalties to groups and organisations are components of a determinate conception of the good. That complex of intrinsic values, including our final ends, functions as a basis for making major decisions, for determining what is important or unimportant in a human life, and for evaluating whether or not the shape of our life is satisfactory (cf. Rawls 1993: 19–20; Waldron 1993: 160–3).

An essential characteristic of a modern liberal society is the freedom of the citizen to arrange their own life according to a self-accepted conception of the good. But even in a liberal society this freedom is limited, in particular by the liberal-political framework. Certainly, the framework of basic rights and correlating duties is a precondition of having the freedom to live according to one's own ideal of the good. But at the same time the liberal framework restricts that freedom: it is not allowed to practise (and perhaps also to propagate) conceptions of the good that are clearly contrary to this framework. In other words, in a liberal society the political-moral framework ('the Right') takes precedence over determinate conceptions of the good life ('the Good').

Precisely this relation of priority provides an advocate of the ideal of modern liberalism with a good reason to attach great importance to a certain form of critical thinking. Realising that the political ideal of liberalism consists in creating a society in which the liberal-political framework is given priority over conceptions of the good, such a society can only function when citizens have the mental equipment to reflect critically upon their ideals of the good from the standpoint of that moral framework. In other words, in our roles as citizens in a modern liberal society, we are expected to be able and willing to stand back critically from our conceptions of the good in order to see whether they are in conflict with the liberal-political framework (cf. Larmore 1990: 350–1).

Conceptions of the good and their intrinsic value

Relevant publications of liberal philosophers mention still another subject of critical thinking; namely, the *intrinsic value* of determinate or substantial conceptions of the good life. With the addition 'intrinsic value' we mean the following. The liberal-political framework of rights and duties can be regarded as a morality in the narrow sense. That means, among other things, that within such a morality citizens can shape their lives according to a wide diversity of conceptions of the good. That is why the plurality of endorsed ideals of the good life is a striking characteristic of a liberal society. In such a society numerous conceptions of the good are practised which, though often mutually conflicting, are perfectly compatible with the liberal-political framework. Consequently, critically testing conceptions of the good against the liberal framework is one thing, the critical assessment of ideals of the good which are permitted by that framework is quite a different matter. Of course, the latter form of evaluation also appeals to certain criteria. But now these criteria are *ipso facto* not the rights and duties of the liberal-political framework. The question here is not whether our ideals of life are permitted by that framework, but whether certain things in a human life are valuable *at all*, and, if so, *to what extent*. It is this particular form of evaluation that we have in mind when we speak about the critical reflection on the intrinsic value of conceptions of the good.

We argued that critical thinking on political policy and legislation can be conceived as a central component of political autonomy. Distinguished from that, we could consider critical thinking on the intrinsic merit of conceptions of the good to be a central aspect of *personal* autonomy. Someone who is autonomous from a personal point of view does not only assent to a certain view of the good life, but is also willing and able to stand back from their beliefs about what gives value to life and to examine critically whether these beliefs are well justified.

Is there an intrinsic relation between the political ideal of modern liberalism and the educational ideal of critical thinking as a component of personal autonomy? In the camp of liberal philosophers opposite answers are given to this question. Take, for example, some of the publications of Amy Gutmann and William Galston, both strong advocates of democratic or modern liberalism. The former philosopher is of the opinion that 'a democratic state must aid children in developing the capacity to understand and to evaluate competing conceptions of the good life' (1987: 44). More than that, 'communities must be prevented from using education to stifle rational deliberation of competing conceptions of the good life' (p. 45). Galston, on the other hand, defends the view that with regard to this educational aim the liberal state has no responsibility whatsoever. He rejects the idea that such a state 'must (or may) structure public education to foster in children sceptical reflection on ways of life inherited from parents or local communities' (1991: 253; cf. Galston 1995). And he emphatically denies that the liberal state has the right or the duty to intervene when parents hamper the development of the child in the direction of the ideal of critical reflection on conceptions of the good (Galston 1991: 254).

Critical thinking about conceptions of the good: three arguments

Which position is more tenable, the view of Gutmann or that of Galston? In this chapter we will not answer this difficult question. We shall restrict ourselves to some preliminary work by distinguishing three arguments that are produced to defend a position à la Gutmann. The question whether these arguments are valid – that is, whether they really provide advocates of modern liberalism with good reasons to plead for the ideal of critical thinking about conceptions of the good and their intrinsic value – will not be examined.

The support argument

The intrinsic relation between the political ideal of modern liberalism on the one hand, and the ideal of critical thinking on the first and second subject on the other, has a distinctive structure. In both cases the argument is that a vital or flourishing liberal society needs citizens with particular qualities, including critical thinking about the subjects concerned. Without citizens who are able and willing to assess critically political policy and legislation (the first subject), a liberal democracy cannot function properly. And if citizens were not able and willing to examine critically the compatibility of their ideals of the good and the liberal framework of rights and duties (the second subject), the liberal society would be in danger and might perhaps even disintegrate. Such an argument actually gives an instrumental justification of the educational ideal of critical thinking: next to other virtues, critical thinking on the subjects at issue is *functional* for the flourishing and finally even for the continued existence of a modern liberal society. 'All institutions', Israel Scheffler rightly observes, 'operate through the instrumentality of persons' (1973:136). The same is true of the liberal-political institutions. This particular instrumental relation provides someone who endorses modern liberalism with a good reason for also endorsing the ideal of critical thinking. Let us call this good reason, for the sake of convenience, the *support* argument.

The question is whether such an argument also applies to the relation between modern liberalism and critical thinking about the third subject: the intrinsic value of determinate conceptions of the good life. Gutmann answers this question in the affirmative. She considers the critical evaluation of ideals of life, including the one in which we were initiated by our parents, as a central liberal-democratic virtue. These virtues, she argues, 'are necessary for a flourishing liberal democracy' (1989: 79; Gutmann 1993: 8). Galston, however, disputes this application of the support argument. In his view, it is improper to regard critical or sceptical reflection on ways of life as a component of the 'core of civic commitments and competences the broad acceptance of which undergirds a well-ordered liberal polity' (1991:255–6; f. Galston 1995).

The welfare argument

There is another account of the intrinsic relation between the ideal of modern liberalism and the educational ideal of critical thinking about the intrinsic merit of conceptions of the good. A version of this second interpretation has been elaborated and defended by John White (1990: 24–6, 95–105), whose views on this particular subject are based on some ideas of Joseph Raz (1986: 390–5; cf. Siegel 1988: 57–8).

Roughly stated, the idea is that in a modern liberal society a positive relation obtains between human well-being and an autonomous lifestyle, including critical reflection on beliefs about what is valuable or choiceworthy in human life. According to White (and Raz), the major institutions of a liberal society, contrary to those of a traditional one, constitute an autonomy-supporting environment. Realising the political ideal of modern liberalism results in an open society in which citizens are offered optimal freedom of choice. Citizens are free to choose a partner and to arrange their relations according to their own preferences, to determine for themselves where to live, which occupation to engage in and how to spend their leisure, or, generally speaking, to choose their own conception of the good and to structure their lives accordingly (obviously within the limits of the liberal-political framework of rights and duties). Within such autonomy-stimulating institutions, so the argument goes, citizens will most likely thrive when they meet the ideal of personal autonomy, especially when they are able and willing to think critically about what option would be best or which preference should be satisfied. If a person's well-being depends in general on their capacity to find their niche, in a liberal environment personal autonomy is part of that capacity: 'ultimately those who live in an autonomy-enhancing culture can prosper only by being autonomous' (Raz 1986: 394).

From now on we will call this account of the intrinsic relation between the ideal of modern liberalism and the ideal of critical thinking the *welfare* argument. In two respects this argument is different from the support argument. First, the ideal of critical thinking about conceptions of the good is not defended here in terms of a flourishing society but in terms of flourishing *persons*. In both arguments reference is made to an instrumental relation. According to the welfare argument, however, the 'good reason' concerns a functional connection with personal well-being or self-interest and not, as the support argument claims, a functional connection with liberal institutions.

Second, an avowed opponent of modern liberalism will hardly regard the support argument as an appealing reason for recommending the ideal of critical thinking. On the contrary, if critical thinking is of value for maintaining a vital and flourishing liberal society, it is more likely that such a person will consider that connection a good reason for disputing or rejecting the ideal of critical thinking. However, even to an opponent of modern liberalism the welfare argument could be a convincing consideration for supporting the educational ideal of critical thinking. Certainly, such a person will deplore the prevalence of liberal institutions in their society. But if they care for the well-being of their fellow citizens, the fact that within such a society critical reflection is positively related to personal flourishing will offer them a good reason to support the ideal of critical thinking.

The necessity argument

The intrinsic relation between the political ideal of modern liberalism on the one hand, and the educational ideal of critical thinking on the other, can be explained in yet a third way. In this interpretation the value of critical thinking is neither regarded as instrumental, nor conceived as historical-contingent. What this argument boils down to is the logical claim that the ideal of modern liberalism *presupposes* the value of critical thinking about the intrinsic merit of conceptions of the good. To put it differently, appealing to the value of personal autonomy is necessary for justifying the ideal of modern liberalism (or at least some of its essential components). If we are not of the opinion that critical thinking is a valuable ideal, reasons would fail us for supporting or recommending the rights and liberties that are covered by the principle of greatest equal liberty.

Let us call this explanation of the intrinsic relation the *necessity* argument. Unlike the arguments discussed above, no instrumental justification of the ideal of critical thinking is presented. In a way, the necessity argument is the mirror image of the support argument. For this time the value of critical thinking is not regarded as a function of the value of modern liberalism, but, just the other way round, the value of the liberal society is conceived as at least partly derivative from the value of critical thinking. And precisely because critical thinking about ways of life is not now justified in terms of a particular, localised society, as is done in the welfare argument, the value of critical thinking is not relativised. In fact, the necessity argument offers no justification of critical thinking about the intrinsic value of ideals of the good whatsoever. Because it just presupposes the value of this educational aim, the question whether this value is instrumental or intrinsic, historical or universal, contingent or absolute, is completely passed over.

Moreover, it is important not to confuse the necessity argument with the argument that an appeal to the ideal of critical thinking is *sufficient* for justifying the ideal of modern liberalism. To be sure, in either case the justification of critical thinking is not an instrumental one. The latter argument, however, only provides someone who endorses the ideal of critical thinking with a good reason to embrace modern liberalism. It does not, like the necessity argument, offer someone who is committed to the ideal of modern liberalism a good reason for supporting the ideal of critical thinking. And as we wrote in the introductory section, we are only interested in interpretations of the intrinsic relation last mentioned.

The necessity argument is undeniably a demanding argument. It means that, if we want to justify the ideal of modern liberalism, we *must* make an appeal to the ideal of personal autonomy, including critical thinking about conceptions of the good life and their intrinsic merit. Nevertheless, it is an argument that is defended by several authors – for instance, by Will Kymlicka (1989: 13, 17–18, 59–60). In his view, some liberal basic rights and liberties can be justified in terms of the principle of tolerance. In particular, the right of citizens to live their lives in accordance with their own beliefs about value is based on this principle. However, according to Kymlicka, not all liberal rights can be made (entirely) intelligible on the basis of the principle of tolerance. Understanding the full meaning of some cultural freedoms requires an appeal to the ideal of critical thinking too. Especially the liberal concern for freedom of expression, freedom of the press and artistic freedom, can hardly (exclusively) be explained in terms of respectful tolerance for a plurality of ideals of the good. The importance liberal societies attach to these freedoms can only be (fully) understood if reference is made to the value of critically examining and revising beliefs about what is valuable in life. Such basic rights, Kymlicka writes, are '*only* explicable . . . if the assumption of plurality is accompanied by the view of revisability' (1989: 60, italics added; cf. Strauss 1992: 199–201; White 1990: 21).

Other modern liberal philosophers, however, are strongly opposed to the necessity argument. In their opinion a really liberal democracy is based on the above-mentioned ideal of public justification: main lines of government policy and political principles by which all are to live must be justifiable to all reasonable citizens regardless of their particular conceptions of the good. This liberal criterion of political legitimacy is sometimes also called the principle of procedural neutrality (cf. Larmore 1987: 43–7; Arneson 1990: 218–19; De Marneffe 1990). In a modern liberal society reasonable citizens hold different and often conflicting ideals of the good life. An implication of the liberal criterion of political legitimacy is that a government is not allowed to justify its policies in terms of such controversial conceptions of the good. If the government wants to justify its policies towards its citizens, it should appeal to *neutral* values; that is, to values that are acceptable to reasonable people who hold different particular conceptions of the good.

Now, according to these modern liberal philosophers, the ideal of personal autonomy is a typical example of a controversial conception of the good life. Because personal autonomy is an object of reasonable disagreement, it cannot be regarded as a neutral value. Consequently, in a legitimate justification of governmental policy and political principles, including the basic principle of greatest equal liberty, an appeal to the ideal of personal autonomy is not allowed. Liberal political policy and the liberal structuring of society have to be justified in a different, neutral way. And because these philosophers actually consider such a neutral justification to be possible, they reject the idea that an appeal to the ideal of personal autonomy is necessary for justifying the principles of a modern liberal society (cf. Larmore 1987: 51–5; 1990: 342–6; Rawls 1993: 37, 99, 199; Macedo 1995: 473–6).

To this argument it can be objected that it is based on a most artificial distinction between political and personal autonomy. An intrinsic relation between modern liberalism and critical thinking on political matters is acknowledged, whereas such a relationship between liberalism and critical reflection on the intrinsic merit of conceptions of the good is denied. But is not such a conjunction rather implausible? For promoting critical deliberation on public policy and legislation almost certainly has the effect of promoting critical thinking in general, including on the intrinsic value of ideals of the good. This objection, however, will be put aside as being not to the point (cf. Macedo 1995: 477–8). Philosophers who reject the necessity argument normally endorse the principle of procedural neutrality without accepting the principle of *outcome* neutrality. That means that they hold the view that public policies should be neutrally justified without claiming that these policies should have neutral *effects* on the spread and viability of different ideals of the good. In other words, even if they acknowledged that a state policy of stimulating political autonomy would result in the growth of personal autonomy, they would still reject the idea that the state is allowed to justify this policy in terms of the ideal of personal autonomy.

Summary and conclusions

Our central question was: does a person who endorses the political ideal of modern liberalism have good reasons to embrace critical thinking as an aim of education? To find an appropriate answer to this question we considered it advisable first to make a distinction between three different subjects of critical thinking. In our view, liberal philosophers are right that there is an intrinsic relation between modern liberalism and two subjects of critical thinking – namely, the justification of political policy and legislation and the compatibility of ideals of the good with the liberal framework of rights and duties. We called the good reasons that are put forward in this connection the support argument.

We did not answer the question whether an advocate of democratic liberalism also has good reasons to stimulate critical thinking about the third subject – namely, the value of conceptions of the good as such. We argued that this intrinsic relation is defended not only in terms of the support argument, but also by what we called the welfare argument and the necessity argument. The validity of these arguments, however, is strongly contested among liberal philosophers.

Though we did not take a position in this fascinating debate, we can at any rate conclude that a government in a liberal democracy has good reasons to regard critical thinking about the first two subjects as an important aim of education. Such a government is rightly expected to establish and maintain a flourishing liberal-democratic political community. And living up to this expectation involves creating optimal conditions for helping children to become citizens who are able and willing to assess main lines of political policy and legislation in a critical way, as well as critically to attune their ideal of the good to the liberal framework of rights and duties (cf. Spiecker and Steutel 1995: 391–3).

References

Arneson, R. J. (1990) 'Neutrality and utility', *Canadian Journal of Philosophy* 20: 215–40.

Buchanan, A. E. (1989) 'Assessing the communitarian critique of liberalism', *Ethics* 99: 852–82.

De Marneffe, P. (1990) 'Liberalism, liberty, and neutrality', *Philosophy & Public Affairs* 19: 253–74.

Galston, W. A. (1991) *Liberal Purposes: Goods, Virtues, and Diversity in the Liberal State*, Cambridge: Cambridge University Press.

——(1995) 'Two concepts of liberalism', *Ethics* 105: 516–34.

Gutmann, A. (1987) *Democratic Education*, Princeton, NJ: Princeton University Press.

——(1989) 'Undemocratic education', in N. L. Rosenblum (ed.) *Liberalism and the Moral Life*, Cambridge, MA: Harvard University Press.

——(1993) 'Democracy and democratic education', *Studies in Philosophy and Education* 12: 1–9.

Kymlicka, W. (1989) *Liberalism, Community and Culture*, Oxford: Clarendon Press.

Kymlicka, W. and Norman, W. (1994) 'Return of the citizen: a survey of recent work on citizenship theory', *Ethics* 104: 352–81.

Larmore, C. E. (1987) *Patterns of Moral Complexity*, Cambridge: Cambridge University Press.

——(1990) 'Political liberalism', *Political Theory* 18: 339–60.

Macedo, S. (1992) 'Charting liberal virtues', in J. W. Chapman and W. A. Galston (eds) *Virtue. Nomos* XXXIV, New York: New York University Press.

——(1995) 'Liberal civic education and religious fundamentalism: the case of God *v.* John Rawls?' *Ethics* 105: 468–96.

Rawls, J. (1993) *Political Liberalism*, New York: Columbia University Press.

Raz, J. (1986) *The Morality of Freedom*, Oxford: Clarendon Press.

Scheffler, I. (1973) *Reason and Teaching*, London: Routledge & Kegan Paul.

Siegel, H. (1988) *Educating Reason: Rationality, Critical Thinking, and Education*, New York: Routledge.

Spiecker, B. and Steutel, J. (1995) 'Political liberalism, civic education and the Dutch Government', *The Journal of Moral Education* 24: 383–94.

Steutel, J. and Spiecker, B. (1997) 'Rational passions and intellectual virtues', *Studies in Philosophy and Education* 16: 59–71.

Strauss, D. A. (1992) 'The liberal virtues', in J. W. Chapman and W. A. Galston (eds) *Virtue. Nomos* XXXIV: 197–203.

Waldron, J. (1993) *Liberal Rights: Collected Papers 1981–1991*, Cambridge: Cambridge University Press.

White, J. (1990) *Education and the Good Life: Beyond the National Curriculum*, London: Kogan Page.

7

AUTONOMY AS
AN EDUCATIONAL AIM

Christopher Winch

A major theme in the liberal project of the definition and justification of education has been the selection of autonomy or rational autonomy as an aim.[1] The purpose of this chapter is to argue: first, that although there are no a priori grounds for making autonomy a non-trivial educational aim for all societies, there are good grounds for thinking that some form of autonomy has to be an aim of public education in democratic societies; second, that if it *is* accepted as a non-trivial educational aim, then it is quite compatible with a wide variety of different forms of educational practices and curricula; and third, that there are, contrary to the views of many liberal thinkers, grave problems about adopting strong autonomy as an educational aim. In effect, the liberal educational project as it has traditionally been conceived of exclusively as a form of academic education cannot be sustained if autonomy conceived of in a broad sense is a primary educational aim. I will also argue for a minimal sense of autonomy, which is usually ignored by the advocates of autonomy as an educational aim. By a minimal sense of autonomy is meant the degree of independence necessary to fulfil any other aims of education, whatever they may be.

There can, however, be little quarrel with autonomy as a minimal aim of education. If education in any society is, broadly speaking, about the preparation of children for adult life, and adults need to be more independent than children, then it is unavoidable that autonomy in this minimal sense is an aim of any educational process, since children need to be prepared for independent life as adults and education is, in a developed society, one of the main routes, if not the only one, for achieving it. Perhaps 'minimal' is the wrong word here in any case, since it is no trivial matter to be able to make a living, raise a family and play some role in the running of the affairs of a community. Indeed, any education that failed to prepare children for these things would, on the broad definition above, have failed, since it would not, in any meaningful sense, have prepared someone for adult life.

But many of the supporters of autonomy as an educational aim would not regard the 'minimal' definition of autonomy as educationally important. The achievement of autonomy is, for them, a much more significant matter than the ability to function as a member of society. It could include the achievement of rationality or the ability to formulate and carry out a life plan.[2] Some writers in the liberal analytical tradition of the philosophy of education would question whether independence or minimal autonomy is an *educational* aim at all. They would prefer to say that it is a worthy aim but a worthy aim of *schooling* rather than of education.[3]

How can one justify the division of activities that prepare people for adult life into various subconcepts that include *education* and *schooling*? Granted that there are some activities, such as buying a house in which to raise a family, which are not educational in any remote sense, but which are a preparation for adult life, it is not clear that one can separate vocational preparation, religious instruction or safety training from another set of activities called 'education'. It is not clear – that is, unless one accepts a certain definition of education which excludes those activities from its scope. But there is no good reason for doing this unless we are already persuaded that the proposed definition of education is the one to be accepted. But this is what is at issue.

One final point: the context of this discussion is the modern, pluralist democratic type of polity rather than traditional, authoritarian or totalitarian systems. It is taken for granted, therefore, that citizens in such a society are entitled to question at least some of the values on which the society is based. Educating someone in such a society in such a way that they have a basic understanding of how it works, therefore, involves getting them to understand that *some* at least of the values on which the society is based are open to questioning. This much is implied by the 'minimal' conception of autonomy in such societies, since it is a necessary part of citizenship in a democratic society that one understands this. This is not, however, true of all societies and even in some democratic societies there are more limits on what can be legitimately questioned than there are in others.

Autonomy and the complexity of society

A complex society requires a division of labour as well as a set of common knowledge, assumptions and practices. Not everyone can do everything and everyone can only do a limited number of things really well. Because of these constraints, public education systems have to find a way of ensuring that common knowledge, assumptions and practices, as well as a huge variety of specialised occupations, are present in society. This seems to imply that schooling has to make children literate, numerate, reasonably knowledgeable about a core of basic geographical, historical, political and scientific facts and has to give them the wherewithal for some degree of functional specialisation in employment.[4] The parts of society are, therefore, unavoidably *interdependent*. Whatever independence people develop is to be exercised within the framework of a common interdependence if society is not to fragment into a mass of individuals, each of whom can only pursue their individual aims through constant friction with others who may be pursuing contrary goals. These reflections suggest three things. First, that people have to be independent to a certain degree in order to function in a society that expects individuals to work, raise families and take part in the democratic process. Second, since independent action involves association with others, there needs to be a common core of rules, concepts, assumptions and propositions that allow such association to take place without too much misunderstanding. Third, since a complex society requires a division of labour, the preparation that each individual has for adult life cannot be identical. These are the constraints that surround any attempt to specify autonomy as an educational aim in a complex society.

So what do they imply for the specification of autonomy as an educational aim? It seems, as we have already noted, that some degree of autonomy is implied by reflecting on the nature of education in any society, and this degree of autonomy not only requires, but implies, a degree of dependence on others.[5] Furthermore, in a modern democratic society, *some* degree of autonomy about ends as well as means seems to be implied by the foregoing discussion. Beyond this, it is difficult to see how autonomy could be the *exclusive* educational aim. The reason for this has already emerged: any complex society has a number of goals and requires some degree of division of labour in order to function. At the very least, education has to prefigure that division in its own aims, making children aware of the requirements of employment, family life and citizenship, for example, even if it does not, within the schools, actually *prepare* them for these roles.[6] Education has a number of aims, none of which entails more than independence. That, at least, is our provisional conclusion.

Education, autonomy and politics

So how is it possible to specify autonomy as a legitimate and realisable educational aim? And, if it is, what sense of autonomy is meant? In order to answer these questions, it is first necessary to look at the way in which educational aims ought to be determined, for it is only by looking at this process that it will become possible to distinguish between legitimate and illegitimate ways of specifying them. It has been a commonplace since the time of Aristotle that political societies embody various interests which are often in conflict and need to be accommodated.[7] Instead of warfare, pressure, persuasion and compromise are the ways in which different interests seek to pursue their ends within a framework that is not mutually destructive of the interests of all.

There is, however, a problem. All these interests will have ethical commitments, and there is something conceptually incoherent about the supposition that these could be the subject of compromise. Insofar as moral values partly constitute a person's identity and core of their personality, they are not something that can be negotiated away. Were they to be so, this would be a *prima facie* reason for taking them to be something else, like judgements of fashion rather than of moral value. But if this is so, then how could it be possible to accommodate different interests that involved different and mutually incompatible values? The problem is a particularly pressing one for the issues under consideration, since the aims of education are precisely the sorts of things that could reasonably be supposed to embody moral values. If some forms of autonomy are incompatible with some forms of interdependence or dependence, then how can all these be legitimate educational aims without provoking conflict?

The answer lies in accepting the integrity of personal values but coming to some arrangement concerning their implementation in the public sphere. In this way, citizens are not expected to compromise their values (which is an incoherent idea), but to negotiate about the nature and extent of their *implementation*. The public values that a society adheres to ought, to a large extent, to reflect this processs of negotiation and compromise.

Public education will have, among its aims, the promotion of those values or at least the promotion of values consistent with them. It is natural to think of a compromise about values resulting in the adoption of a plurality of desirable or at least acceptable values, and that public education would tend towards the promotion or at least the informing of young people about them. A democratic society committed to the promotion, or at least tolerance, of a variety of values would normally allow its public system of education to give future citizens choice over which values to adopt and which ways of life expressive of those values to follow.

For example, a society would probably wish to promote the value of mutual cooperation and would thus educate future citizens to become socially useful and productive members of their communities.[8] But there are many different ways of doing this: through paid employment, through voluntary work, through the pursuit of domestic life and so on. Even within these categories there are many choices to be made (for example, between different forms of employment), and within a lifetime choices may be made about whether to work in paid employment or to leave work to bring up a family or to retire and engage in voluntary work. It is thus evident that, within the set of values promoted or tolerated, there are numerous and difficult choices that each individual has to make in order to promote both personal and social well-being, and education would, at the very least, provide some of the tools to make these choices.

However, *independence* in the sense outlined above could not be sufficient for the fulfilment of aims which involve the kinds of choices required. Someone could be independent in this sense and yet live a life of complete heteronomy, having all the major decisions in life taken by someone else. It is probably more accurate to say that independence is a necessary or near-necessary condition for living a life which involves successfully making the kinds of choices alluded to above. So education in a democratic society seems to entail that something stronger than independence ought to be a primary educational aim, and a natural candidate for such an aim is that individuals should be properly equipped to make those choices that allow them to be both happy and productive members of society. They should, in one relatively uncontroversial sense of the term, become autonomous.

So far, the argument has established that a public education system has good reason to promote a variety of different goals in life which its citizens can autonomously choose from. This conception of autonomy is sometimes known as 'weak autonomy' and is contrasted with 'strong autonomy'.[9] It is worth noting that weak autonomy is a form of autonomy about ends; it does not *prescribe* ends or only allow choice regarding the means to achieve those ends: it invites citizens to choose from a variety of approved and tolerated ends. It incorporates minimal autonomy, and thus entails that someone who is weakly autonomous nevertheless understands that *some* at least of the values on which their society is based are properly open to questioning and that they have some responsibility for choosing which values to adopt. The conclusion we have now reached is a stronger one than that reached at the end of the previous section.

But this is not sufficient for the proponent of *strong autonomy* who tends to be sceptical about the idea of an imposed common good that lies behind the set of values that a public education committed to weak autonomy supports. It will be my argument that not only does weak autonomy not commit itself to any developed notion of a common good, but is the most liberal conception of autonomy that is consistent with the idea that education is, in some sense, about promoting both social and human flourishing.

Strong autonomy as an educational aim

What do advocates of strong autonomy suggest? We have seen that they, like weak autonomists, support the idea that citizens should be able to choose their own route through life. Unlike weak autonomists, however, they would prefer not to prescribe a set of ends from which the citizen would be entitled to choose. The weak autonomist is not committed to the idea that society itself should not be strongly autonomous; that is, that it cannot choose and promote those ends which it determines — indeed, the stance of weak autonomy as it has been outlined here suggests that the values that a society wishes to promote and tolerate are a matter of negotiation among citizens. The citizens, though, are constrained by the *outcome* of that process of negotiation. Neither are weak autonomists concerning education necessarily committed to the view that individuals should not be strongly autonomous; they can, in consistency, say that an individual should be free to choose to live a life that meets with the disapproval of most of society. Indeed, weak autonomists might even concede that a child might be *educated* to be strongly autonomous in some circumstances (see the next section). What they cannot concede is that a *public education system* should have strong autonomy as one of its aims.

Most strong autonomists would argue that strong autonomy is a legitimate aim for a public education system. The argument could go along the following lines. In a democracy, it is no part of society's remit to tell people what kind of life they should adopt. Citizens have rights which cannot be violated; among the most important of these is that of choosing what kind of life they should lead. These rights impose a duty on society to respect them, and it follows that public education, as an agent of society, should also respect those rights. This seems to entail that a public education system should at least not *proscribe* strong autonomy as an educational aim. However, if one of the major aims of education is to allow young people to make informed choices, then schools can hardly avoid pointing out that there is a wider range of choices available than those approved of by society. If it is one of the aims of public education to allow citizens to make informed choices, then it is a *duty* of the system to ensure that future citizens be given the wherewithal to do so. Since the ability to make informed choices in the widest possible sense is the ability to choose ends unchosen by society itself, then it is tantamount to strong autonomy. Acceptance of citizen's rights appears, therefore, to entail that a public education system has the *duty* to adopt strong autonomy as an aim.

The flaw in this argument results from a misinterpretation of the premiss that individuals have inviolable rights to choose what kind of life they should lead. This principle must be subject to some limitation if it is not to lapse into incoherence. Since individual rights have implications for the rights of others, they impose duties on those others. In particular, the duty of A not to violate the rights of B is entailed. Therefore individuals can only have rights which do not themselves violate the rights of others. Not even a strong autonomist can, therefore, take the view that *any* social value is subject to question. It would not be open to a strong autonomist to say that *as a matter of right* it is allowable for someone to choose aims that involve constraining the rights of others, because, unless one distinguishes between the degree of rights of different citizens, the proposal would render the claim to such rights incoherent. *A fortiori,* it would not be allowable for a public education system to pursue such aims since they would compromise the weak autonomy of some citizens.

Furthermore, *public* education systems are funded by citizens for the purpose of realising certain aims that have been mutually agreed. Typically, in a democratic society, this will include a range of aims to do with culture, citizenship and occupation, together with the aim that citizens should be weakly autonomous. Funding is usually given on the basis of an understanding that it be put to use in carrying out the purpose for which it was initially allocated, in this case to pursue a variety of educational aims, which include, as one of them, the recognition that some values at least, are susceptible to doubt and criticism. It could not be the case that such a system allowed *all* values to be subject to doubt and criticism for two reasons. The first has just been alluded to; were the proposition that people's rights are not to be violated to be questioned, then weak and even minimal autonomy would come under threat. The second is that an aim would be promoted which had not been sanctioned as a result of the process of negotiation alluded to earlier, since an outcome of any negotiation of that sort would be that a finite set of aims would be promoted which would in turn lead to the promotion and toleration of a finite set of values, rather than a questioning of all of them. Third, the proposing of strong autonomy would suggest that the system by which a consensus about aims is arrived at would no longer be stable, thus undermining the basis on which strong autonomy as an aim could legitimately emerge. When held as a political aim, strong autonomy in its strongest form, which suggests that all socially held values are no more than non-mandatory options, is a position that contains the seeds of its own incoherence.

Autonomy in a stronger sense than independence emerges as a necessary condition of choosing among societal ends (independence does not entail this condition – one could independently pursue someone else's chosen end). But the aim of independence entails a richer and more diverse set of aims than does weak autonomy by itself. If independence is to be achievable, the aims of education must include some form of preparation for work, for family life and for citizenship. Weak autonomy would allow one to choose the right mix of these aims for different phases of life.[10]

Strong autonomy and the aims of independent education

Strong autonomy is, quite possibly, a legitimate aim for an individual in a democratic society. Many such societies tolerate views which are inimical to the values and assumptions on which the society is itself based, even if they do not actively promote them. Provided that the holding of such views is compatible with non-violation of the rights of fellow citizens, then it may be tolerated. However, where strong autonomy entails that the *pursuit of certain chosen ends* violates the rights of other citizens, then there are grounds for legally curtailing it. This is not an exclusive feature of strong autonomy; any action, even if it results from the activity of a weakly autonomous or merely independent person, is subject to the same constraint. But we have seen that it is logically incoherent to suppose that a public education system could promote strong autonomy because to do so would undermine the assumptions and procedures on which that system is based.

On the face of it, this constraint does not apply to non-publicly funded education; if a group of parents were to decide to finance an education for their children that promoted strong autonomy, then those who were educating their children would, on the accountability criterion mentioned earlier, be *obliged* to pursue that aim. Furthermore, the only negotiation about aims that would need to take place would be among those who were providing the resources for the education in the first place and, if these could agree on strong autonomy as an educational aim, that would seem to be the end of the matter.

But this brings us to another aspect of accountability that has not so far been touched upon. So far the discussion has proceeded as if it were purely a matter of finance. But our interests in our fellow citizens extend beyond our concern as to how they spend our money; their behaviour in other respects affects our well-being. If others in our society fail to flourish or flourish in an inappropriate way, then this has repercussions for us. The interests of others affect us more directly as well, through the allocation of positional goods; if there is a desirable position in society which can be filled by only a limited number of people, then whoever fills it other than oneself affects one's own ability to fill it.

Traditionally, parents have educated their children independently for one of four principal reasons. First, to enable them better to acquire coveted positional goods such as jobs and status (the British public schools exist largely to fulfil this purpose); second, to provide a secure *grounding* which, they fear, cannot be provided by what they see as a decadent public education system; third, to promote *heteronomy* of ends (schools dedicated to various forms of confessionally based religion are an example; independent Catholic schools in France exist largely because of the secular nature of French public education). Fourth, they exist to promote various forms of strong autonomy (like the 'progressive' independent schools found in Britain, such as Summerhill or Dartington Hall).

For the reason mentioned above, no society could be indifferent to the existence and nature of an independent education sector, but the question arises as to whether or not it would wish to regulate or even restrict its operation. There is no one answer to this question; one major issue is that of parental rights – to what extent should parents be the interpreters of their children's long-term interests? Should they be allowed to educate them in such a way, for example, as to promote strong heteronomy? Alternatively, should they be allowed to promote very strong autonomy when it is felt that strongly autonomous individuals might undermine social cohesion? In a democratic society, any decision to restrict parental rights has to be made as part of a balance of judgement as to the damage to civil society and to democratic values of such a decision. Even within a Lockean framework of thinking about children's rights, there is much scope for differences of opinion on these matters.[11]

What does seem clear, however, is that if we grant that parents cannot be strongly autonomous in relation to the upbringing of their children, then there may come a point when society may wish to place limits on the education that they provide, or enter into some form of negotiation with such parents as to what aims they might choose that would be compatible with the aspirations of the rest of society.[12] The point applies as well, of course, to parents who choose to educate their children in such a way as to promote strong heteronomy, although in many cases there will be considerations of religious freedom which will need to be taken carefully into account in any such process of negotiation. If, though, it is accepted that people as citizens in a democracy have further interests in the well-being of their fellows than purely financial ones, then, however they educate their offspring, that will have an impact both on the society and on the individuals within that society. If politics is about the negotiation and accommodation of differing and sometimes conflicting interests, then the aims of independent education are a matter of legitimate political interest, no matter that it be funded independently of the rest of society.

Conclusion

We started with the notion of accountability in public education systems as a financial consideration; is the money spent on education being spent in accord with the negotiated aspirations of social partners? This led us to the view that, although independence and autonomy in relation to a range of ends is likely to be an aspiration for the education of children in democratic societies, a form of autonomy that encouraged people actively to question or undermine the institutions which allow such negotiation of the spending of public money would not be tolerated unless the society was already sceptical about the value of its democratic institutions. A healthy and self-confident democratic society would, then, quite properly be unwilling to prescribe strong autonomy as an educational aim.

There is more, however, to accountability than finance. If we all have interests in society, then the behaviour of others, including the way in which they educate their children, is going to affect those interests. If some, at least, of our rights are grounded on our interests, then we have rights to enter some form of negotiation with parents who wish to educate their children independently, as to what aims they may choose for their children's education.[13] Their freedom to choose strong autonomy as an educational aim will thus be a matter for negotiation. What the fine detail of the outcome of any such negotiation should be is a matter for different societies and is beyond the scope of this chapter. That there should be such negotiation is what I have been seeking to establish.

Similar considerations of non-financial accountability apply in the public sector of education; the negotiation of aims must take into account the ramifications of the pursuit of certain aims on different interests. But to say that is to say no more than that the negotiation of aims for public education is more than just a matter of whether or not such aims can be afforded; it is a question of how to balance the interests of different groups and individuals in order to bring about outcomes that are satisfactory to all.

Notes

1 See, for example, J. P. White, *The Aims of Education Restated*, London: Routledge, 1982; *Education and the Good Life*, London: Routledge, 1990; R. F. Dearden, *Means and Ends in Education*, London: Routledge, 1984.

2 R. S. Peters, *Ethics and Education*, London: Allen & Unwin, 1966; P. H. Hirst, *Knowledge and the Curriculum*, London: Routledge, 1974; J. P. White, *The Aims of Education Restated*, London: Routledge, 1982.

3 Cf. R. Barrow, *Common Sense and the Curriculum*, Harvester Wheatsheaf, 1981; see pp.26ff.

4 It is not sufficiently realised that this is an *epistemic* rather than a political constraint. Since the learning of some facts and skills presupposes mutual understanding, those facts and skills that are necessary to mutual understanding need to be learned first. Cf. E. D. Hirsch, Jr. 'The primal scene of education', *New York Review of Books* XXXVI(3): 29–34.

5 The idea that autonomy and heteronomy are incompatible opposites seems to be a consequence of Kantian theorising about ethics, with its deterministic view of the phenomenal world. Rejection of this rigid framework allows us to get a clearer view of the relationship between autonomy and heteronomy. See I. Kant, *Groundwork of the Metaphysic of Morals*, available in H. J. Paton, *The Moral Law*, London: Hutchinson, 1948.

6 For a sensitive discussion of this issue, see H. Entwistle, *Education, Work and Leisure*, London: Routledge, 1970.

7 Cf. Aristotle, *The Politics*, especially Books III and IV, edited by Stephen Everson, Cambridge: Cambridge University Press, 1988.

8 Note that this does not entail any particular view about the nature of the common good, but expresses a minimal condition for a self-sustaining form of mutual association and interdependency.

9 Cf. J. P. White, *Education and the Good Life*, London: Routledge, 1990, p.102; R. Norman, '"I Did it My Way": some thoughts on autonomy', *Journal of Philosophy of Education* 28(1) (1994): 25–34.

10 In this sense it would allow young people to form a life plan, which is one of the require-

ments of autonomy drawn attention to by J. P. White (*Education and the Good Life*, London: Routledge, 1982).

11 J. Locke, *Second Treatise of Government*, London: Dent, 1924 (first published, 1690). See chapter VI.

12 There is nothing unusual in the idea that the independent sector should be regulated; the issue here is whether or not the aims of independent education should be subject to some form of regulation.

13 For a discussion of interest-based accounts of rights, see D. N. McCormick, *Rights in Legislation*, available in P. M. S. Hacker and J. Raz (eds) *Law, Morality and Society*, Oxford: Oxford University Press, 1977.

References

The references are to: John Stuart Mill, *On Liberty*, ch. 2; Immanuel Kant, *Critique of Judgment*, First part, Second book; David Hume, *Enquiry Concerning Human Understanding*, Section 10; René Descartes, *Rules for the Direction of the Mind*, Rule 3; and for Socrates on the examined life, Plato, *Apology* 38A. The image of the cave appears in Plato, *The Republic*, Book 7.

8

CRITICAL THINKING
AS AN AIM OF EDUCATION

William Hare

The emergence of the ideal

Critical thinking has come to be perceived by many as desperately needed in education in the late twentieth century; it is seen as an ideal which can and should transform the manner of teaching and the learning of students. As a result, critical thinking has received far more attention over the past two decades than any other educational aim. Clearly, many factors are responsible for its emergence as a fundamental educational standard, but these would surely include:

1   an awareness, resulting from much-publicised reports, that there remain countless classrooms where mindless rote learning persists, where serious inquiry is all but lost in a 'rhetoric of conclusions', where students are unable to apply what they know to the solution of problems, and where students are not respected and treated as persons capable of intellectual independence;

2   belated recognition, provoked by concerns over bias, prejudice and intolerance, of the need for a critical form of moral education in pluralistic societies which would avoid the traditional pitfall of indoctrination yet resist the slide into relativism which has plagued values clarification and similar programmes; and

3   a growing sense that students entering an uncertain future and rapidly changing work environment need the adaptability, resourcefulness and autonomy which critical ability would seem to promise.

The current obsession has created the impression that we have suddenly, and at long last, seen through the deficiencies of traditional education which have blinded us for so long to the insight we have now achieved. We have stumbled out of the cave into the daylight. If, however, critical thinking really is a central aim of education, it would be remarkable indeed if this were a discovery of the late twentieth century, having somehow eluded philosophers for more than 2,000 years.

In fact, the history of this ideal can be traced back through philosophy to the earliest times. That account would include references to Mill on keeping one's mind open to criticism, Kant on thinking for oneself, Hume on proportioning belief to the evidence, Descartes on the need to assess (not simply to be acquainted with) the views of other philosophers, and on through the history of philosophy to its origins, in the Western tradition at least, in the Socratic emphasis on the examined life.[1] These ideas are central to any account of the intellectual virtues, including wisdom, judgement and open-mindedness, and it is within this family of concepts that critical thinking emerges as an ideal.

Dewey, Russell, Whitehead and many others in the early decades of the century pursued these themes vigorously and developed a conception of education which stressed the importance of thought, inquiry and intellectual independence. The basic idea of critical thinking was alive and well in a multitude of discussions in the first half of the century dealing with reflective thinking, the scientific method, inert ideas, rote learning, authoritarianism and propaganda analysis.[2]

By mid-century, critical thinking had found its name and a regular if not yet commanding place on the agenda of educational theorists. Critical thinking tests started to appear in the 1940s; philosophers began to see in informal logic a tool for developing critical skills; those with an interest in curriculum asked how school subjects might be infused with critical thinking; and an emerging literature on indoctrination clearly had the threat to critical thinking very much in mind.[3] There was, in short, a sufficiently high level of interest that it took just a few really influential discussions to bring matters to a head.[4]

Critical thinking, as a philosophical and educational ideal, has now been embraced by theorists and practitioners alike. Executive Order 338 made formal instruction in critical thinking compulsory throughout the California State University system in 1980. The American Philosophical Association adopted a statement in October 1984 urging its members to use their expertise to help boards of education and testing agencies to develop new curricula and tests in the area of critical thinking. Another development helping to bridge the traditional gap between theory and practice has been the increasingly influential philosophy for children movement, pioneered by Matthew Lipman, which has also consistently viewed critical thinking as central to its objectives.[5]

One explanation of the appeal of critical thinking is the fact that it is a comprehensive notion encompassing both attitudes and skills. Robert Ennis, for example, has set out a large number of skills and abilities which a critical thinker would possess, and his taxonomy has invited consideration of *practical* ways in which critical thinking competency can be developed and tested.[6] John Passmore has persuasively argued that attitudes and virtues, both intellectual and moral, must also be seen as a vital part of what it is to be a critical thinker, if we are to do justice to the idea of the critical spirit.[7] Israel Scheffler made critical thinking central to a conception of teaching in which the teacher's reasons are submitted to the student for evaluation and judgement, and this intimate association of teaching with critical thinking helped bring the notion to centre stage in education.[8] Critical thinking has succeeded, where many other ideals have failed, in crossing the theory/practice divide. We shall see, however, that it too is not without its critics.

What is critical thinking?

We should be wary of succinct definitions, especially when dealing with a rich and fertile notion. It has been said that when one feels the need of a definition, it is a good idea to lie down until the feeling passes.[9] It is tempting, of course, to try to find one comprehensive formula which captures the essence of critical thinking, but the chances of success are slim; critical thinking comes into so many contexts and takes such different forms that it is enormously difficult for any *summary* account to do justice to the ramifications of the idea. Consider the following examples taken from the recent literature:

1   'Critical thinking is the conscious, deliberate rational assessment of claims according to clearly identified standards of proof.'[10]
2   'Critical thinking is the appropriate use of reflective scepticism within the problem area under consideration.'[11]
3   'Critical thinking is thinking which appropriately reflects the power and convicting force of reasons.'[12]
4   'Critical thinking involves calling into question the assumptions under-lying our customary, habitual ways of thinking and acting and then being ready to think and act differently on the basis of this critical questioning.'[13]
5   'Critical thinking is thinking that facilitates judgment because it relies on criteria, is self-correcting, and is sensitive to context.'[14]

All of these provide some insight into critical thinking, often capturing in a succinct way general ideas which have been in circulation for some time.[15] We can learn from each of these without feeling that we have to decide which one gives us *the* definition. Critical reflection might unearth limitations in these very accounts and, at the same time, illustrate certain aspects of the ideal.

For example, the first one above comes, perhaps not surprisingly, from a short guide to studying philosophy, written for beginning students, and emphasises rational assessment according to clearly identified standards of *proof*. No doubt, and for good reason, the author wanted to put students on notice that the mere expression of one's opinion is not philosophy. It would be very surprising, however, if a review of a book or a film in the arts section of the newspaper attempted any proofs or refutations, but it might yet be a fine example of critical thinking. We recognise a critical review without thinking that anything must be *proven*. The definition does not work well for all branches of philosophy. Do we have clearly identified standards of proof in ethics? Does anyone expect to find a *proof* emerging in the abortion debate? Proof, in short, is not invariably appropriate or possible; the critical thinker needs a sense of when proof is the objective and when it is not.

Consider also the important suggestion that critical thinking involves the use of reflective scepticism. When James Randi investigates the claims of various charlatans, and shows how a clever magician can readily duplicate such performances, his judicious scepticism surely manifests critical thinking. With certain topics such as parapsychology, or alleged encounters with aliens, reflective scepticism *is* no doubt the appropriate attitude for the critical thinker. Without it our would-be 'critical' inspection will very likely end in credulity and gullibility.[16] If, on the other hand, a student comes up with a possible interpretation of a difficult passage in a piece of philosophy or in a poem, it is not clear that reflective scepticism is necessarily involved. There was, perhaps, no prior interpretation to be sceptical about, and one may see at once that the proposed account itself is helpful. Again, critical thought can produce a *further* reason for believing in a theory which had already been given some support, rather than a reason to doubt the theory. We should, perhaps, be reflectively sceptical about this definition.

With respect to the account in terms of the power and convicting force of reasons, it is again clear that critical thinking *is* closely connected with the appeal to reason and evidence. A scientist who is thinking critically may see, for example, that such and such constitutes counter-evidence to the theory in question, and may wonder if an account which does justice to all the evidence can be found. In another context, a critic recognises that a word or metaphor counts against a certain interpretation and looks for some way of making sense of the whole text. Such examples, however, presuppose a notion, albeit vague, of something *problematic* in the background, a notion that will vary according to context.[17] The moves we now make with relative ease once required critical thought but familiarity and practice have reduced them to virtually an automatic response.[18] I am appropriately moved by reasons when I add together the amounts on two cheques I am about to deposit, but this does not earn me *any* credit as a critical thinker because there is nothing problematic for me here.[19]

We may agree that a critical thinker should be able, and disposed, to identify and examine *assumptions* which lie hidden. Those educators who are particularly concerned about hegemony, the hidden curriculum, bias and the taken-for-granted in our lives, will want to emphasise this aspect of critical thinking in the context of teaching. Important as this is, however, it hardly captures the whole of critical thinking. If we were to think critically about this account of critical thinking, we *might* ask about the assumptions it makes; alternatively, however, we might try to find a counter-example, to formulate a different account, to look for ambiguities or vagueness, and so on. Critical thinking takes a variety of forms; looking for hidden assumptions is just one, albeit rather important, task. It is a task which those who are concerned with critical pedagogy are particularly interested in because, as Dewey pointed out, unrecognised assumptions exercise control over us.

Notions like proof, scepticism, reasons and assumption finding help to illuminate the nature of critical thinking to some extent, but they do this in the manner of a flashlight rather than sunlight. They show up a small area quite clearly but leave much else in shadows. It is useful, I think, to view these various accounts as partial and complementary, and to be aware of their limitations. What the comments on the definitions suggest is that if one changes the context in some way, by changing the subject matter, the individual involved, his or her purpose or interests, what seemed so natural and central in the account becomes less convincing.

The fifth definition cited earlier, from Lipman's work, needs to be fleshed out by referring to aspects of the ideas just discussed, but it has the great merit of emphasising *judgement* (how critical thinking takes us beyond that which we can routinely calculate), the importance of *context* (how rules and principles have to be adapted to situations), and the *self-referential* character of critical thinking (how such thinking needs to be applied to whatever critical thinking principles and criteria we currently endorse).

Skills and attitudes

Inspired by the above definitions, we may tentatively suggest that a critical thinker has the following sorts of dispositions, supported by relevant abilities and attitudes:

1   to examine and evaluate claims to knowledge, normative principles, theories, policy recommendations, and other matters where judgement is called for;

2   to determine if what is presented as evidence and relevant argument merits being so considered, and to what extent it is biased, inadequate, misleading or in other ways deficient;

3   to resist efforts by others to impose ideas on him or her, and to avoid being being imposed upon by ideas which are taken for granted in the prevailing intellectual and social climate;

4   to regard situations and issues conventionally deemed to be straightforward as potentially problematic and controversial, to try to attend to the unusual when attracted by the familiar, and to imagine ways in which the existing framework might be transcended.

One can readily see how the critical thinker needs skills and relevant critical principles if these dispositions are to be displayed; but a commitment to critical thinking also requires the presence of certain attitudes.

Perhaps because skills can be more easily measured than attitudes, and because they are perceived as practical and directly useful, discussion of critical thinking often deals exclusively with skills and techniques. One sees this, for example, when critical thinking is equated with informal logic; critical thinking and critical thinking skills become virtually synonymous. A distortion results here, because skills need to be *combined* with certain attitudes and virtues. This is not, however, to give any undeserved support to the claim that acquiring certain skills, such as the ability to detect and avoid fallacies, is irrelevant to critical thinking; nor is it to support the view that what is called the teaching of critical thinking skills would, paradoxically, be better termed teaching conformity and passivity. A comment about each of these suggestions is in order.

Some critics complain that there is no clear theory of fallacy, that there are simply endless ways in which reasoning can go astray, and that skilled practitioners of history, physics and other disciplines can in any case recognise fallacious reasoning without having to learn special labels.[20] All of this is intended to debunk attempts to teach critical thinking skills, especially the skills of fallacy avoidance. These arguments are not impressive. In the absence of a general theory, one can still learn, through practice, to identify examples of well-known fallacies; and to learn *some* such examples is worthwhile even if a complete list could never be drawn up. It is possible, of course, to recognise a mistake which one cannot name, but this does not show that it is not *useful* to *have* a name for a particular mistake. If one wants to listen critically to a political speech, for example, some familiarity with fallacious arguments will not be a handicap.[21]

This, however, brings us to the second of the doubts just mentioned; namely, that what passes for critical thinking in education and textbooks is a training in conformity, where students are not encouraged to question what is being presented *as* a good reason or a fallacy.[22] The skills learned, it is alleged, help one simply to adapt to the situations one finds oneself in; in other words, they provide the benefits offered by the Sophists. The examples presented in critical thinking textbooks are said to create an oversimplified set of alternatives, and students are not invited to imagine other possibilities. No doubt such criticisms sometimes apply to the way in which critical thinking is *taught*, but one cannot argue on this basis against learning critical skills in general. The skills we learn may in time, and with suitable encouragement and opportunity, be turned against the very examples on which the skills were first practised; and the skills we acquire may be used subsequently to sharpen or modify the skills themselves, as when our skill at detecting oversimplification leads us to see that some of our critical skills and tools are *themselves* oversimplified.[23] We need to ask now how these richer possibilities may be encouraged.

At any pedagogical moment, we are being introduced to what our teachers think of as worth learning. The fact of human fallibility means that, together with the knowledge, rules, skills and reasons which we acquire, certain attitudes are required to ensure that what we have learned does not itself come to be *held* uncritically. Whitehead reminded us that it is often the fate of a bright idea to turn into an inert one. Need one add that the ideas we learn from our teachers are not always bright ones to begin with? Critical thinking is capable of self-correction, always ready to be applied to what we take to be our best principles, rules, distinctions and so on. Some are inclined to recommend a sceptical attitude as a component of critical thinking,[24] and we have seen that this notion is even built into certain definitions of critical thinking. The trouble with the notion of scepticism as a generally desirable aim, however, is that it fails to do justice to the idea of coming to a definite conclusion when the evidence is overwhelming; and it seems to cast doubt on the wisdom of having *any* settled views at all. The notion of scepticism only exacerbates the negative element which many already associate with critical thinking.

The attitude needed, I suggest, is open-mindedness rather than scepticism. Open-mindedness suggests a willingness to take relevant evidence and arguments into account in forming our beliefs and values, and being willing to consider what can be said against the views which we now hold, altering or rejecting them where necessary. Of course, it can only come into meaningful play if we also possess the relevant abilities and understanding which *enable* us to review the evidence and arguments intelligently, or at least the ability to develop or hit upon the necessary tools to do so. One might, however, possess the *ability* to review one's position and never do so because one lacked the disposition, and the attitude of open-mindedness captures this vital point.[25]

This attitude also addresses the concerns just mentioned of those who fear a dangerous conformity in teaching for critical thinking, because an open-minded individual will also have to bear in mind the possibility that the very *framework* of critical principles and distinctions being acquired is itself problematic. A student might be invited to analyse an example to which a certain distinction is thought to apply. The example, however, might reveal that the distinction itself is by no means as clear or unproblematic as one had thought. Where critical thinking is genuine, there can be *no* mere exercises; the situation remains problematic, and open-mindedness helps to keep this insight alive.[26]

Open-mindedness does not mean that we never come to any definite opinion, only that the ones we form remain subject to revision and rejection in the light of further reflection.[27] It serves, therefore, to introduce a certain humility which can temper any tendency in the direction of arrogance and rigidity that might be fostered by a sense of one's emerging critical skills and increasing knowledge. Open-mindedness is relevant to Passmore's distinction between critical *skills* and a critical *spirit*; we would not regard a person as open-minded who allowed his or her reflections to be determined by other considerations, such as self-interest, or who used their skills to pervert the course of the inquiry. Open-mindedness stands opposed to bias and prejudice, and thus serves to prevent the deliberate misuse of critical skills.[28]

Objections to critical thinking

Despite widespread endorsement of critical thinking as an educational ideal, various misgivings are expressed. First, there is the complaint hinted at above that critical thinking, by association with 'being critical', is essentially negative, a process of finding fault, pulling things apart, with no positive or constructive features. Critical thinking may, of course, result in negative comments, though the identification of error may also be the beginning of a search for a better answer. A critical appraisal, however, may show that a work is fine, that an argument is valid, that a policy is justifiable; there is no reason why an appraisal must be unfavourable. Anthony O'Hear, by contrast, in defending what he himself describes as an authoritarian approach to education, speaks of the need for students to *learn* things *rather than* acquiring a universal *scepticism*, a comment which occurs in the context of his opposition to inducing a spirit of criticism in the young. One sees how readily and misleadingly a negative connotation surfaces.[29]

A related objection is that critical thinking represents a defensive stance, an argumentative form of discourse, which gives pride of place to truth as the objective, thereby minimising and endangering the aim of people working together to solve problems based on receptiveness and caring. At least as an initial response, it is argued, the argumentative mode should be replaced by a narrative mode which would encourage conversation and cooperation.[30] This objection, however, does not count against critical thinking as such, only against a certain approach to critical thinking which is hostile and aggressive. The tone and style which is appropriate will vary from context to context. In the face of Holocaust denial, a hostile critical response might be desirable. On the other hand, it may be entirely appropriate in many contexts to defer temporarily a critical assessment until one has established a relationship and an atmosphere which is supportive and cooperative.

Also of concern is the accusation that critical thinking ignores the importance of creative and imaginative thinking, and puts undue emphasis on just one aspect of thinking. We should certainly remind ourselves of the dangers of either–or thinking, and resolve to give both criticism and creativity our attention. We can go still further, however, and recognise an important *connection* between them.[31] Imagination is needed to come up with a critical judgement since one is going beyond what is given and not merely offering a stock response. In *imagining* how a position might be supported or countered, one exercises creative ability. Similarly, the critical examination of arguments and policies may suggest unanticipated and novel possibilities; creative ideas do not come out of nowhere. At some point, they too will require critical assessment.[32]

A further doubt arises with the view that there is really no such thing as critical thinking in general, only good thinking in the context of some particular subject or discipline. Critical thinking, on this view, is not, as it might appear to be, the name of a *general* ability which can be developed and then applied. In saying that critical thinking is important, the objection goes, we are only encouraging belief in an imaginary capacity, and minimising the importance of hard work in the particular subjects which make up the curriculum.[33] It is certainly true that critical thinking presupposes a body of knowledge to draw on, and philosophers of education in the twentieth century have largely concurred in this.[34] There is no way to avoid the implication of R. S. Peters' aphorism that 'content without criticism is blind, but criticism without content is empty'.[35] It does not follow from this view, however, that generally useful critical skills cannot become part of one's non-specialist repertoire. One always needs to know enough to understand what is going on in a debate; very often, however, our general knowledge will allow us to *follow* a discussion, and we can see at a certain point that something is going wrong. Not all principles of argument are subject-specific; useful distinctions can be learned in a context-free way, and drawn on in *any* context where they are relevant.[36]

The importance of content as a necessary condition of critical thinking also gives rise to the objection that critical thinking has no place in early education since children must spend many years acquiring that basis in knowledge which would make critical reflection possible. Some, including

Richard Rorty, maintain that critical thinking is not an appropriate aim before the university level.[37] The main problem with this argument is that it assumes that an *exclusive* focus on content mastery must *precede* any attempt to foster critical thinking. What is neglected is the point that a critical attitude may be imparted in the way in which content is presented. As Quinton puts it, teachers need to learn to attach a critical question-mark to the propositions they affirm.[38] Passmore, moreover, has pointed out that sensible teachers intersperse the teaching of content with opportunities for critical reflection.[39]

Finally, we may consider the objection that critical thinking is gender-biased.[40] Its connection with rationality, objectivity and autonomy makes it genderised in favour of males; it serves to devalue intuition, feelings, relationship and one's inner voice. Certainly, it is important to acknowledge that genderised traits have traditionally placed girls and women in what Jane Roland Martin calls a 'double bind': they have been derided for acquiring traits, such as critical ability, which have been genderised in favour of males, and not properly valued for acquiring traits genderised as female.[41] The educational objective, however, should be to make the ideal of critical thinking equally available and attractive to males and females, to find ways of transcending the dichotomy reflected in the traditional stereotypes. We should not encourage the view that there is an alternative path to knowledge for women which does not draw on critical thinking.[42] In this connection, it is important to be clear that the empirical evidence is that females are not less disposed nor less competent to engage in critical thinking than males.[43] Girls at school need to be encouraged to develop critical thinking skills and attitudes; their interests are not well served by leading them to believe that intuition is a viable substitute for reason, or that logic is inherently male and alien to women. The importance of intuition in science and other inquiries does not mean that we can ignore the need to assess critically those ideas which come intuitively. Moreover, critical thinking, with its appeal to reasons and objectivity,[44] is indispensable if we hope to identify and expose the bias and discrimination which produce sexism. Critical thinking does not involve the naïve view, as some suggest, that the critical thinker attains objectivity; it involves a striving for objectivity, and this is in no way at odds with attending to one's inner voice.

Is critical thinking important?

Turning now directly to the importance of critical thinking, there are three main lines of justification. First, there is an *ethical* justification. Human beings have potentialities which other animals do not possess. It was this difference which suggested to Socrates that the matter of choosing a teacher for one's children was charged with great significance. One potentiality is to

develop into an adult capable of a self-determined existence, where fundamental decisions and choices which affect one's life are made by the person
themself. It is equally possible to bring up a child in such a way that he or
she remains incapable of such decisions and choices, becoming permanently
dependent upon some other person or institution. In this case, the individual has been harmed because they have been deprived of a vital aspect of a
meaningful and fulfilling life. The ethical wrong is simply that the child
has not been treated with the respect due to someone *capable* of growing
into an autonomous adult with a distinctive point of view. If, as Jacques
Barzun has put it, the whole aim of good teaching is to turn the young
learner into an independent, self-propelling creature,[45] then good teaching
requires that our educational aims include the development of critical
thinking.

There is, however, another, more *pragmatic* line of argument. Students
often complain that the schools fail to provide the job training that they
desperately need. The problem with this point of view, however, is that the
schools simply cannot know what jobs will be available in the future, and
students will not be well served if they are narrowly trained for *particular*
jobs which may well disappear completely. When the time comes, as it
almost certainly will, to move into another line of work, students will need
the flexibility and resourcefulness to adapt to something new. They will
need to learn what the new job requires, and they will need the sort of
attitude which permits them to see themselves in some other capacity. An
emphasis on critical, independent thought in their schooling will be all to
the good.[46]

Finally, there is a purely *intellectual* justification suggested by Descartes'
remark mentioned at the outset. To become a philosopher, scientist, histo-
rian and so on, it is not enough to be familiar with what others have said on
one's subject. There is a useful distinction between learning about the
subject and learning to do what the subject involves. To participate in the
conversation is to be able to contribute to it, and this requires being able to
draw upon what one knows and use it effectively. This, I believe, was
Whitehead's point in his famous account of education as the acquisition of
the art of the *utilisation* of knowledge.[47] This intellectual justification does
not presuppose that everyone is capable of critical work at the forefront of
the discipline; in many areas, we will be relatively dependent on experts.
Critical thinking, however, exists at different levels; to aim at critical
thinking in teaching is to attempt to wean students away from the mere
acceptance of beliefs which others tell them are true, and to encourage them
to try to assess the credentials of those who present themselves as experts.

Concluding comment

Properly conceived, critical thinking is crucial in teaching at all levels, serving to thwart various forms of miseducation which always threaten to undermine our efforts. Teachers need to think through their aims in education to see how the ideas implicit in the general ideal of critical thinking may capture important aspects of their overall objective. Most important of all, they need to ask what it would mean to teach in a critical way,[48] and to find ways of expressing the ideal in classroom practice.[49]

Notes

1 The references are to John Stuart Mill, *On Liberty*, ch. 2; Immanuel Kant, *Critique of Judgement*, First part, Second book; David Hume, *Enquiry Concerning Human Understanding*, Section 10; René Descartes, *Rules for the Direction of the Mind*, Rule 3; and for Socrates on the examined life, Plato, *Apology* 38A. The image of the cave appears in Plato, *The Republic*, Book 7.

2 For comments on Dewey, Russell and Whitehead on critical thinking, see my paper 'Content and criticism: the aims of schooling', *Journal of Philosophy of Education*, 29(1) (1995): 47–60; reprinted in *Inquiry* 14(3) (1995): 13–27. For other examples of early discussions, see Victor H. Noll, 'The habit of scientific thinking', *Teacher's College Record* 35(1) (1933): 1–9; L. Susan Stebbing, *A Modern Introduction to Logic*, London: Methuen, 1933, especially ch. 1, and her *Thinking to Some Purpose*, Harmondsworth: Penguin Books, 1939; and Howard R. Anderson (ed.) *Teaching Critical Thinking in the Social Studies*, Washington, DC: National Council for the Social Studies, 1942.

3 The Watson-Glaser Critical Thinking Test appeared in 1940; Max Black, *Critical Thinking*, New York: Prentice-Hall (1946); Mary Jane Aschner looked at critical thinking in the context of high school English in 'Teaching the anatomy of criticism', *School Review* 64(7) (1956): 317–22; and numerous papers on indoctrination appeared in the 1960s, many reprinted in I. A. Snook (ed.) *Concepts of Indoctrination*, London: Routledge & Kegan Paul, 1972.

4 See especially Israel Scheffler, *The Langauge of Education*, Springfield, IL: Charles C. Thomas, 1960; Robert H. Ennis, 'A concept of critical thinking', *Harvard Educational Review* 32(1) (1962): 81–111; and John Passmore, 'On teaching to be critical', in R. S. Peters (ed.) *The Concept of Education*, Routledge & Kegan Paul, 1967: 192–211.

5 See Matthew Lipman, *Philosophy Goes to School*, Philadelphia: Temple University Press, 1988. For an account of Lipman's achievement, see Ronald F. Reed and Ann E. Witcher, 'Matthew Lipman: restoring the connection between education and philosophy', in James J. van Patten (ed.) *Academic Profiles in Higher Education*, Lampeter: Edward Mellen, 1992: 203–28.

6 The list of relevant abilities is very extensive and includes skills of identification, clarification, judgement, deduction, generalisation, inference, evaluation, definition and fallacy avoidance. For one fairly comprehensive account, see Robert H. Ennis, 'A taxonomy of critical thinking dispositions and abilities', in Joan Boykoff Baron and Robert J. Sternberg (eds) *Teaching Thinking Skills: Theory and Practice*, New York: W. H. Freeman, 1987: 9–26.

7 See Passmore, 'On teaching to be critical', in R. S. Peters (ed.) *The Concept of Education*, London: Routledge & Kegan Paul, 1967; Ennis, 'A taxonomy of critical thinking dispositions and abilities', in Joan Boykoff Baron and Robert J. Sternberg (eds) *Teaching Thinking Skills: Theory and Practice*, New York: W. H. Freeman, 1987, where Ennis lists fouteen

relevant dispositions, including such virtues as open-mindedness, intellectual honesty, sensitivity to others, and a concern for relevancy and clarity; Neil Cooper, 'The intellectual virtues', *Philosophy* 69 (1994): 459–69; and my *Teaching and the Socratic Virtues*, St John's Nfld: Memorial University, 1995.

 8 Sheffler, *The Language of Education*, Springfield, IL: Charles C. Thomas, 1960. Also Sheffler, *Reason and Teaching*, Indianapolis: Bobbs-Merrill, 1973. See also my paper, 'Reason in teaching: Sheffler's philosophy of education', *Studies in Philosophy and Education* 16(1–2) (1997): 89–101.

 9 William Kennick, 'Teaching philosophy', in *Teaching What We Do*, Essays by Amherst College Faculty, Amherst, MA: Amherst College Press, 1991: 163–81. And Peter Geach has reminded us that there is much that we can identify which we cannot readily define. See his 'Plato's *Euthyphro*', *The Monist* 50(3) (1966): 369–82.

10 Douglas J. Soccio, *How to Get the Most out of Philosophy*, Belmont: Wadsworth, 1992: 37.

11 John McPeck, *Critical Thinking and Education*, Oxford: Martin Robertson, 1981: 7.

12 Harvey Siegel, 'The role of reasons in (science) education', in William Hare (ed.) *Reason in Teaching and Education*, Halifax, NS: Dalhousie University School of Education, 1989: 6; reprinted in William Hare and John P. Portelli (eds) *Philosophy of Education: Introductory Readings*, 2nd edn, Calgary: Detselig, 1996: 107–23.

13 Stephen D. Brookfield, *Developing Critical Thinkers*, San Fransisco: Jossey-Bass, 1988: 1.

14 Matthew Lipman, *Thinking in Education*, Cambridge: Cambridge University Press, 1991: 116.

15 For example, Brookfield's account in terms of detecting assumptions puts one in mind of Dewey's argument for the value of philosophy itself, given the prejudices we are all prone to, which is 'to enable us to get a conscious mastery which will change them from assumptions which control us to tools of inquiry and action'. See John Dewey, 'Why study philosophy?' in Jo Ann Boydston (ed.) *John Dewey, The Early Works 1882–98*, vol. 4, Carbondale: Southern Illinois University Press, 1971: 62–5. A similar theme emerges when Susan Stebbing discussed cherished beliefs which cannot withstand critical questioning. See *Thinking to Some Purpose*, Harmondsworth: Penguin Books, 1939: 39.

16 Any issue of *The Skeptical Inquirer* will illustrate these points.

17 The problematic aspect was stressed by Susan Stebbing in her discussion of reflective thinking. See *A Modern Introduction to Logic*, London: Methuen, 1933: 9.

18 R. S. Peters observes that if someone successfully applies elementary rules, we do not ascribe a sense of judgement to that person. See his 'Michael Oakeshott's philosophy of education', in Preston King and B. C. Parekh (eds) *Politics and Experience: Essays Presented to Michael Oakeshott*, London: Cambridge University Press, 1968.

19 Similarly, deciding reasonably what to do in a certain situation may call for nothing more than common sense. Deciding to call an ambulance to the scene of a traffic accident does not normally require critical thinking. Thus Ennis's account in terms of 'reasonable, reflective thinking' is also too broad.

20 These points have been made in various places by John McPeck. See, for example, his *Critical Thinking and Education*, Oxford: Martin Robertson, 1981, and his paper 'What is learned in informal logic courses?' *Teaching Philosophy* 14(1) (1991): 25–34.

21 See my review of McPeck's *Critical Thinking and Education* in *Canadian Journal of Education* 7 (4) (1982): 107–10.

22 See, for example, Laura Duhan Kaplan, 'Teaching intellectual autonomy: the failure of the critical thinking movement', *Educational Theory* 41(4) (1991): 361–70.

23 See my discussion of Kaplan in *What Makes a Good Teacher?* London, Ont: Althouse Press, 1993.

24 Carl Sagan, 'The burden of skepticism', *The Skeptical Inquirer* 12(1) (1987): 38–46.

25 See my *Open-mindedness and Education*, Montreal: McGill-Queen's, 1979; *In Defence of Open-mindedness*, Montreal: McGill-Queen's, 1985; and 'Open-mindedness in the classroom',

Journal of Philosophy of Education 19(2) (1985): 251–9.

26 See Passmore, 'On teaching to be critical', in R. S. Peters (ed.) *The Concept of Education*, London: Routledge & Kegan Paul, 1967.

27 See William Hare and T. H. McLaughlin, 'Open-mindedness, commitment and Peter Gardner', *Journal of Philosophy of Education* 28(2) (1994): 239–44.

28 Not, of course, that it is the only desirable attitude. One will also need courage to take a critical stances, a sympathetic imgination if one is to understand the views being critically assessed, and so on.

29 Anthony O'Hear, *Education and Democracy*, London: The Claridge Press, 1991: 33.

30 See Stephen P. Norris, 'Sustaining and responding to charges of bias in critical thinking', *Educational Theory* 45(2) (1995): 199–211. I should add that Norris makes it clear that he does believe that the argumentative mode is also important.

31 See my discussion in *What Makes a Good Teacher?* London, Ont: Althouse Press, 1993.

32 Cf. John Dewey, *Construction and Criticism*, New York: Columbia University Press, 1930. For an excellent contemporary discussion, see Sharon Bailin, 'Critical and creative thinking', *Informal Logic* 9(1) (1987): 23–30; reprinted in William Hare and John P. Portelli (eds) *Philosophy of Education: Introductory Readings*, 2nd edn, Calgary: Detselig, 1996: 73–82.

33 Again, this view has been conspicuously, though by no means exclusively, associated with the work of John McPeck. For a recent statement of his views, see his *Teaching Critical Thinking: Dialogue and Dialectic*, New York: Routledge, 1990.

34 See my 'Content and criticism: the aim of schooling', *Journal of Philosophy of Education* 29 (1) (1995).

35 R. S. Peters, 'Education as initiation', in R. D. Archambault (ed.) *Philosophical Analysis and Education*, London: Routledge & Kegan Paul, 1965: 104.

36 For other examples of the view that critical principles may be subject-neutral, see Harvey Siegel, 'The role of reasons in (science) education', in William Hare (ed.) *Reason in Teaching and Education*, Halifax, NS: Dalhousie University School of Education, 1989 – reprinted in William Hare and John P. Portelli (eds) *Philosophy of Education: Introductory Readings*, 2nd edn, Calgary: Detselig, 1996; and Paul Hager, review of Robin Barrow, *Understanding Skills*, *Educational Philosophy and Theory* 23(2) (1991): 108–13.

37 Richard Rorty, 'Education without dogma', *Dissent* 36(2) (1989): 198–204; reprinted in William Hare and John P. Portelli (eds) *Philosophy of Education: Introductory Readings*, 2nd edn, Calgary: Detselig, 1996: 207–17.

38 Anthony Quinton, 'On the ethics of belief', in Graham Haydon (ed.) *Education and Values*, London: Institute of Education, 1987: 44.

39 John Passmore, *The Philosophy of Teaching*, London: Duckworth, 1980.

40 See, for example, Barbara Thayer-Bacon, 'Is modern critical thinking theory sexist?' *Inquiry: Critical Thinking across the Disciplines* 10(2) (1992): 3–7; reprinted in William Hare and John P. Portelli (eds) *Philosophy of Education: Introductory Readings*, 2nd edn, Calgary: Detselig, 1996: 95–106.

41 Jane Roland Martin, 'Becoming educated: a journey of alienation or integration?' *Journal of Education* 167(3) (1985): 71–84; reprinted in William Hare and John P. Portelli (eds) *Philosophy of Education: Introductory Readings*, 2nd edn, Calgary: Detselig, 1996: 219–32. A genderised trait is one which is appraised differently when possessed by males rather than females, and conversely.

42 For a critique of this position, see Susan Haack, 'Knowledge and propaganda: reflections of an old feminist', *Partisan Review* 60(4) (1993): 556–64; and Noretta Koertge, 'How feminism is now alientating women from science', *Skeptical Inquirer* 19(2) (1995): 42–3.

43 See Deanna Kuhn, *The Skills of Argumenet*, Cambridge: Cambridge University Press, 1991: 280–1. Which is not to say that the intellectual achievements of women have not been minimised or trivialised. See Anne Eisenberg, 'Women and the discourse of science',

Scientific American (July 1992): 122.

44 Linking critical thinking to Truth and Certainty, as Thayer-Bacon does, deliberately ignores fallibility conceptions of knowledge widely represented in the literature, which have emerged as a result of critical work in epistemology. See Barbara Thayer-Bacon, 'Is modern critical thinking theory sexist?' *Inquiry: Critical Thinking across the Disciplines* 10(2) (1992); reprinted in William Hare and John P. Portelli (eds) *Philosophy of Education: Introductory Readings*, 2nd edn, Calgary: Detselig, 1996: 95–106.

45 Jacques Barzun, *Teacher in America*, Boston: Little, Brown & Company, 1946: 21.

46 See John Passmore, 'Educating for the 21st century', The Fourth Wallace Wurth Memorial Lecture, University of New South Wales, 22 April 1985.

47 A. N. Whitehead, *The Aims of Education*, New York: The Free Press, 1967: 4 (first published 1929).

48 See John P. Portelli, 'The challenge of teaching for critical thinking', *McGill Journal of Education* 29(2) (1994): 137–51; reprinted in William Hare and John P. Portelli (eds) *Philosophy of Education: Introductory Readings*, 2nd edn, Calgary: Detselig, 1996: 55–71; see also Shelagh Crooks, 'Developing the critical attitude', *Teaching Philosophy* 18(4) (1995): 313–25.

49 A version of this chapter was delivered as a public lecture at the University of Cyprus, November 1996.

9

THE PLACE OF
NATIONAL IDENTITY
IN THE AIMS OF EDUCATION[1]

Penny Enslin

Should the teaching of national identity have a place in the aims of education? Although national identity, nationalism and nationality have recently enjoyed renewed interest and sympathetic treatment, both in terms of their ethical and cultural significance (Miller 1993; Tamir 1993) and in relation to education (White 1996; Tamir 1992), I argue in this chapter against the promotion of national identity in schools. My central claim is that the teaching of national identity is likely to undermine the educational aims of autonomy and democratic citizenship.

Like most published work in philosophy of education, much of the recent debate about nationalism has taken place in, and is about, liberal democracies. But nationalism and national identity vary according to context. As Anne McClintock observes, 'there is no single narrative of the nation . . . nationalisms are invented, performed, and consumed in ways that do not follow a universal blueprint' (1993: 67). Some current expressions of nationalism appear to be quite benign, when contrasted (for example) with the nationalism of ethnic cleansing. In taking current debate about nation building in South African education as my example, the concerns which I raise in this chapter about national identity as an aim of education are more suited to education in societies without strong liberal traditions, especially post-colonial ones with heterogeneous populations and authoritarian traditions. But these concerns do none the less also point to the dangers of nationalism to education in liberal democracies.

For the purposes of this discussion I shall follow Liah Greenfeld's example and treat nationalism as an umbrella term 'under which are subsumed the related phenomena of national identity (or nationality) and consciousness, and . . . nations' (1992: 3). I understand identity to be a sense of self, one's understanding of who one is in relation to others in a particular place and time. While little detail has been offered by proponents of education for nation building in South Africa (Mkwanazi and Cross 1992; McGurk 1990) of what such a process would involve, I take it that, when schools set out to teach a particular national identity, they set out firstly to persuade children to see themselves as belonging to one nation, which is a constituent part of their understanding of who they are. This has a second, moral implication: children's identity as members of a nation acquires a moral authority in terms of which ties of loyalty to the nation will influence in a fundamental way their behaviour towards one another, and ultimately the character of the political life in which they will participate. Accepting a certain national identity would persuade people to believe that they belong to the nation and that this membership imposes on them moral obligations to their fellow nationals. Presumably this implies, thirdly, that the school curriculum would include ingredients which explicitly set out to persuade children that they belong to a particular nation.

In arguing that teaching a national identity is likely to undermine the educational aims of autonomy and democratic citizenship, and taking South Africa as my case study, I will begin by showing in the next section the extent to which persuading children that they belong to a South African nation requires the development of a myth or illusion of nationhood. Two features of this illusion will then be explored: in the third section the teaching of myths about the past – a central feature of nationalism – will be shown to be at odds with the educational aim of rational autonomy; and in the fourth section the illusory inclusiveness fostered by national identity will be shown to exclude women from equal access to democratic citizenship. These problems, I shall argue in the fifth section, raise more fundamental considerations of how schools should approach the teaching of identities in general. If we aim to teach people to be autonomous members of democratic societies, an educated understanding of given and chosen identities precludes teaching national identity, indeed it should expose the illusion of the nation.

National identity and myth

While South Africa has a history which is distinctive in some respects, it is an example of a post-colonial society in which the unifying idea of nationhood is advocated by some as part of a process of building democracy. As South Africa addresses the task of transforming a divided and unequal educational system, a process of education for nation building has been proposed by some as a strategy for creating unity from diversity (Mkwanazi and Cross 1992; McGurk 1990).

But while creating unity by the assertion of ties of loyalty to co-nationals might seem necessary, how realistic is it to posit a common national identity in a society as divided as South Africa? For the people living permanently within the borders of this country do not conform to a significant extent to the normally cited criteria of nationhood, analyses of which emphasise the difficulties involved in characterising it (Ree 1992: 3; Gellner 1983). Let us take the features of nationality or national identity cited by two authors as examples. For David Miller (1988: 648), who emphasises its subjective quality, nationality is constituted by a set of people's shared beliefs, that they belong together, that this sense of belonging together emerges from a common history and that it will endure in the future. In Miller's account the members of the nation share both a common loyalty and features that distinguish them from others, from whom they enjoy some political autonomy. They are prepared to make personal sacrifices for the good of the nation. Anthony Smith suggests that the fundamental features of national identity include:

> the idea that nations are territorially bounded units of population and that they must have their own homelands; that their members share a common mass culture and common historical myths and memories; that members have reciprocal legal rights and duties under a common legal system; and that nations possess a common division of labour and system of production with mobility across the territory for members.
>
> (1991: 13–14)

Whether these features of nationality and national identity are taken as a subjective set of beliefs or as objective features attributable to a group of people, it is striking that most of them are not applicable to South Africa. Let us accept that since the democratic election of 1994 political autonomy, a historical territory, common legal rights and duties and a common economy with territorial mobility for its members are characteristics of this society. What about the other features?

The members of the 'nation' do not share distinctive characteristics; the society is culturally and linguistically heterogeneous, with some of its citizens sharing more distinctive characteristics with groups of people elsewhere than with many of their compatriots. While the majority share a common loyalty to the political community, the relationship of this disposition to the history of the country is deeply problematic. This is a history which is only partly describable as one of living together; it is also a history of colonialism and conquest, of conflict, expropriation, oppression and exploitation. As a result members of the society have very different sets of memories and myths, in which other members are often depicted as enemies rather than compatriots. It is difficult to locate a common sense of nationhood here. Although apartheid abused the concept of culture for cynical racist ends, it remains the case that South Africans cannot be described as culturally homogeneous or as sharing distinctive characteristics, although there are elements of culture which are shared. There are deep divisions which make it understandable that many do not share a sense of belonging with their compatriots, and which would require extensive, inventive efforts at myth making to counter them.

These problems of applying the usual characteristics of nations to societies like South Africa should not be taken to imply that other 'nations', which do reflect more of these features, have come to do so naturally, or that they are nations in some objective sense. Defenders and opponents of nationalism might raise at this point Ernest Gellner's observation that 'It is nationalism which engenders nations, and not the other way round' (1983: 55).

As Miller observes:

> it is characteristic of nations that their identities are formed not through spontaneous processes of ethnic self-definition but primarily according to the exigencies of power – the demands of states seeking to assure themselves of the loyalty of their subjects. Nationality is to a greater or lesser degree a manufactured item . . . a work of invention, in particular the invention of a communal national past.
>
> (1988: 656)

That nationalism is a political programme which has taken various forms (Smith 1986) is recognised by its defenders. Theorists of nationalism conventionally observe that nations are 'imagined communities', as Benedict Anderson has put it (1983). The ties of national attachment that bind compatriots to one another may be fictitious, but they are valuable as a source of community.

Two recent responses to Anderson's influential account of the nation as an imagined community pose a challenge to his claim that Gellner is wrong in attributing falsity rather than invention to nationalism. Both John O'Neill (1994) and Ross Poole (1991) prefer to describe the community invented by nationalism as illusory rather than imagined, on the grounds of the myths it tells of both its past and its supposed present unity. What is important in this objection for my argument in this chapter is not that it doubts the sense of community that some members of nations might derive from seeing themselves as members of nations. But the illusory quality of the nation as myth has important implications for education, and for the question of whether national identity should have a place in its aims. I will now explore the two senses of illusion attributed to the idea of the nation by Poole and O'Neill, confirming their claims and showing their implications for education.

Nationhood, education and democracy

The idea that education should include the manufacture and teaching of myths and inventions as part of a process of learning a national identity is problematic, both from an educational point of view, and for the democratic project too. Both education itself and education for democratic citizenship necessarily require the development of autonomy – the ability to think for oneself, a capacity for rational, critical thinking in which one is able to achieve some independence from those who seek to influence one's opinions.

Miller notes that ties of national allegiance are unable to withstand rational reflection, which threatens to destroy the community as an object of allegiance by revealing its imaginary quality. 'Whether a nation exists depends on whether its members have the appropriate beliefs; it is no part of the definition that the beliefs should in fact be true' (1988: 648).

The teaching of national identity has occupied a significant place in the history of South African education. The celebration in 1938 of the centenary of the Great Trek was a time of retrospective mythologising among Afrikaner nationalists (McClintock 1993: 69–71). From this period of invention of community there emerged, as part of a nationalist strategy, the Christian National Education (CNE) Policy of 1948 (Rose and Tunmer 1975). As well as explicitly excluding blacks from the nation, the Policy proclaims certain myths of nationhood, of which two are particularly pertinent here. Invoking occupation of a particular territory, it declares: 'We believe that every nation is rooted in its own soil which is allotted to it by the creator,' thus concealing South Africa's history of conquest and expropriation of the land of the original inhabitants. Turning to historical myths and memories, the Policy proclaims: 'We believe that history must be taught in the light of the divine revelation and must be seen as the fulfilment of God's decree for the world and humanity' (ibid.: 123). The hand of God can be invoked as justification for the oppression and exploitation of those who are not members of the nation.

For education conceived of as the development of autonomy, such myths are obviously problematic. The problem is not that education should promote only knowledge and not belief; for if I know something I must at the same time believe it. And while we cannot plausibly expect the educated person to have at their command only true beliefs, autonomy requires that their beliefs rest on reasons or evidence for holding them to be true, and they would also be held provisionally, in case rational reflection on some new evidence or argument were to persuade them to reconsider. We must be alarmed at the idea that the educated individual should embrace certain myths manufactured about their 'nation' and its history as if they were true and not subject to critical scrutiny. This is particularly so of history, for, as Hobsbawm puts it: 'Unfortunately, the history that nationalists want is not the history that professional academic historians, even ideologically committed ones, ought to supply. It is a retrospective mythology' (1992: 23). While the retrospective mythologising of Afrikaner nationalism has lost its political influence, creating a myth of the nation for post-apartheid South Africa appears also to require a retrospective mythologising in which the truth is secondary to the myth, in this case a myth which must offer an illusion in which past division is concealed.

I am not suggesting that education is only a matter of enabling people to acquire knowledge and belief held rationally, and that there is no place for imagination and invention in education. Imagination and creativity have their place in all disciplines. Crucially, if activities such as imagining what it was like to be present at significant historical events contribute to the development of autonomy and the growth of democratic values, education should encourage democratic citizens to exercise political imagination, including considering an issue from the point of view of others. What distinguishes such examples of the development and exercise of imagination from belief in the nation as imagined or illusory community is, first, that as part of the educational process the individual person is exercising their own imagination, even if prompted by teachers. They are not being manipulated as a result of others exercising their imaginations. Second and relatedly, the educational experience helps them to learn to know the difference between imagining and other activities, like knowing, defending, questioning and proving. This points us to a crucial characteristic of being educated: that there is willingness on the part of the learner (Peters 1966: 45). By this I don't mean to suggest that children in particular are always and from an early age aware of the rationale for the activities in which they engage while at school. Rather, I suggest that education enables us, eventually, to adopt our beliefs because we choose to, rather than as a result of manipulation of which we are unaware, and that we have an understanding of the process we have undergone.

I take the development of rationality to be central to autonomy and to education, in which we try to help students to learn the skills of rational inquiry and encourage them to exercise those skills. While this does not mean that education is only about learning to engage in rational inquiry – it also legitimately promotes imagination and creativity – it does imply that education should not encourage pupils to embrace false beliefs. Indeed, education and particularly education for a democratic way of life must include directing pupils' attention to the exposing of false beliefs, especially the myths which political and commercial entrepreneurs would have them embrace.

The democratic way of life could occasionally require that pupils and citizens publicly renounce the nation's values and deeds. But loyalty to the nation is expected of its members; 'identity' in this context implies both a sense of who one is and an obligation to 'identify' in the sense of agreement with doctrines and policies. While nationhood is often expressed as a demand for autonomy for the nation, this does not usually imply autonomy for its members. It is typically claimed by nationalists that every nation is unique, yet commonly that each individual member of the nation must subsume themselves under the category of the nation, surrendering their individual uniqueness in order to have an identity as a member of an organic whole, firmly identifying with and celebrating a given heritage. As Michael Walzer puts it when discussing the question of what sort of institutions provide the most supportive environment for the good life, nationalism, as 'most characteristically an ideology of the right . . . requires no political choices and no activity beyond ritual affirmation' (1992: 96). He adds that for nations ruled by foreigners (or, one might add, people oppressed by minorities) nationalism requires self-sacrifice as well as ritual affirmation as individuals seek autonomy for their people rather than for themselves. After liberation, nationalists are more likely to settle for vicarious participation.

Nationalism offers little by way of inspiration to democratic deeds and procedures, nothing to prompt debate. It serves a purpose in liberation struggles, as it has indeed done in South Africa, but offers little thereafter. It is a form of association that promotes community, but typically lacks commitment to democratic participation. Informed by a sense of history which is a combination of forgetting and retrospective mythologising, nationalism does not foster the exercise of reason and informed, critical imagination and questioning of authority which are central to the practices developed by education. Nationalism is more likely to pre-empt the exercise of democratic reason and imagination by discouraging open-ended public debate on alternative political possibilities, and exploration of proper rational grounds for action.

Mother of the nation

'All nations,' as McClintock has observed, 'are gendered' (1993: 61). Nationhood is standardly expressed in terms of what have traditionally been regarded as masculine exploits, ideals and concerns, as is illustrated in the celebration of nationhood by commemorating battles and conquests, the bravery of heroes and the singing of martial anthems. The myths and symbols of militarism, the capacity to coerce by military means, were central to the development of the idea of the nation state. Indeed, in some cases the growth of the nation state and the development of its military capacity were closely interrelated (Held 1992).

This feature of nationalism has two implications for democracy, and for education. The first is that the values of militarism – of force as a strategy and of hierarchical structures of authority – do not foster the exercise of reason in public debate and the exercise of individual autonomy. Second, fostering national identity as an expression of militaristic masculinity excludes women from its image of citizenship. The nation apparently includes all citizens. But, as has been observed by O'Neill (1994: 140) in respect of language groups, classes, ethnicity and religion, this inclusiveness is illusory. I will explore gender, as an example of the illusory inclusiveness offered by national identity, again taking as my example South Africa, where women have been accorded a similar political status in the concept of the nation in the languages of both Afrikaner nationalism and that of the liberation struggle against it.

The place of the woman in Afrikaner nationalism was expressed in the idea of the *'volksmoeder'* or 'mother of the nation'. In common with some other male-dominated societies, Afrikaner women have been allocated a role which purports to accord them status and respect while subordinating them to male control. This idea established 'a clear role model for Afrikaner women. It was a deliberately constructed ideal, [mainly] the work of male cultural entrepreneurs who deliberately promoted a set of images surrounding women; these centred mainly on their nurturing and homemaking roles' (Brink 1990: 290). This image of Afrikaner women was based on popularised accounts of their role in the Great Trek and their suffering in the concentration camps established as part of the scorched earth tactics of the British during the Second Anglo-Boer War. While these accounts stressed the courage and resistance shown by the women, the notion of the *volksmoeder* was incorporated into a nationalism that was male-dominated and emphasised her qualities of self-sacrifice, resilience, suffering, virtue and of nurturing both her own family and the nation itself.

The themes of nurturing, suffering and courage in the concept of the Afrikaner *volksmoeder* are also present in the discourse of the national liberation struggle, where the ideal of the 'mother of the nation' appears again. Cherryl Walker comments:

> In societies in which the boundaries of 'the nation' are most fiercely contested . . . women are frequently granted [the role of] symbol of the nation or ethnic group. It is a symbolism that has nothing to do with citizenship and everything to do with Woman as Mother: mother of the nation, mother of heroes and martyrs, mother, above all, of sons. . . . 'Mother of the Nation' often has very little to do with tangible benefits.
> (1990: 43)

While there are similarities between the mother of the nation in Afrikaner nationalism and in the nationalism of the liberation struggle – the metaphor of the mother in both portrays her as a political subject rather than a political agent – there are also important differences. First, while Afrikaner nationalism is based on a concept of the nation which is racially exclusive, the nationalism of the African National Congress (ANC), the central force in the liberation struggle, is in principle inclusive and non-racial. Second: 'In the case of Afrikaner nationalism, motherhood is seen as an essentially home-centred, supportive and ultimately passive activity, whereas in the nationalism of the ANC, by contrast, motherhood has assumed a very different character: it is militant, politically focused' (Walker 1990: 65).

Yet although this latter image is that of a woman struggling for change, Walker also raises the problem of the actual role and influence of black women in the liberation movement, noting as others have done their minimal role in the negotiations which preceded the 1994 elections, and in most of the organisations associated with the struggle. And although there are now more women than before in positions of authority, equal citizenship, including domestic equality, is a long way off.

A notable common feature of both Afrikaner nationalism and that of the liberation struggle is that both incorporate ideals of masculinity. During the rise of Afrikaner nationalism the '*volk*' which women were supposed to serve was a masculine phenomenon (Cloete 1992: 291). The national liberation struggle is also commonly depicted in terms of masculine pride and assertiveness (Bozzoli 1983: 170). Not only was the popular image of the nationalist struggle against apartheid typically a masculine one; socialisation of the youth – black and white – has also been 'into a militarist masculinity which is reinforced by a gender defined sense of social solidarity, a brotherhood of combatants' (Cock 1993: 53).

Thus, while the idea of the nation suggests unity and inclusiveness, as well as neutrality between members who share and benefit equally from belonging to the nation, its depiction of citizenship excludes some, with two likely consequences. First, if some members of a society are marginalised in its depiction of citizenship, they are less likely to benefit from its political and social programmes. Second, this unequal depiction of citizens, in which some are more active than others, threatens the development of autonomy, especially if it is taught as part of a process of developing national identity in schools. This raises the issue of how identities in general ought to be approached in education.

Conclusion: educating identities

I have argued, taking South Africa as my example of a diverse society at a moment of transition, against the teaching of national identity. But national identity is one of several identities whose acquisition could be included among the aims of education. Consideration of the place of national identity in the aims of education requires attention to the more fundamental issue of the teaching of identities in schools, and to the need to develop an educative response to the learning of identities taught by a range of institutions and influences, such as families, religious institutions, the media and advertising.

In societies where regular schooling is available, schools have been ready to claim the constitution of identities as one of their tasks, indeed as a prerogative. This role has not always been performed benignly. Schools prefer to inculcate identities that make their charges easier to control and in doing so have favoured traditional gendered, class and racial identities. While not always an explicit ingredient in the curriculum, these identities have often proved oppressive and have been taught as if they are given, natural and unproblematic. For example, the teaching of what are suppos- edly given gendered identities standardly assumes masculine and feminine identities which are determined by traditional, homophobic ideologies of gender. National identities too are presented as given and natural, rather than as invented outside schools by elements in the surrounding society like cultural organisations, political movements and the state, all of which have agendas of their own in which education as the development of autonomy does not necessarily figure. In their turn these national identities reinforce oppressive qualities of other identities such as gendered ones (Stromquist 1995: 435). The identities ascribed to students, not only by schools, fix their social roles and correspondingly their expectations in life, including expectations of schooling itself; for girls, blacks and working-class children, this has commonly meant lowered expectations, ambitions and goals.

As feminist writers have emphasised (Friedman 1989; Mendus 1993), the identities we acquire may be chosen and created, as well as given and discovered. While schools teach identities as if they are unproblematically and unavoidably given, the acquisition and exercise of identities is far more complex and variable than this. At different times in our lives we may discover aspects of our identities which were unnoticed or unvalued before. Ascribed identities may be adopted with little awareness that one does so, and with varying degrees of understanding of their origins and significance. If these observations are true, then a feature of developing autonomy as one of the aims of education is to help learners to develop an understanding of given identities, and to provide opportunities to choose or create new ones, including identities which emerge from doing certain kinds of work, membership of a profession, of a group with common leisure interests, different lifestyles, and chosen goals and projects. This requires abandoning the idea that schools are legitimately places where persons are told who they are. If instead schools are regarded as places where persons learn to be autonomous members of a democratic society, their role in relation to identity is to provide students with as much opportunity as possible for self-definition. This would require that the curriculum enable them to study their location at a particular time and place, and to develop a sense of the self as a participant in a democratic way of life which includes understand- ing and respecting the identities of others.

The development of an educated sense of self is likely to be undermined by the promotion of national identity in schools. If the illusion of the nation hinders the development of autonomy as an aim of education, and if it conceals the effective exclusion of some from full democratic citizenship, then national identity ought not to be given a place among the aims of education.

Note

1 Material for this chapter has been drawn from Enslin (1993–94, 1994a and 1994b).

References

Anderson, B. (1983) *Imagined Communities*, London: Verso.

Bozzoli, B. (1983) 'Marxism, feminism and South Africa studies', *Journal of Southern African Studies* 9(2): 139–71.

Brink, E. (1990) 'Man-made women: gender, class and the ideology of the *Volksmoeder*', in C. Walker (ed.) *Women and Gender in South Africa to 1945*, Cape Town: David Philip: 273–92.

Cloete, E. (1992) 'Afrikaner identity: culture, tradition and gender', *Agenda* 13: 42–56.

Cock, J. (1993) 'The place of gender in a demilitarisation agenda', *Agenda* 16: 49–55.

Enslin, P. (1993–94) 'Education for nation-building: a feminist critique', *Perspectives in Education* 15(1): 13–25.

—— (1994a) 'Should nation-building be an aim of education?' *Journal of Education* (University of Natal) 19(1): 23–36.

—— (1994b) 'Identity, democracy and education', Fourth Biennial Conference of the International Network of Philosophers of Education, Leuven (August).

Friedman, M. (1989) 'Feminism and modern friendship: dislocating the community', *Ethics* 99: 275–90.

Gellner, E. (1983) *Nations and Nationalism*, Oxford: Blackwell.

Greenfeld, L. (1992) *Nationalism: Five Roads to Modernity*, Cambridge, MA: Harvard University Press.

Held, D. (1992) 'The development of the modern state', in S. Hall, and B. Gieben (eds) *Formations of Modernity*, Cambridge: Cambridge University Press: 72–119.

Hobsbawm, E. (1992) *Nations and Nationalism since 1780*, 2nd edn, Cambridge: Cambridge University Press.

McClintock, A. (1993) 'Family feuds: gender, nationalism and the family', *Feminist Review* 44 (Summer): 61–80.

McGurk, N. (1990) *I Speak as a White: Education, Culture, Nation*, Johannesburg: Heinemann.

Mendus, S. (1993) 'Different voices, still lives: problems in the ethics of care', *Journal of Applied Philosophy* 10(1): 17–27.

Miller, D. (1988) 'The ethical significance of nationality', *Ethics* 98: 647–62.

—— (1993) 'In defence of nationality', *Journal of Applied Philosophy* 10(1): 3–16.

Mkwanazi, Z. and Cross, M. (1992) 'The dialectic of unity and diversity in education: its implications for a national curriculum in South Africa', National Education Policy Investigation, Mimeograph.

O'Neill, J. (1994) 'Should communitarians be nationalists?', *Journal of Applied Philosophy*

11(2): 135–43.

Peters, R. (1966) *Ethics and Education*, London: Allen & Unwin.

Poole, R. (1991) 'The illusory community: the nation', in *Morality and Modernity*, London: Routledge.

Ree, J. (1992) 'Internationality', *Radical Philosophy* 60: 3–11.

Rose, B. and Tunmer, R. (1975) *Documents in South African Education*, Johannesburg: Ad. Donker.

Smith, A. (1986) *The Ethnic Origins of Nations*, Oxford: Blackwell.

—— (1991) *National Identity*, London: Penguin.

Stromquist, N. (1995) 'Romancing the state: gender and power in education', *Comparative Education Review* 39(4): 17–27.

Tamir, Y. (1992) 'Democracy, nationalism and education', *Educational Philosophy and Theory* 24(1): 17–27.

—— (1993) *Liberal Nationalism*, Princeton, NJ: Princeton University Press.

Walker, C. (1990) Review of *Woman-Nation-State*, *Agenda* 6: 40–8.

Walzer, M. (1992) 'The civil society argument', in C. Mouffe (ed.) *Dimensions of Radical Democracy*, London: Verso.

White, J. (1996) 'Education and nationality', *Journal of Philosophy of Education* 30(3): 327–43.

10

SELF-DETERMINATION AS AN EDUCATIONAL AIM

James C. Walker

Implicit in every educational decision is a fundamental choice. Are students, of whatever age, to be enabled to become more self-determined in their learning? Or are they to be disempowered, their learning subjected to the purposes and presumed interests of others, whether government, industry, educational institutions or indeed students' own parents and families?

The second option is not only morally and politically questionable; it is also, arguably, self-defeating. Economic prosperity, political stability and family harmony are likely best served by a population of human individuals capable of spontaneous self-expression, independence of thought and autonomous decision making. Unless our young people are becoming more self-determined and capable of communicating their views and knowledge and awareness of the problems of our world and our societies, then education in the twentieth century will have largely failed to deliver. Meeting the need for self-determination of our children and young people in the twenty-first century is a precondition for, not in competition with, meeting the needs of government, economy and society. At any rate, this can be argued, and would strongly support an educational philosophy highlighting self-determination as an educational aim.

Be that as it may, in this chapter I outline a philosophical case for self-determination as *the* fundamental educational aim, a case which is consistent with contemporary theory of human development and knowledge about the conditions for optimal learning. I present an account of self-determination as constituted by the dispositions to authentic self-expression, management of one's own learning, and creation of the conditions for further, enhanced self-determination. Since the third disposition, I shall argue, entails creating the conditions for enhancement of others' self-determination, my account of self-determination is communitarian rather than individualistic. In as much as self-determination is an aim for educators and educational institutions, educational policy and practice will be geared to the fostering of each of these three dispositions. Students will acquire the capacities for each and education will provide environments conducive to the development of each.

Education for self-determination does not entail the use of any particular educational method. Which methods facilitate self-determination, and in what respects, are matters for further inquiry. Direct instruction, for example, serves some purposes but inhibits others; likewise, inquiry learning, groupwork and so on. On the other hand, it is also important not to confuse the issue of particular methods with the more general methodological question of whether self-determination as an educational aim is best pursued by methods which, taken together, reflect self-determination as a procedural principle, encouraging students to act in self-determined ways. I argue that the pursuit of the aim requires adoption of the procedural principle; that the conditions for the development of self-determination are the same as the conditions for its exercise. In education this means the creation of free associations of people in learning communities.

Self-determination, freedom and autonomy

In contemporary English-language educational philosophy there has been little or no discussion of self-determination as an educational aim. (I am not aware of any treatment in another language.) There has, on the other hand, been considerable discussion of the related issues of freedom and autonomy in education. This may be explained by the philosophical ancestry of relevant problems and theories prominent in contemporary philosophy of education. For instance, *liberty*, an Enlightenment ideal, has persisted for two centuries of liberalism of all forms, particularly as applied to individual liberties, including human rights. *Autonomy* has a more specific history deriving, in contemporary moral, political and educational philosophy, from the work of Kant, whose primary concern is the moral autonomy of the responsible moral agent, and its relation to the moral law, or *nomos* (Kant 1956). An autonomous person wills his or her own moral law, just as a *polis* in ancient Greece itself *(autos)* made its own laws *(nomoi)*.

Isaiah Berlin provides another way of understanding autonomy and liberty, characterising two different but related forms of freedom or liberty (he uses the words interchangeably) as 'positive' and 'negative'. The latter, negative liberty, 'is involved in the answer to the question "What is the area in which the subject – a person or group of persons – is or should be left to do or be what he is able to do or be, without interference by other persons?"' Whereas positive liberty (or autonomy), 'is involved in the answer to the question "What, or who, is the source of control or interference that can determine someone to do, or be, this rather than that?"' (Berlin 1969: 121–2).

Following Berlin's characterisation, we may say that when the source of determination on one's doing or being is oneself, one is self-determined and possesses positive liberty in Berlin's sense. One controls, and influences, oneself. Two questions arise: what is the self? and what is self-determination – is it inherited or acquired, and if acquired, how? If the conditions for the development of self-determination are identical to the conditions for its exercise, then freedom from control or interference is one of those conditions. It then becomes critical to know which aspects of the individual are to be free or controlled by others: thoughts, desires, actions – or all of these?

It is on this issue that educational philosophers of 'the London school', particularly Richard Peters, Paul Hirst and Robert Dearden, have been influential in thinking about personal autonomy among contemporary philosophers of education. Their view, which I call 'liberal rationalism' (Walker 1981) holds, following Kant, that one's autonomy depends on the exercise of one's reason, in which one is aware of rules as alterable conventions which structure one's social life, subjecting them to reflection and criticism in the light of principles, such as impartiality and respect for persons (Peters 1973: 124). This is not a matter of following one's own desires, but of freely accepting the discipline of the principles of reason, which include moral principles transcendentally deduced, in the manner of Kant, from the nature of reason itself (Peters 1966). Thus, when Dearden says 'a person is "autonomous" to the degree that what he thinks and does cannot be explained without reference to his own activity of mind' (Dearden 1972: 453), by 'explanation' he does not mean causal explanation; he means an account of conscious, rule-governed thought where outcomes are determined by reasons the person has for beliefs and actions. The development of reason does not occur in the natural world of cause and effect: reasons are not causes, and explanation by reference to reasons is logically distinct from causal explanation which cannot account for purposive, rule-following action (Peters 1958). We understand human action through the conceptual schemes of common sense, not science. Indeed, causal explanation in psychology applies properly only to the 'limbo of lapses' from genuinely free, self-determined action. Empirical psychology is relegated by Peters to the exploration of this limbo (Peters 1969).

Liberal rationalism locates the development of reason, and therefore of personal autonomy, in a liberal education consisting of initiation into and mastery of putatively logically necessary forms of knowledge (Hirst 1965; Hirst and Peters 1970). The historical context of this view is significant. The connection between personal autonomy and forms of knowledge was made, during the *floruit* of liberal rationalism some thirty years ago, with a view to more than a philosophy with implications for the curriculum and an argument for the professional authority of the educators who are masters of the forms of knowledge. There were polemical purposes as well. Armed with their rationalist doctrine of autonomy as a function of mind, and a radical distinction between mind and emotion, the liberal rationalists attacked 'progressivist' notions of autonomy which emphasised the self-expression of the child and required conditions of liberty (negative freedom) for this to develop, thus taking a position contrary to my suggestion that there is an equivalence between the conditions for development and exercise. In his preparation for an attack on the equivalence view of progressivists, Peters (1973: 119) rejected 'the presupposition implicit in the writings and practices of educators . . . that some desirable state of mind or character trait will be best developed by an institution whose workings reflect the principle, which is thought desirable when personalised as a character trait'.

For the liberal rationalist answer is there is a development/exercise dichotomy rather than a development/exercise equivalence. Elsewhere I have argued that this position, commonly adopted in our schooling systems, is logically unsustainable (Walker 1984). This does not mean that students do not accept the authority of a teacher, nor that the teacher does not need to exercise control. It raises the question of when authority should be exercised through control. I argue that this is so when it is necessary for securing the conditions for the development of self-determination, and that this can only be so when there is agreement between student and teacher. If so, the educational institution promoting self-determination as a desirable principle will always reflect that principle in its own workings.

As to the question of the nature and identification of the self, in the liberal rationalist theory of personal autonomy, 'the self who owns and rules in the autonomous life', as Eamonn Callan puts it, 'is located in the reflective powers of the individual, as opposed to whatever might seem to fix identity prior to rational reflection'. Other views locate the self elsewhere. For example, Callan (1994: 35), followed by Aharon Aviram (1995: 63) identifies a voluntarist view, evident (for instance) in the thought of David Hume, for whom personal autonomy is evident in the 'unhindered expression of the will and desires'. The role of reason, for Hume (1959) is to be slave of the passions. Rousseau's view in *Emile* (Rousseau 1969), reflected in certain versions of educational progressivism, is similar. There is no sense to the idea that self-expression can or should be rationally regulated.

Callan (1988, 1994) and Aviram (1995) canvas a third possibility, voluntarist-rationalism, an earlier version of which is found in John Stuart Mill (1954). Whereas Mill holds the self's desires to be innate and organised by the autonomous person into a rational pattern and life plan, for Callan desire is socially embedded, if not determined; but for both of them what is constitutive of the self precedes rational reflection (see also Lindsey 1986).

Self-determination, authenticity and the self

The theory of self-determination I advocate includes, but goes beyond, what is understood by the various theories of personal autonomy. In particular, it espouses a compatibilist account of the determination of free human action, the classical advocates of which are Locke, Hume and Mill (Flanaghan 1984: 48), the predecessors of contemporary naturalism in philosophy and philosophy of education (Walker 1996). Human freedom, in both of Berlin's senses, is compatible with causation, and free actions are to be explained causally. Free action is not uncaused; it is determined by certain types of cause present in the conscious mental life of the person, including beliefs and desires, reason and emotion. What are these self-determined causes, then, and how is the self to be understood? To develop a satisfactory answer to this question we need, contrary to the liberal rationalists, to blend our philosophising with relevant psychological theory and research. Research on personality and cognition is particularly important.

First, consider the identification of the self. One way to approach this is to differentiate the self from the non-self, both within and outside the human person. Some aspects of our personality are self-determined and some other-determined. In a review of psychological theory and research on personal identity differentiation and maintenance, Polster (1983) draws attention to the capacity of the individual to differentiate between characteristics of one's own self and characteristics of other selves, to be able to draw a boundary between the former and the latter. The point is not that the boundary is never crossed, that characteristics of others are not taken on and assimilated into the self – on such an account no learning from others as models, a universal feature of human growth and development, would be possible – rather that, somewhat analogously to consuming healthy food rather than poison, what is absorbed promotes the well-being of the self rather than debilitating or destroying it (Whitfield 1993: 1–2). Moreover, the self grows and changes throughout life (autonomously rather than heteronomously, in political-legal language) in a self-determined fashion.

In this respect both versions of voluntarist-rationalism just discussed are, although on the right track, a little one-sided. Mill's view that the authentic desires of the self are innate is half true: there is no reason that desires cannot be authentically acquired in a way which honours and succours what is innate. Likewise Callan's assertion of the necessary social embeddedness of all authentic desires cannot account adequately for what is innately unique to each of us. Incidentally, it is not necessary that we are able to distinguish the innate from the acquired in all cases – that would be to re-run the tortured heredity/environment, nature/nurture debate. Rather, what is necessary is to establish social relationships and educational processes which enable the individual person to be aware of what is conducive to self-determined growth and to decide, accordingly, what action to take.

There is a range of psychological theories suggesting different ways of describing self-identity differentiation and maintenance. For example, developments from ego psychology through to object relations theory (Guntrip 1973) are in agreement that healthy development of the self begins with the infant child's initial separation of self from parents and independent exploration of the environment. This is a gradual process which is stunted if for some reason the child becomes trapped in 'all or nothing' thinking ('splitting') – for example, that saying no is always bad – rather than sometimes good and sometimes bad – but advanced if the latter lesson is learned, along with the correlative independent behaviour (Kohut 1971).

The sense of self necessary for self-determination is learned in the first place in the family if there is a sensitivity and practical support for identity differentiation and independent exploration. For self-determination to take root and flourish during childhood, a social setting, a community of individuals modelling self-determination, beginning with the family and extending beyond, is required. Eventually, after the child discovers the main similarities between self and others, during adolescence the individual moves to separate from parents and family, the successful autonomous achievement of which is a condition for adult independence and intimate relationships. There is also considerable clinical evidence that the capacity to understand and manage the boundary between self and others is a critical factor in determining both individual and family health and avoidance of illness (Minuchin 1974). Psychotherapists are working within a conceptual framework which stresses the integrity of the self and prevention or reversal of processes of fusion of self with others. In each of these stages and situations there is an equivalence between the conditions for development of self-determination and for its exercise.

Some psychologists, echoing the distinction between authenticity and inauthenticity, have distinguished between a 'true self' and a 'false self' (or ego) (Whitfield 1993: 54–9). I operate from my true self when I set my own boundaries, determining, aware of my beliefs and desires, what I will absorb and what not. The decisions and actions involved range all the way from saying 'yes' or 'no' – 'yes' to offers to assist me in pursuit of my goals and 'no' to invasions of my privacy – to active involvement in emotional, intellectual and professional relationships with others which either enhance or detract from my capacity for self-determination. If, as a child, I have believed my survival to be dependent on subjecting myself to the unwelcome incursions of my parents or others, whether extreme such as incest or subtle such as implied denigration of my integrity, and this subjection becomes an established

117

strategy for relating to others, my self-determination, although present in the original decision, is compromised by the consequences, and establishes a false, or other-determined, self. Unless I re-establish my authentic or true self as my driving force, my chances of enhanced self-determination across the various spheres of my life are diminished. Even though I may become highly self-determined in one sphere of my life, such as the intellectual, to the extent that I am unable authentically to express my true self in my activities and relationships my self-determination is limited.

The self-determined learner in a learning community

Given this understanding of the consequences of the child's suppression of his or her authentic responses, desires and beliefs, it follows that a condition for the continuing development and exercise of authentic self-expression is trust between adult and child. Trust takes root when the adult respects the child's wishes and seeks agreement for joint adult/child activities, such as formal educational processes. An agreement is a relation between individuals, whether or not they enter it individually or collectively. It may be explicit and formalised, or implicit in the relationship itself. Where the relationship is one of mutual trust and respect, there will be little or no need for explicit formal agreements, especially when there is a prior, underpinning agreement to a role relationship, such as teacher/student; although sensitive and effective teachers will constantly monitor the state of trust and consent between them and their students.

Self-determined learning can occur only in a situation where there is agreement to participate (Walker 1995). Where there is no agreement, there is no self-control in respect of the learning itself. A student in disagreement with a teacher may well exercise self-control, in the sense of self-discipline, by restraining negative emotional reactions which are not in their own interest. This self-discipline is indeed self-determined: it is geared to survival, and acknowledges the power structure of the unfree situation. This self-control, however, masks, through suppression, relevant aspects of the student's true self and so hinders authentic self-expression.

The liberating power of education comes from agreements between people to learn together. Keeping these agreements, in turn, requires self-control and social control. The situation must be maintained and people not keeping the agreement prevented from destroying the creative partnership between those who do. This may require coercion on the part of the teacher or indeed of other students (contrary to the libertarian view of freedom and autonomy for which the liberal rationalists rightly criticised some progressivists – Walker 1981). Every teacher has the responsibility to impose control in such a situation, where the prior right is created by agreement from all, including the student who has broken the agreement. To enter an agreement is to make a commitment, to oneself and to others. The commitment to oneself is one of honour; it is a basis for self-respect. It is a moral act, a promise. The commitment to others recognises the mutual need to support each other in our individual self-determination, and is the basis for creation of community.

From this it is evident that agreement to community, based as it is on recognition of each other as individuals – that is, valuing authenticity by embedding the conditions for its expression in social practice – is necessary for there to be hope for the future, *within that social situation.* If there is no agreement to community, the result will be despair, whether it is expressed as alienated resignation, or resistance and rebellion reflecting the belief that the only hope for self-determination lies in escaping from the present situation. The classrooms in our schools reflect countless examples of each kind of response. A condition for self-determination is the enhancement of the conditions for further self-determination.

This requires commitment to and caring for each other. The communitarian view I am putting is to be distinguished from views which oppose community to autonomy, seeing autonomy as detached separation from others (for example, Stone 1990) or as undermining our capacity to care for each other (Cuypers 1992). (For a critique of these views, see Morgan 1996.) Thus it is a mistake to believe that it is not possible to love another person and still retain one's autonomy because of the supposition that the autonomous person would preserve a degree of distance from all such emotional attachments, and any attachments formed would have a somewhat provisional nature and be constantly subject to critical scrutiny and review. Such versions of communitarianism are mistaken, confusing love with attachment. Love is care and commitment which might sometimes lead to breaking attachments where they compromise self-determination. As I have argued, it is not possible to exercise such care and commitment without maintaining healthy boundaries.

Community, based as it is on agreement, cannot be imposed; it has to be created by people working together. To create it they will need to learn about each other, to discover each other's true selves and support each other in expressing them. When students are readily and as a matter of course in agreement with their teacher, when there is a classroom community, there will be few 'discipline problems' and the students will spontaneously accept the teacher's authority. Teachers who know their students and their subjects well enough to create quickly such communities of agreement are often described as possessing 'natural authority', and this is an apt phrase. The authority is natural because it flows from the authentic expression of the students and the teacher. Such knowledge of students is commonly constituted of intuitive as well as formalised knowledge, and is expressed in affinity for and empathy with students.

This affinity is also a condition for effective communication, including the communication of the teacher's aims and purposes to the students. The educational purposes of the teacher and the school cannot be communicated effectively unless there is knowledge and appreciation of the purposes of the students. Moreover, very frequently students need to be assisted to discover, decide or formulate their purposes, whether they be quite specific and contextual ('What would you like to do this morning?') or long term and developmental ('What would you like to do when you leave school?'). When there is an understanding of each other's purposes and a framework of agreed classroom practice where these purposes can be cooperatively pursued, there is a flow of communication and learning, and a co-determination which is co-created out of a united set of self-determinations. When this is achieved, there is no need for the imposition of control by coercion. It is not that control is absent – that would be to equate control with coercion – but that control is exercised individually and collectively through the agreed social practices.

This requires skill, not just will, on the part of the teacher; and also on the part of students. The teacher's skill derives as much from mastery of the content of the curriculum as it does from knowledge and understanding of the students. The knowledge of subject matter is not crudely or simply applied to the teaching of the students. In teaching mathematics, for instance, affinity for the students means understanding how they think and the levels of understanding they have achieved. This is an epistemic synthesis which is at the core of the expertise of the successful teacher, and has been described by Lee Shulman (1987) as 'pedagogical content knowledge'. Shulman suggests that it is at the heart of teaching's professional knowledge base. It varies, of course, with the age and prior educational experience, and often with the gender and culture of students. Acquiring it requires formal learning as well as sustained practical experience working with students. Effectively mixing the two is a perennial problem for teacher education.

Research in cognitive science, particularly cognitive psychology, is now demonstrating how teachers' expertise consists in deploying pedagogical content knowledge to students' self-managed learning (Leinhardt and Smith 1985; Leinhardt and Greeno 1986), as they assist students to progress from the status of novice to expert in a range of curriculum fields. Thanks to recent syntheses of research by Perkins (1995) and Bruer (1993), we are now developing an understanding of how self-determined learning in one field can be built into more empowered learning overall. Similar thinking in organisational psychology is demonstrating how the points I have been making about community translate into successful management of organisations, including schools (Argyris and Schön 1996; Senge 1992).

No teacher is perfectly skilled, and no learning community is perfect. (If this were the case there would be nothing to learn.) There will be occasions when a teacher's affinity fails, and occasions when students do not sustain their commitments to each other and the teacher. This is not only a normal feature of healthy community life, but itself an essential condition of self-determined learning. Community has to be constantly recreated, and self-determination, never an all-or-nothing affair, strengthened and developed. Problem solving, trial and error, learning from mistakes, testing hypotheses and discovering what we want to do individually and together, are at the heart of education, as they are at the heart of science. The difference between a learning community of self-determined individuals and a coercive, alienated situation is that in the former there is agreement that it is not only inevitable and acceptable that people make mistakes, but that it is desirable because this is a major way in which learning occurs. People will be detached about their errors, and welcome them as opportunities for further learning. There will be safety for people to reveal their lack of knowledge, their misconceptions, and their real level of skill. Needless to say, this has implications for assessment as well as pedagogy. It will be acceptable, too, for the teacher to make mistakes, and to be supported by students as fellow human beings in learning from them.

Self-determination: the fundamental educational aim

If this account of self-determination is sound, then self-determination is not only the fundamental outcome of educative learning and characteristic of educated people, but securing self-determined learning is also the fundamental procedural principle of well-directed education. This is as it should be, given the argument that the conditions for the development of self-determination are identical to the conditions for its exercise. The naturalistic position I am advocating inclines us, unlike the liberal rationalists, to look to science, as well as practical experience, to understand the causal basis for education for self-determination, and for the development of suitably effective pedagogy, curriculum and assessment, and professional education for teachers. Progress towards these achievements would be reflected in the choice, made in every educational decision, to the empowerment of our students and of their contribution to our social health and prosperity.

References

Argyris, C. and Schön, D. S. (1996) *Organizational Learning II: Theory, Method and Practice,* Boston: Addison-Wesley.

Aviram, A. (1995) 'Autonomy and commitment: compatible ideals', *Journal of Philosophy of Education* 29(1): 61–73.

Berlin, I. (1969) 'Two concepts of liberty', in *Four Essays on Liberty,* London: Oxford University Press.

121

Bruer, J. T. (1993) *Schools of Thought: A Science of Learning for the Classroom,* Cambridge, MA: MIT Press.

Callan, E. (1988) *Autonomy and Schooling,* Kingston, Ont: McGill-Queen's University.

——(1994) 'Autonomy and alienation', *Journal of Philosophy of Education* 28(1): 35–53.

Cuypers, S. E. (1992) 'Is personal autonomy the first principle of education?' *Journal of Philosophy of Education* 26: 5–17.

Dearden, R. F. (1972) 'Autonomy and education', in R. F. Dearden, P. H. Hirst and R. S. Peters (eds) *Education and the Development of Reason,* London: Routledge & Kegan Paul.

Flanaghan, O. (1984) *The Science of the Mind,* 2nd edn, Cambridge, MA: MIT Press.

Guntrip, H. (1973) *Psychoanalytical Theory, Therapy and the Self: A Basic Guide to the Human Personality,* New York: Basic Books.

Hirst, P. H. (1965) 'Liberal education and the nature of knowledge', in R. D. Archambault (ed.) *Philosophical Analysis and Education,* London: Routledge & Kegan Paul.

Hirst, P. H. and Peters, R. S. (1970) *The Logic of Education,* London: Routledge & Kegan Paul.

Hume, D. (1959) *A Treatise of Human Nature,* London: Dent.

Kant, I. (1956) *Groundwork of the Metaphysic of Morals,* trans. H. J. Paton as *The Moral Law,* 3rd edn, London: Hutchinson.

Kohut, H. (1971) *The Analysis of the Self,* New York: International University Press.

Leinhardt, G. and Greeno, J. G. (1986) 'The cognitive skill of teaching', *Journal of Educational Psychology* 78(2): 75–95.

Leinhardt, G. and Smith, D. (1985) 'Expertise in mathematics instruction: subject matter knowledge', *Journal of Educational Psychology* 77(3): 247–71.

Lindsey, R. (1986) *Autonomy,* Houndmills: Macmillan.

Masterson, J. F. (1988) *The Search for the Real Self: Unmasking the Personality Disorders of our Age,* New York: Free Press/Macmillan.

Mill, J. S. (1954) *On Liberty,* in *Utilitarianism, Liberty and Representative Government*, London: Dent.

Minuchin, S. (1974) *Families and Family Therapy*, Cambridge, MA: Harvard University Press.

Morgan, J. (1996) 'A defence of autonomy as an educational ideal', *Journal of Philosophy of Education* 30(2): 239–52.

Perkins, D. (1995) *Outsmarting IQ: The Emerging Science of Learnable Intelligence*, New York: The Free Press.

Peters, R. S. (1958) *The Concept of Motivation,* London: Routledge & Kegan Paul.

——(1966) *Ethics and Education,* London: Allen & Unwin.

——(1969) 'Motivation, emotion and the conceptual schemes of commonsense', in T. Mischel (ed.) *Human Action,* New York: Academic Press.

——(1973) 'Freedom and the development of the free man', in J. F. Doyle (ed.) *Educational Judgements,* London: Routledge & Kegan Paul.

Polster, S. (1983) 'Ego boundary as process: a systemic contextual approach', *Psychiatry* 46: 247–57.

Rousseau, J. J. (1969) *Emile,* London: Dent.

Senge, P. M. (1992) *The Fifth Discipline: The Art and Practice of the Learning Organization,* New York: Random House.

Shulman, L. (1987) 'Knowledge and teaching: foundations of the new reform', *Harvard Educational Review* 57(1): 1–22.

Stone, C. (1990) 'Autonomy, emotions and desires: some problems concerning R. F

Dearden's account of autonomy', *Journal of Philosophy of Education* 24(2): 271–83.

Walker, J. C. (1981) 'Two competing theories of personal autonomy: a critique of the liberal rationalist attack on progressivism', *Educational Theory* 31(3–4): 285–306.

——(1984) 'The development/exercise dichotomy', in C. W. Evers and J. C. Walker (eds) *Epistemology, Semantics and Educational Theory* (Occasional Paper 16), Sydney: University of Sydney Department of Education.

——(1995) 'Self-determination in teaching and learning: an essay review of W. Louden's *Understanding Teaching*', *Curriculum Inquiry* 25(1): 101–10, 115–16.

——(1996) 'Practical educational knowledge: a naturalist philosophy of education', in D. N. Aspin (ed.) *Logical Empiricism and Post-empiricism in Philosophy of Education*, London: Heinemann.

Whitfield, C. (1993) *Boundaries and Relationships: Knowing, Protecting and Enjoying the Self*, Deerfield Beach, FL: Health Communications.

11

THE NATURE OF
EDUCATIONAL AIMS

Paul H. Hirst

Central to the history of Western educational thought has been the constantly developing notion of a liberal education. Rooted in beliefs propounded by classical Greek philosophers, this conception of education has been progressively reconstructed under many different influences, not least Cartesian dualism, British empiricism, Kantian rationalism and nineteenth-century liberalism. Its most recent detailed characterisation has been by philosophers of education much influenced by twentieth-century analytical philosophy. The resulting formulation, with its sharply focused aims and attendant philosophical underpinnings, has in fact widely determined at least the framework of almost all discussion of educational aims up to very recent times. But of late, the major philosophical beliefs behind the approach have been severely attacked, so much so that this whole formulation and not just its details now seem in need of radical reconsideration. In this chapter, via an examination of certain of these fundamental beliefs, I shall argue for a new and, it is to be hoped, more adequate approach to characterising the whole domain of educational aims.

I shall take it as axiomatic that the term 'education' labels those activities of learning aimed at enabling individuals to live good lives. Clearly, the term is frequently used for areas of activity that can only contribute in some limited way to such a life. But in its general sense I shall take it that education is directed at the development and promotion of a person's good life as a whole. The liberal education tradition has certainly taken such an overall view, and, given that aim, has sought repeatedly to spell out in detail what it entails in contemporary terms.

Manifestly, any such attempt demands both some conception of what it is to develop and live a human life and the making of certain value judgements that will mark out a good life and its distinctive features. In these terms the late twentieth-century form of liberal education has taken human beings to be entities capable, by virtue of certain naturally given capacities, of making sense of themselves and their world and of engaging in autonomous action. Granted such a view of human nature, a good life has been held to be one autonomously determined in all its aspects by reason – that is, by the proper exercise of a person's capacities to achieve knowledge and understanding – to make rational choices and to act accordingly. Liberal education is then seen as fundamentally an initiation into the nature and content of knowledge and understanding, into 'the best that has been thought and said'. On that foundation, given capacities for autonomously determining all other personal characteristics, individuals are judged able to fashion for themselves their own rational lives. Insofar as educational aims go beyond the pursuit of knowledge and understanding they focus on facilitating the making of rational choices in its application, acting in accordance with such choices and developing the personal qualities and skills these entail. At the heart of all these additional aims, however, lies the knowledge that gives them their character and meaning.

This formulation of the aims of education as the development of rational autonomy is clearly grounded in particular doctrines about human nature and about the character of reason. It is these doctrines I wish to consider critically, and in the light of their inadequacies to suggest more defensible notions so that we might better construe what constitutes a good life and hence reformulate the aims of education. There are two directions in which the autonomy of individual persons is generally held to be secured. First, it is asserted that there exists within each of us a distinct self, or domain of the self taken as a whole, that operates independently of the rest of the person. It is by virtue of this 'autonomy of the self', as I shall call it, that we are self-determining and self-directing, able to achieve rational understanding, make rational choices and take rational actions. But, second, it is also asserted that we are independent individuals whose relations with others are of our own determination. This 'autonomy of the individual' means that we exist as individual persons prior to and independently of our social relations. These two forms of autonomy have received many different formulations in detail but in some form or other are fundamental to the aims espoused by liberal education.

The 'autonomy of the self' marks out operationally, and perhaps even metaphysically, our generation of objective, disinterested knowledge, our rational choice of ends and means and the rational will to act accordingly. It distinguishes these achievements from all our particular embodied needs, desires, interests, feelings, dispositions and behaviour. In this way our individual experiences, beliefs, ends, means and relationships, indeed all the substantive elements of our personal lives, are open to review and reformation in the light of the demands of autonomous reason and will. The good life is thus the substantive expression and application of autonomous reason in our individual lives. But the assertion of such a division within us seems increasingly indefensible. We are surely fundamentally natural entities with given needs and capacities that are physical, psychological and social in character. It is by virtue of these attributes that we are capable of developing knowledge and understanding, of making rational choices and acting on them. But to dissociate from our naturally given substantive attributes what would seem to be achieved by the very exercise of these in some particular way and then giving these achievements a determining status and power over our natural lives in all other respects increasingly seems a speculative interpretation of experience that lacks adequate justification.

Rather than accept the metaphysical claims or transcendental arguments on which this account dubiously rests maybe we would be better served by careful analysis of the operation of all our capacities in the generation and deliberative re-formation of the substantive content of our lives. We are constituted as individual persons by what we are by nature and what we achieve across the whole range of our beliefs, knowledge, desires, interests, dispositions of thought and behaviour, relationships, values and so on. The list comprises all those attributes that are distinctive of human lives. What matters in this whole complex conglomeration is how these many elements are of their very nature related to each other, and objective knowledge and rational principles for action must not be given a detachment and effective command over other elements of what constitute the person that on analysis is unjustifiable. The very intellectual abstraction from all other aspects of the person that is necessary to the concepts in which objective knowledge and principles must be built surely renders the knowledge thus achieved so limited in scope and significance as to make it of minor value in the deter-mination of the complex decisions in huge areas of human experience. Indeed, it will be argued later that the activities of reason here invoked are quite inadequate to the job assigned them. Such knowledge and principles have a place within an individual's constitutive self, not outside it, and what that is needs careful specification. In particular, claims for the efficacy of such elements in determining action and character 'by will' seem to run counter to much personal experience. That the substantive self can be, let alone should be, developed or re-formed on objective rational grounds as this account claims has certainly begun to look implausible.

What I have labelled 'the autonomy of the individual' is now also widely regarded as unacceptable. The claim is that our existence as autonomous persons is essentially an individual given, common characteristics contin-gently making possible the social creation of language, institutions and relationships of enormous instrumental value in the development of our rational lives. The exercise of our capacities of reason and will are held to operate independently of all social relationships and indeed determine all rationally ordered social bonds. As persons we are thus seen as fundamentally atomic individuals, our social relationships being secondary. Yet surely careful consideration reveals that we are beings with not only physical needs that are shared with others but also with social needs and interests, needs for social relationships that are constitutive of us as persons. To be a person and not merely an individual being is to live and act in relationships with others in which shared activities, concepts, beliefs and so on crucially define us as the persons we are. It is in fact only by engaging in shared practices that our individual capacities can be so exercised that we achieve identity as substantive persons. We are our thoughts, beliefs, knowledge, skills, feelings, habits, social roles, relationships and so on. But these elements all derive their specific character from being features of the public social practices in which we come to engage.

By a social practice I mean a pattern of activity established traditionally or by deliberate institution that is engaged in for achieving the satisfaction of our needs and interests. Engaging in this involves elements of knowledge, belief, judgement, action, criteria of success and failure, principles, skills, dispositions, feelings, indeed elements encompassing the activity and achievements of all our capacities. In any particular practice these elements are locked together, each taking its distinctive character in part from its relationship to other elements, the whole constituting the very nature of the practice. Practices range from the primarily physical to the primarily theoretical, from simple skills to complex professional and interpersonal activities. They are typically 'nested' with simple practices subsumed under more complex wholes which are never merely the sum of their parts.

Of their nature practices develop in the doing by trial and error and in the light of previous experience, their development involving changes in the different interlocked constitutive elements. In such development new and alternative forms of satisfaction for our needs and interests arise. Interests and satisfactions that lack the necessity of basic natural needs emerge as possibilities in social and personal life. But it is by engaging in established practices and related exploratory possibilities that our individual lives are constituted as personal 'narratives' formed in relation to the vast web of social practices to which we are heirs. Our beliefs, skills, values, dispositions, emotional patterns and so on are progressively laid down with differing degrees of stability and revisability. The significance for each of us of particular practices or elements in them may vary considerably in relation to our natural endowments and individual contexts. Yet it is in the satisfaction of our developing needs and interests in relation to the network of developing practices available that our individual lives make sense. Not that we are rigidly determined by those practices. Rather, we are formed in response to them, embracing them in varying degrees, modifying them or acting in opposition to them. But it is the web of social practices that gives meaning to our lives and it is only in response to them that our individual identities as persons are established.

In rejecting the 'autonomy of the self' and the 'autonomy of the individual' on which the concept of rational autonomy has come to be based, I have clearly begun to articulate what I consider a more adequate concept of a person. I have suggested that we exist as individual entities with given inter-related physical, psychological and social needs and with parallel wide-ranging capacities. It is then in the exercise of those capacities in the satisfaction of our diverse needs that we progressively construct social practices of great complexity in relation to which our personal lives become coherently structured. In this sense we are socially constructed as individual substantive persons. Society is not the product of voluntary collaboration between pre-existing substantive persons, for it is only in relation to social practices that our lives take on determinate individual form. If persons are understood in these terms, then what constitutes their good can best be seen as the fulfil-ment achieved in the satisfaction of their needs and interests. That good is then something that can only be discerned in experience, not something first understood in propositional truths. Social practices are seen to be the essential means to the achievement of such satisfactions, and it is through these alone that we can individually come to fashion a good life. At any given moment what constitutes our good can be hard to discern and equally hard to pursue. But what emerges is surely that for each of us a good life must be one that seeks overall, across our needs and changing interests, the greatest fulfilment in the long run, given all we inherit individually and socially.

From this point of view the idea that a good life is one of rational autonomy is both inadequate and mistaken. The achievement of knowledge and understanding and the making of choices on abstracted rational grounds are in fact the satisfaction of certain very particular psychological needs and interests, those concerned to pursue abstracted, universal proposi-tional truths, and principles. This pursuit is then being set above all others in a demand that all other forms of satisfaction, physical, psychological and social, be found only in practices that such propositional claims can formally justify. To so define what is good in all areas of life is simply to fail to understand adequately the full potential significance of all other naturally given needs and desires. It results in the radical distortion of the conduct of life and the development of personal character in the interests of certain intellectual practices and their achievements.

But if a good life is to be found in the satisfaction of needs and interests in relation to the social practices available to us, how are we then to under-stand the activity of reason in this pursuit? Its operation can be seen to originate when, in seeking the satisfaction of our needs and interests, we exercise our cognitive capacities to distinguish objects, situations and events for their significance in these practical searches. In our necessary relations with others we thus create shared conceptual schemes in which we make essentially practical judgements of success and failure, expressing these in practical discourse. The concepts, propositions, rules and principles we construct have conative and affective as well as cognitive meaning. The knowledge and understanding expressed in the discourse is thus essentially the know-how of attaining satisfactions. We thus discover, by trial and error in practice itself, what activities we have reason to pursue. Progressively, therefore, we socially develop rational practices as precisely those pursuits that bring about the satisfaction of our needs and interests. But the rules and principles of such rational practice expressed in practical discourse are the outcomes of successful practice, not the determiners of it. They have validity in other situations only into . . sofar as the concepts employed have valid application in all their rich meaning. Yet it is by such discourse alone that practices can be analysed and critically assessed and potentially more rational activities proposed. Rational practices are practices justified in practice itself, and their creation, conduct and development are possible only by virtue of the exercise of reason in this practical mode.

It is in the exercise of practical reason, then, that we have developed such sophisticated practices as those of technology, industry, politics, law and economics for the satisfaction of our diverse human needs and interests. These being of their nature constructed for the achievement of what constitutes our good and the necessary shapes of our substantive lives, it is in relation to them alone that we can fashion our individual good lives. For each of us what that is can only be discerned in practice, by engaging in those most rationally developed practices available to us. And that engagement is in itself a rational practice that we must learn to pursue, the practice of critically reflective exploration as we seek to master what the practices can contribute to our composing a satisfying life overall and in the long run. In this sense the good life is a rational life, provided that is understood as a life of practical reason.

In this account of the operation of practical reason I have sharply distinguished it from that of theoretical reason, by the latter meaning the creation and use of conceptual schemes for the achievement of propositional truths as abstracted from all non-cognitive needs and interests. Theoretical knowledge and understanding is, I suggest, of its nature incapable of generating rational practices. Abstracted understanding of dismembered aspects of ourselves and our world cannot be reassembled to provide the operational understanding that is constitutive of practical knowledge. Yet theoretical knowledge is not irrelevant to social practices. The universal understanding it provides sets out necessary limiting characteristics of the very framework in which practical reason must operate and in which rational practices can be pursued. In all areas of practice the knowledge of theoretical disciplines cannot provide the 'material' from which practical knowledge can be built.

But it can orientate most profoundly the direction in which successful – that is, rational – practices can be constituted. The sciences, social sciences and the humanities are vital to the effective experimental generation of rational practices in such areas as technology, medicine, politics and the conduct of personal relationships.

For us individually the character of the good life possible for us clearly depends on the rational practices available in our society. In this sense the pursuits of theoretical reason in the disciplines are of great importance for us all in contributing to the social creation of those practices. But that importance does not make them significant pursuits for us all in personally constructing good lives. Practical reason, not theoretical reason, is what a rational life directly requires. It involves participation in the many complex elements in those practices best able to satisfy our given needs and developing interests, including their practical discourse. In that very process those practices structure and develop the personal capacities they engage. But proper participation demands critically reflective assessment of the judgements and actions taken and their consequences for ourselves and others. It demands reflective initiative as we seek the satisfaction of our needs and interests overall and in the long run. It involves critical reflection and initiative too in relation to alternative and newly emerging forms of practice as the circumstances of our lives develop.

A good life is in these terms a rational life, but one ordered by the demands of practical reason, not those of theoretical reason as the advocates of rational autonomy have understood those. Nor is it a life characterised by autonomy as they have understood that. Such a life certainly involves the exercise of many given capacities that generate knowledge, choices and actions, but in no way does it posit their existence or operation in any way outside or independently of the individual's substantive self. Indeed it sees the exercise of all capacities and their achievements as elements within the life of the constitutive self. In form and content what have been seen as expressions of autonomy are now seen as features of social practices when they are engaged in with the critical reflection their proper rational conduct requires. And that critical reflection is itself a form of practice that is socially formed and socially sustained.

If, as I originally proposed, the general aim of education is the development and promotion of good lives, how is that now to be conceived? Fundamentally, it must be progressive initiation into those social practices in relation to which each individual can find their greatest satisfaction and fulfilment. It necessitates critically reflective response to those practices both internally and in their wider relationships. There must develop too a critically reflective awareness of alternative practices. And there must be developed a constant sense that it is in one's overall and long-run satisfaction that one's good is constituted, not in satisfactions on a narrow front and in the short term. In this picture, education's focus is on the practices that provide its content. But engagement in those results in the development of the individual's substantive character as a rationally ordered person and the achievements of life narrative.

In any given social context there will be existing practices that are clearly necessary for any good life and which must therefore figure in the education of all. Many will relate to rationally given needs and capacities, physical, psychological and social, in, for instance, the management of oneself in one's physical environment, the establishment and sustaining of personal and other social relationships and the conduct of effective communication. Others relate to more complex and sophisticated needs and interests that have emerged in society to do with, say, finance, law or politics. Beyond these are less necessary practices which may be desirable if optional and take alternative forms, as in the arts, religion, industry or sports. The place of this last group in education may vary according to individual differences in abilities and in social circumstances. Wide opportunity for exploration and engagement among diverse practices is, however, clearly essential. One point of importance must be added. I argued earlier that academic disciplines, being practices concerned with theoretical knowledge, are in general of only indirect significance in the conduct of a good life. They are primarily relevant only to the social development of practices and not individual conduct in relation to them. It follows that such disciplines are important only as optional practices in education in general, appropriate for those who can find significant personal satisfaction in them or in their contribution to the development of other, non-theoretical, practices.

No matter what practices provide the content of education, initiation into them necessitates involvement in the full range of their elements. Those include concepts, judgements, knowledge, activities, discourse, principles and dispositions as these operate in the conduct of those practices. But vital too is the critical reflection that is attentive to the achievement of the satisfaction of needs and interests for which the practices exist. Not only is that reflection necessary to the conduct of any particular practice, but it also constantly brings to the fore the basic motivating force that must operate throughout the educational enterprise, the individual's personal experience of the satisfaction and fulfilment that these practices can bring as part of a developing good life.

How best distinct areas of practice can be demarcated to structure the content of education is a far from easy question. The divisions I have followed in referring to practices are those that have emerged progressively in our society as relatively distinct areas. These divisions are already not unknown as curriculum units and practically orientated 'subjects', and it would seem desirable to follow these in the first instance.

What practices should be pursued and when are equally complex questions. At the very early stages of education they will usually be

131

answered by parents. What is then needed is sensitivity to the differing needs and interests of children and to the social world in which they live. But as children's needs and interests become articulated and their capacities develop, they increasingly become the best judges of their own educational requirements. What matters throughout, however, is that rational choice, choice informed by practical reason, be made so as to further the construction of a good life for the individual throughout the whole enterprise. After all, education at all stages must be a rational practice.

But it is not my purpose in this chapter to pursue such practical questions about the content and processes of education. What I have sought to do is argue that certain mistaken philosophical – that is, theoretical – beliefs about the nature of persons and the character of reason have determined the very framework of our understanding of the aims of education. If I am right, what we must now do is radically reconstruct in the light of more defensible beliefs our practical concept of what is involved in living a good life and thence our understanding of what education must do to develop and promote that. My central conclusions are that:

1   a good life is to be understood as a life determined by practical and not theoretical reason;
2   practical reason is expressed in social practices developed in critical reflection for the satisfaction of human needs and interests;
3   a good life is a critically reflective life developed in relation to such practices for the satisfaction of one's own developing needs and interests overall and in the long run;
4   the overall aim of education is to be understood as initiation into those practices in which such a good life can be developed; and
5   initiation into those practices is itself a social practice that must be developed in critically reflective practice.

It is my contention that, holding to the central importance of propositional knowledge for a good life, education has for far too long been mistakenly dominated by the content and character of academic theoretical disciplines. For the good of us all we must now begin to see the good life and the aims of education in terms of rational social practices by which alone we can find the satisfaction and fulfilment which constitute our good, individually and collectively.

12

WELL-BEING AS AN AIM OF EDUCATION[1]

Roger Marples

A system of schooling may be designed for many reasons, not all of which are morally acceptable. Children have been forced to attend schools whose specific intentions included producing Christian gentlemen or committed communists where any reference to the potentially liberating possibilities afforded by schooling have met with incomprehension or hostility. Those who have wished to indoctrinate the young into particular conceptions of well-being have all too frequently found schools willing to accommodate them.

The reaction against such systems has been accompanied by an unwarranted scepticism concerning the role of teachers in assisting children with the task of determining where their well-being might lie. This is in no small part due to the contemporary moral and political climate which derives support from subjectivism and individualism. Those teachers who see their job as having something to do with helping pupils appreciate the implications of, and values associated with, certain forms of life (especially if this is seen in terms of something more than either merely equipping them with the capacity to decide for themselves the values by reference to which their decisions are determined, or with helping them to formulate strategies for satisfying their desires) may well leave themselves open to the charge of indoctrinating others with their own, subjectively chosen, *Weltanschauungen*.

Whatever it is that we are aiming to achieve through compulsory schooling and whatever curriculum is considered appropriate as a means to such achievement, we have to acknowledge that some conception or other of what is good for both individuals and society at large – what, in other words, it is to flourish as persons and as citizens - underpins all that we do. It is all too easy to despair of providing an acceptable theoretical underpinning to educational practice with any claims to objectivity in terms of which charges of indoctrination or perfectionism may plausibly be rebuffed, but it is incumbent on those who are dissatisfied with the subjectivism on which so many accounts of well-being appear to rely, to endeavour to provide such an alternative.

Subjectivism accepts that values are self-chosen and ultimately a matter of individual preference. Flourishing, on this view, amounts to nothing more than success in providing coherence, together with a hierarchical structure to one's desires, it being an impertinence to suggest that one could both succeed in this enterprise and fail to achieve personal well-being. This chapter aims to go some way towards exposing the shortcomings of subjectivism associated with desire-satisfaction accounts of well-being, and in so doing takes issue with John White's continued insistence on reducing well-being to some form of desire-satisfaction. Much of what follows is an attempt to cast serious doubt on this form of reductionism.

Although White's position changed between the publication of *The Aims of Education Restated*[2] and *Education and the Good Life: Beyond the National Curriculum*[3] (hereinafter referred to as *AER* and *EGL* respectively) in that he provides an account of well-being in terms of what he calls 'post-reflective-desire-satisfaction' in the earlier book while his more recent *EGL* relies on more familiar 'informed-desires', both accounts remain bedevilled by a tenacious attachment to the significance of satisfied desires. Like all such accounts, these rely on a view concerning the relationship between value and desire which refuses to grant at least *logical* priority to the former. Any attempt to secure well-being on more objective foundations has to provide for such a possibility and this is attempted in the second part of this chapter.

In spite of the change of emphasis, White's thesis is premised on the belief that values are chosen rather than discovered, and he remains oblivious to the distinction between satisfaction of *desire* and satisfaction of *self* which results in conclusions and recommendations that are both counter-intuitive and educationally suspect. Apart from serious questions relating to both the conception of rationality employed and its associated neutrality with respect to possible ends of rational choice, White's explanation of 'reflection' in post-reflective-desire-satisfaction is as flawed as his reliance on the polarisation of 'ethical experts' on the one hand and individual choice on the other is unwarranted.

Once it is acknowledged that we are not mere bundles of desires confronted with the task of getting them into some sort of order of priority, we are forced to acknowledge that desires have a certain rationale; we come to desire x rather than y for reasons to do with the aspect under which we see them. It is in virtue of so-called desirability-characteristics possessed by x and absent in y that we acknowledge its value and admit the possibility that my satisfied *desire* may leave *me* thoroughly unsatisfied; I may end up feeling ashamed or guilty or simply indifferent. I may not actually mind, in retrospect, if my desire had been frustrated altogether. Rational persons reflect upon the extent to which a satisfied desire is likely to satisfy them, and do not stop short in the way suggested by White to the effect that 'reflectiveness . . . subserves desire-satisfaction'.[4]

Although White appears not to recognise the distinction between desire-satisfaction and self-satisfaction, its force becomes apparent in his example of a pupil who is asked to reflect upon the merits or otherwise of a career in the civil service. White wants the pupil to ask questions like 'Is the secure life of a civil servant found to prove satisfying to me in the long term?' and would caution the pupil to think this through in the full knowledge of *what he or she is*.[5] But looked at within the context of well-being as post-reflective-desire-satisfaction, it is impossible to grant that there is any more to all this than making a choice of career in the light of those desires the pupil would like satisfied, or, which is more or less the same thing, which desires left unsatisfied will cause them most frustration. Well-being on this view is little more than a species of contentedness. But there is more to *being* satisfied with something than merely enjoying a state of quiescence whereby one is not dissatisfied with something or other; to say as much would beg the question of what it is to be dissatisfied *with* something.

The importance of reflection in determining the value of things has long been recognised by White. In his *Towards a Compulsory Curriculum*,[6] he argues that intrinsic value is identifiable with what a person would on reflection want for its own sake, and it is reflection which enables a person to determine which of all possible options they prefer and which is essential in the weighing of relative importance of various ways of life.[7] The problem, of course, is one of adjudicating between those considerations which are relevant to the formulation of priorities and those which are hindrances to such decision making. White, however, is adamant: 'The individual himself must make the ultimate decisions,'[8] but the basis on which decisions are made is the result of a very special kind of reflection: 'he has to dig beneath his surface inclinations, steel himself against unthinking acceptance of ideals of life which he has picked up from others, *penetrate to more fundamental levels of his* being, *to his "deepest needs"*'.[9] The italicised phrase fits uneasily with mere desire-satisfaction. After all, the satisfaction of desires and acting in accordance with my needs are frequently impossible to reconcile, and in what follows White seems altogether too vague about the nature of the reflection in question. 'Suppose,' he says, 'there is nothing at the bottom of the barrel. Can we *discover* our deepest selves? Or is self-*creation* . . . a more appropriate description? It is nonsense to say that we create ourselves *ex nihilo*, . . . But ours are still the ultimate choices.'[10]

White's insistence (which is at least consistent with his overall thesis) that 'we should do the things we most want to; that is what life-planning is all about'[11] is simply unacceptable. Until more has been said about *what* it is that one discovers through reflection, it is difficult to indicate in what respects the statement misleads. In reflecting, I am concerned with not merely *believing* that I am flourishing, but with actual flourishing. White gives up too soon. His supposition that 'one cannot, finally, say what one's well-being *is* as distinct from what one *thinks* it is'[12] would, if it were true, mean that there would be no reason why I should care about being misled over the issues involved. I should have no reason to care about my life being worthless as long as I had worked out a hierarchy of desires all of which were consistent, combined with the assurance of seeing at least some of them satisfied. On White's account the only room for *mistaken* evaluation is an evaluation that is unreflectively arrived at. Given the subjectivist premiss with which he begins, there is no distinction in reality. It is this premiss which needs refuting if we are to provide for the possibility of genuine human flourishing.

If we were to ask White what he thought the point of all this reflection amounted to, he would say that it is to enable pupils to make choices with respect to possible ways of life. And there is more to this than mere plumping. 'One chooses against a background of wants which one already has. . . . Choosing is weighing relative importances.'[13] The importance of this in White's account cannot be overestimated. Having gone through a period of compulsory schooling, the ideal pupil to emerge is the autonomous reflective chooser, and it is an ideal which, in my view, is in need of considerable modification before it is acceptable as an aim of education. It assumes a model of man which is deficient in many respects, a model which fits uneasily with something White says immediately afterwards. In all this reflecting about the life I am to choose, 'I can only think this through in the full knowledge of what kind of creature I am'.[14] Now this is either chosen or it is not. If it is, then 'what am I' is hardly a constraint upon my reflective choices; if it is not, there are limits to choice of which the free and autonomous person needs to be aware. The picture that emerges from White's book is not of a person constrained in this way. Nature and human culture only assist in helping pupils to establish their priorities; in the end '*the individual must make the ultimate decisions*'.[15] There is a tension here which is troublesome, the significance of which seems to go unrecognised by White, yet an exploration of this tension will prove not only illuminating as far as a proper understanding of the limits to individual choice is concerned but will also be helpful in providing a basis from which to construct an alternative picture of human well-being.

Practical knowledge may well be possible but only where there is a measure of self-knowledge whereby particular courses of action are imbued with significance within a particular scheme of things. The truth of this becomes apparent when we consider what it would be like to commit oneself to values on the basis of desire-satisfaction alone, ignoring one's fundamental evaluations. The satisfied desire is, trivially, my desire, but for that desire to be part of me in the sense that it is *me* that is satisfied and not merely the desire, a view of the self is required which is not in endless pursuit of desire-satisfaction however reflectively arrived at.[16] As Iris Murdoch reminds us, the reduction of individuality to an abstract and lonely will 'makes no sense of [a person] as continually active, as making progress, or of her inner acts as belonging to her or forming part of a continuous fabric of being'.[17] Decisions made by reference to desire-satisfaction alone without reference to what matters to one militates against an appreciation of the full significance of what one might be doing. In short, for there to be any possibility of practical knowledge, the scope for individual choice must of necessity be restricted.[18] This claim, together with its implications for individual well-being, merits careful examination.

From their earliest days a child chooses within the context of a particular culture with concepts and traditions of its own. These are inherited and are as much a part of their self-identity as any desire they might have or choices they might make. Indeed, it is impossible to see how the child could come to want anything at all without reference to this shared and common framework. Not only does it determine their whole conception of themselves, it provides them with the wherewithal for the adoption of those ideals in accordance with which they are able to conclude that it is better to do one thing rather than another. To appreciate this is to begin to appreciate what is involved in the social nature of human beings.

The significance of this has been carefully spelled out by John Kekes, who draws our attention to the fact that a setting or tradition is required in order to provide human actions with any intelligibility.[19] Composers are able to write down any note they decide, but for these notes to add up to anything remotely meaningful they are restricted by the tradition of which they are but a small part, such as that involved in the creation of a string quartet. Intelligibility is not a function of their will but something that depends on a familiarity with the language of music. If they are fortunate, there will be a certain inevitability in their notation. But it is not only within the confines of art that reference to choice is misleading. Within the bounds of logical and physical possibility I can do almost anything I choose and yet the significance of what is done is outside my control, for this is something requiring a shared conceptual framework. This is especially true, according to Kekes, in morality:

'Choosing an action is rarely, and only exceptionally, a conscious active process of deliberation. An agent acts as a matter of course given the past, his ideals, his perception of the situation, and the practical exigencies. This is why concentration on choice obscures the real texture of moral life. To appreciate that texture one must start with how a person sees the situation in which he is to act. '*Sensitive perception is the crux of the matter*'.[20]

According to Kekes, one's sensitivity to a moral situation depends on what he calls the 'moral idioms' available. These are provided by the language, tradition and culture, and they include such descriptive appraisals as considerate, honest, courageous, conscientious, cruel and suchlike. Their significance is only partly culturally dependent; significance is also a function of the breadth and depth of understanding a moral agent brings with them to a situation. Thus it is that Kekes believes that one's sensitivity to a moral situation is dependent on the significance one attaches to the moral idioms at one's disposal. Where one is able to employ moral idioms successfully in the characterisation of a situation, the requisite course of action is generally straightforward. This is why the choice of action is far less problematic than the selection of idioms and thus where reflection is particularly important. Its function is to give breadth and depth to the employment of moral idioms:

> to see both that our moral idioms are the conventional products of the social context we happen to live in, and that underlying the various conventions there is an abiding concern with benefit and harm and with living a good life.[21]

Reflection enables one to make important discoveries; it is necessary if we are to develop a greater moral sensitivity, whereby we are able to recognise that what we had hitherto taken to be a correct understanding of a situation was superficial and incomplete. The deeper comprehension, which is the outcome of reflection, is not itself a matter for individual choice. Discoveries of this kind, Kekes maintains, are not like those of a tone-deaf man suddenly acquiring musical appreciation, but more akin to a musical person coming to appreciate a particularly difficult work.

Expressed in this way, it may look as though one is advocating an account of the way in which values come to be assigned which is excessively deterministic. If one were entirely passive with respect to discoveries of this kind, the characterisation of a situation in terms of one moral idiom rather than another would rest on a purely causal relation between the experiences to which one was subject and the language in which one's evaluations were formulated. The result would be an individual who was no more than a passive register of competing desirability-characteristics and, as such, totally bereft of that requisite degree of personal autonomy for any life-plan to count as authentically their own. Such a person would be no more than what Martin Hollis refers to as 'plastic man' whose behaviour is explicable in terms of a programme he did not write.[22] And yet such a system of values, whatever else it is, is not something which is simply adopted at will.[23] Having acquired a conceptual vocabulary with which to make sense of the world, one is in a position to render articulate one's evaluations and in so doing take on a measure of responsibility for failure to re-evaluate one's decisions. As such, one's behaviour cannot be explained as the mere end product of a complex causal chain, which means that we are not entirely passive with regard to what we judge to be of value. Moral idioms are selected not on the basis of a some Kantian-like will but on the basis of deeper and more fundamental evaluations which are bound up with one's entire self-identity.

The relationship between the notions of 'choice' and 'discovery' is exceedingly complex, as Alan Montefiore clearly demonstrates in emphasising the fact that one's own reality, while depending in part on one's choices and present and future decisions, requires us 'to accept as our own at each particular moment of our lives a reality which for all that it may not be wholly determinate, is nevertheless at that moment given to us'. Invoking Charles Taylor's notion of strong evaluation, he insists that 'our choices and evaluations remain . . . superficial if they are not rooted in the inner – and outer – reality out of which we are choosing. And this must include the recognition that there must always be more to these roots than whatever we may believe ourselves to have discovered so far.'[24]

All this is profoundly relevant to the teacher's task, for children clearly learn how to want. As our familiarity with moral idioms grows, our ability accurately to characterise and evaluate the plethora of possibilities before us is deepened. In the very young there will inevitably be an element of hit and miss in all of this. It is a mark of maturity, however, that a person is able to take on a greater measure of responsibility for what kind of person to be henceforward. But the reasons underpinning commitment to a set of values are not themselves self-chosen. They are in part due to choices made in the past by reference to reasons which are public and non-arbitrary. Opportunities should be therefore granted to children, within certain prudential and moral boundaries, to make their own decisions about what to believe and what to do, for it would be absurd to expect them to make important discoveries relating to their well-being without them. If personal education is to amount to anything at all it must address itself to exactly this. Pupils must be provided with the opportunity to discuss their most deeply held convictions and have them exposed to critical assessment. They need this if they are to be helped in the difficult process of re-evaluating those things which really matter to them and which appear to provide point and purpose to their lives. In so doing their autonomy is strengthened and within the security of the classroom they are engaged in that all-important process of self-discovery and self-affirmation.

In *EGL,* White construes well-being as the satisfaction of 'informed-desires' or those desires one would have were one in possession of information enabling one to appreciate the implications of satisfying a particular desire.[25] Recognising that desires have a hierarchical structure – which for Griffin provides the criterion for informed-desire – does not, White quite rightly maintains, imply a neat and tidy desire structure. We are all too familiar with desires which we are intent upon satisfying but for a variety of reasons, largely to do with the brevity of life, we are unable to fulfil. Unfortunately, White moves too speedily from his rejection of a post-reflective-desire-satisfaction account of well-being to what appears to him as the only alternative namely, an informed-desire account. Before examining what informed-desires are supposed to be and why their satisfaction might be thought to be synonymous with personal well-being it is worth reminding ourselves of what it is about the satisfaction of actual (as opposed to informed) desires which makes it so unsatisfactory as an account of well-being.

First, and most obviously, many of our desires, however authentic they may be, are for things which are either harmful or trivial. The satisfaction obtained may be altogether incompatible with our well-being or have so little consequence as to contribute nothing whatsoever. Second, and of particular significance for teachers, people may well desire all kinds of things on the basis of inadequate or totally false information. As they become more informed about the object of desire and, importantly, about themselves and the relationship between the two, they may well find that they no longer desire any such thing. Education has an indispensable role in helping children to formulate and reformulate their desires in accordance with increasing self-knowledge and understanding. As such, it is instrumental in creating desires we never had and never would have in a state of ignorance. A person's desires (or lack of desires) may not only be due to lack of relevant information, they may be due to lack of appropriate concepts in terms of which desires are formulated. Without the appropriate conceptual apparatus one cannot even imagine that certain things are suitable 'objects' of desire. Again, teachers have a crucial part to play here, not only to open children's eyes to the number and variety of desirable things and actions from which to choose but, as White himself insists, to help children organise their burgeoning desires by imposing some sort of hierarchical structure on them by reference to which conflict between them may be minimised. Finally, attempts to reduce interests or well-being to states of mind are equally implausible. 'Pleasurable feelings' may well be a mark of a thing's value but such a value cannot be reduced to any such state.[26]

In contrast to an actual-desire account of well-being the *prima facie* attraction of the informed-desire account is obvious. Assuming that one is aware of the implications of satisfying certain desires whereby one has a clear understanding of the objects of one's desire, one is less likely to be confronted with unresolved conflict and certainly less likely to fall victim to one's desires. The informed-desire account would also appear to accord very nicely with the view that there is no universally applicable *summum bonum* to which we should all aspire. People vary in their interests and enthusiasms, their characters and dispositions, tastes and convictions, and personal well-being varies accordingly. Recognition of individual differences would thus appear to sit quite comfortably with an account of well-being in terms of informed-desires and preferences. In reality, however, the whole idea of informed-desire is more problematic than people like White and Griffin would have us believe.

First of all, there is the problem of rendering the account of well-being in terms of informed-desire intelligible. How, for example, are we supposed to decide, given two incompatible courses of action, which one would lead to most desire-satisfaction? Our desires are far from constant whether they be for career, partners or specific pleasures.[27] Second, there are numerous occasions where the satisfaction of one's informed-desires (for something like tobacco, say) is manifestly incompatible with well-being. The informed-desire theorist cannot escape by pretending to restrict informed-desires to only those desires a person *would* have were they properly to appreciate the information, unless they can provide us with an account of what it is to 'appreciate' such information that is not circular.[28] Griffin concedes as much in his appeal to 'our rough notion of well being in deciding which informed-desires to exclude from [his] account of well-being,'[29] but I confess to finding his account of how such circular reasoning might be avoided both unclear and unconvincing. If something is in accordance with my well-being, it is in virtue of something other than the fact that I have an informed preference for it. It is precisely because we see things in a certain light – as something *worth* obtaining or avoiding (Griffin's own example is that of 'accomplishment') – that we end up having some informed preferences rather than others. While Griffin parts company with Hume in seeing understanding (cognition) and desire (appetite) as distinct existences, he denies that 'one can explain our fixing on desirability features purely in terms of understandings'[30] and insists that there is still a strong case for saying that the order of explanation is from *desire* to *value*. Suffice it to say that the issues are extremely complex and cannot be pursued here, but there is a growing literature lending support to the view that desire *as an independent element* in the explanation of actions is altogether redundant.[31]

Having cast serious doubt on attempts to account for well-being in terms of desire-satisfaction I now wish to develop an alternative and less subjective account by invoking the notion of 'real-interest'. Once we begin to appreciate that people have interests, and not only desires, we shall be in a better position to understand how personal well-being is not as subjective as a desire-satisfaction theorist would have us believe. The immediate problem facing anyone wishing to construct an objective account of value or what is in our real-interests is confronted with the ugly spectre of authoritarianism thought to be embedded in any such attempt. After all, is not the whole point of 'real' in 'real-interests' designed to show that a particular policy or course of action may well be contrary to a person's interests even if they have an expressed interest in it.

However, the charge of authoritarianism may be rebutted in a number of ways. First, the fact that something is seen in a certain light (such as possessing desirability-characteristics of various kinds) is, in itself, insufficient to enable one to decide what to do on a particular occasion. Actions are at least in part justified by reference to their significance within the context of the unity of one's life as subjectively conceived and evaluated, and one may well have good reasons for not doing that which from a certain point of view one might readily acknowledge to be worthwhile. Second, although my interests are subjective insofar as they are my interests and not (at least not necessarily) yours, they are not, and could not be, subjective to the point of being entirely idiosyncratic; there are features of human nature which entail that whatever form of life we adopt we will be harmed (which is another way of saying that we cannot flourish) unless we find room for certain fundamental requirements which may be subsumed under the heading of 'real-interests'. And there is nothing incompatible in this with a respect for individuality and the acceptance of a plurality of values. The form of objectivism I wish to sustain is that there are objectively determined limits to what may legitimately count as human well-being and, by parity of reasoning, to what may count as harm or serious damage to persons and their development. In spite of the difficulties associated with specifying an uncontested account of human flourishing, I believe that we can demonstrate that certain things are fundamental prerequisites of normal functioning, given our physical, psychological and social make-up by reference to which a particular life enjoys dignity.

We are able to envisage alternatives to the *status quo* and to adopt standpoints in accordance with which alternatives are evaluated. We have opinions concerning what is right, bad, to be avoided or pursued. We can formulate ambitions by reference to which our actions cohere. We take delight in art, relationships, exploration, work; and we find some things uninteresting, dull and boring. Our natural curiosity prompts us to seek an understanding of the world and our place within it. We can laugh and cry and experience events as comical, tragic or absurd. We form conceptions of ourselves in terms of which we develop our self-respect and self-esteem. Such conceptions are in large measure the result of social intercourse which provides opportunities for conviviality, friendship and love. Our lives are governed by a whole catalogue of emotions, forcing us to adopt strategies in order to avoid their domination and instead acknowledge their rightful place within our rational orderings.

All of this requires systematic analysis for a proper understanding of human nature, but it serves to remind us that human characteristics of this kind explain the value we attach to things like truth, meaningful work and autonomy. Acceptance of what would appear to be indisputable about human nature commits one to the conclusion that there are features common to any minimally worthwhile life. If desirability is indeed ultimately reducible to preference, then the possibility of discovery of what is of value is impossible. However, we can admit to wanting things in virtue of a recognition of who and what we are on the one hand, combined with an appropriate employment of the language of contrastive evaluation on the other, which provides a strategy for accounting for well-being by reference to more objective criteria than desire-satisfaction theories would admit.

Well-being might be explained in terms of the 'fit' between the direction in which our individual lives are given shape and purpose and the presence of those values which are not merely self-chosen but which are objective in being determined by our common humanity and which we may be said to have a genuine stake in nurturing.

Notes

1 An earlier version of this chapter was presented to the Philosophy of Education Society in San Francisco in April 1995 and subsequently published in *Philosophy of Education*. I am grateful to the editors of *Philosophy of Education* for their kind permission to allow an earlier version of 'Well-being as an aim of education' to be printed here. The earlier version appeared as 'Education and well-being: beyond desire satisfaction' and appeared in *Philosophy of Education*, 1995.

2 London: Routledge & Kegan Paul, 1982.

3 London: Kegan Paul, 1992.

4 *AER*, p. 57. An account of rational choice which ignores the relationship between it and a person's *good* (or real-interest), concentrating exlusively on their chosen goals is, in my view, radically misconceived.

5 Ibid., p. 52 (my emphasis).

6 London: Routledge & Kegan Paul, 1973.

7 *AER*, p. 52.

8 Ibid., p. 54.

9 Ibid.

10 Ibid., pp. 54–5.

11 Ibid., p. 57.

12 Ibid., p. 55.

13 Ibid., p. 52.

14 Ibid.

15 Ibid. (my emphasis).

16 The idea is not easy to spell out but it receives elegant articulation in Michael Sandel's *Liberalism and the Limits of Justice*, Cambridge: Cambridge University Press, 1982, p. 55.

17 I. Murdoch (1970) 'The idea of perfection', in *The Sovereignty of Good*, London: Routledge & Kegan Paul, p. 39.

18 For reasons why this is so, see R. Scruton (1981) 'The significance of a common culture', *Philosophy* 54: 66.

19 See his 'Moral sensitivity', *Philosophy* 59: 3–19.
20 Ibid., p. 7 (my emphasis).
21 Ibid.
22 M. Hollis (1977) *Models of Man: Philosophical Thoughts on Social Action*, Cambridge: Cambridge University Press.
23 In his article 'On seeing things differently', in *Radical Philosophy* I (1971): 6–14, Richard Norman ably demonstrates that although the figure in Leeper's Ambiguous Lady Illusion can be seen as a picture of a young woman, or an old woman, this is entirely subjective. What is there imposes limitations on what is seen. As Norman says: 'What is possible for us to see depends upon how it is possible for us to conceptualise our experience'. And he draws a parallel between ways of seeing such pictures and *Weltanschauungen*: 'the possible ways of seeing man's nature and his place in the universe are made available by the moral and intellectual traditions within one's culture. . . . The available traditions do not confine us once and for all; new ways of seeing can be developed and extended – *but not arbitrarily*' (p. 11, my emphasis).
24 A. Montefiore, 'Self-reality, self-respect and respect for others', *Midwest Studies in Philosophy* 3: 200.
25 The notion of informed-desire was employed as long ago as 1907 by Henry Sidgwick in his *Methods of Ethics*. Its most recent defence is in James Griffin's *Well-being: Its Meaning, Measurement and Moral Importance*, Oxford: Clarendon Press, 1986, sections i–iv.
26 For reasons provided by Robert Nozick, who invites us to contemplate being plugged in to an experience machine capable of giving us any experience desired. Those who find such a prospect inviting should read his *Anarchy, State and Utopia*, Oxford: Blackwell, 1974, pp. 42–5.
27 To the suggestion that it is desires at the time of satisfaction which count, Richard Brandt has doubts raised by the following example:

> a convinced sceptic who has rebelled against a religious background wants, most of his life, no priest to be called when he is about to die. But he weakens on his deathbed, and asks for a priest. Do we maximise his welfare by summoning a priest? Some would say not, in view of his past desires. The programme also ignores future regrets.

See his *A Theory of the Good and the Right*, Oxford: Clarendon Press, 1979, p. 250. I admit to sharing Brandt's scepticism about the inteligibility of such a programme in spite of what Griffin has to say later in the book.
28 As Garrett Thompson puts it:

> it is circular to define 'appreciation' in terms of our informed preferences matching what is valuable, e.g. a person appreciates what he prefers if and only if he prefers Y to X only when Y is more valuable than X. . . . Without an independent grip on the . . . notion of appreciation in the phrase "what a person would prefer if he appreciated what it is like to have what he prefers', it advances us no further to define prudential value in terms of this phrase.
>
> (G. Thomson (1990) *Needs*, Oxford: Clarendon Press, pp. 46–7)

29 Op. cit., p. 22.
30 Ibid., pp. 27–9.
31 See, e.g., M. Platts (1979) *Ways of Meaning*, London: Routledge & Kegan Paul; and R. L. Arrington (1989) *Rationalism, Realism and Relativism: Perspectives in Contemporary Moral Epistemology*, Ithaca, NY: Cornell University Press.

13

AIMING FOR A FAIR EDUCATION

What use is philosophy?[1]

Morwenna Griffiths

Aims? Whose aims?

Aims for education are not hard to find. They appear in schools' mission statements, in party policies for the state, in policy statements from local government, and in the writing of educationists and of social theorists. Aims are formulated by teachers, parents, individual LEA officials, inspectors, employers, pressure groups, NGOs, university tutors, school governors – and all their organisations. In Africa, nation-building ideas may be emphasised, and in the West, individual autonomy. The world over, there is concern about the need for a skilled workforce. In this chapter I concentrate on schools and teachers, but with the proviso that it has to be understood within the wider context.

It might seem that there is a great deal of agreement in schools about the aims of education. Here is a deputy head of a city secondary school in England talking about aiming for fairness[2] in school:

> If you look at the aims of all the schools I've worked in and I suspect most schools, somewhere they will have something like 'to achieve the full potential of all pupils'. They will also have something about 'respecting everybody'. That's something to do with social justice that's built into every school. What happens to the aims is what's very different in schools. I think in many schools they are the aims that are written in the school brochure and they are, if you like, tucked in a drawer, but they actually mean nothing in the school. That's where the school can have a big influence, if they mean something in the school. I

think the idea of treating everyone equally, we actually try to put into practice.

If everyone agrees, what happens? Why do such statements remain tucked in a drawer? Faced with this question, what is a teacher, headteacher, adviser or educationist to do? Can philosophy help? This chapter presents an argument about the relationship of philosophy and philosophers with schools and schoolteachers.

There is a pervasive self-image of philosophy in which the philosopher is the spectator (for example, Aristotle's contemplator); or the legislator (such as Plato); or the one able to bring the insights of critique: the exercise of reason at the same time as seeing the limits to that reason (for instance, Kant). All of these require a certain lofty removal from the world. Hutchings summarises Arendt's critique of philosophers in relation to the *vita activa*, human activity:

> For Arendt, Heidegger and Plato represent the two aspects of the threat that philosophy poses to politics. Heidegger is the philosopher who turns away from the world and in gazing at the stars risks Thales' fate of falling down the well at his feet. Plato is the philosopher who turns towards the world and in an effort to make it safe for philosophy conceptualises the world as both inferior and manageable.
>
> (Hutchings 1995: 82)

In this chapter I take up Adriana Cavarero's suggestion that we see what we can learn from the maidservant from Thrace (who laughed at Thales), and from others immersed in everyday life, like Penelope, when we read about them against the grain of philosophy's own self-understanding:

> The Thracian maidservant laughs at the philosopher . . . who pays no heed to her derision, holding theory as a higher value than the world of ordinary experience . . . [p.32] [Penelope] continued to weave the individual whole made up of body and mind that had already appeared in her *metis*: the reality where to live is most of all to be born and then only at the end, also to die. The interweaving of intelligence and the senses is where all humans exist as part of their gender, not as eternal souls fallen into a body like many other bodies, regardless of species or sex. [p.30]
>
> (Cavarero 1995)

In this chapter I argue that philosophers and teachers take up the suggestion of a new way of doing philosophy which will not attract the derision of the maidservant of Thrace. I also argue that we need to do so in the idiom of our contemporary world in which telecommunication is commonplace, and in which maidservants in Thrace or ladies in Ithaca can do things (including doing philosophy) in ways which are not determined by their gender, class or ethnic background.

Getting there: an educational journey

The power of an argument is often lodged in metaphor.[3] It is for this reason that I address the question of the metaphor of this argument explicitly. Part of the argument of the chapter is that the metaphors by which we understand our practices, as in education, may be beginning to outlive their usefulness, even when used ironically and against the grain to subvert some of their original meanings. I begin the argument with a set of metaphors drawing attention to their subversive possibilities. I then go on to question them later in the chapter (in the section beginning on page 150).

My guiding metaphors are of landscape, maps and journeys. The particular metaphor I am playing with is drawn from Donald Schon's metaphor of the swamps of practice contrasted with the high ground of theory (Schon 1983). This is a rich, ambiguous metaphor which includes in its imagery the hierarchy between theory and practice, thinking and doing, so pervasive of Western thinking. I try to subvert this, mimetically, by drawing attention to the richness and fertility of the low ground (where we all live) while acknowledging the appeal of the barren, high peaks and the beautiful views we get from them.

In this chapter I refer to bogs and mountains, to hedges and fields. I also refer to the fogs and clouds which can cling to them. This is a dream landscape, but it is one that had its inspiration in Britain, this corner of North-western Europe, with its patchworks of fields, its moors and highlands, and its pervading dampness. Anyway, as I shall argue, dreaming is not an optional part of improving our educational practices.

Understanding justice in/for schools

In this section I ground the general discussion by using the specific example of self and society and what to do about it. This is a question of justice as an aim in education; that is, the contribution that education makes to the right ordering of society and to the well-being of the individuals within it. A central question is how it is that the personal, individual, private aspects of a self interrelate with the political, collaborative, public struggle to establish social justice through education. I consider this question first from the perspective of philosophy and then from the perspective of teaching.

Self and social justice: philosophers

In seeking to understand the question of the self and its relation to social justice, there are starting places in the high ground, even if we are liable to find ourselves beguiled by star-gazing, or with our heads in the clouds. (This high up, in this rarefied atmosphere 'it seems an appropriate pronoun. In the high discourse of universal humanity, gender gets lost.) The question seems to require mapping the boundaries of the self in its relation to the rest of the world. Drawing such a map might require a distancing, a discovery of the underlying features of the terrain in order to make sense of the confusing jumble of natural and human features down below: hedges, ditches, streams, bogs, motorways and woods.

Descartes did his best to withdraw from his social life in order to abstract an understanding of a self. From the high ground above the busy, everyday world below, he drew a map that has been influential ever since. The self for him was a unity, because it was that which thought. It could introspect itself, and see what it was. This view is a source of the self-legislating consciousness, which is the ultimate source of all knowledge. It is a view which has come in for criticism by some other thinkers – including both structuralists and post-structuralists – on neighbouring peaks, who see that history and language are an essential part of the terrain they survey. Descartes apparently did not notice the discourse which was a human construction independent of him, but which he needed in order even to formulate 'I think, therefore I am'. His language was bound by the discourses he inhabited, and which lie in a number of discursive relations to each other. He might have solved an epistemological problem but in terms of personal identity it is a hollow solution. That kind of introspection reveals very little about an individual self and its relation to others. Moreover, as Mary Daly pointed out, it is the identity of a severed head (Daly 1984).

Mar'a Lugones, an Hispanic-American philosopher, has written about the experience of what she terms '"world"-travelling'. She analyses what it is that makes her at ease in the different worlds she inhabits, some of them Latin-American and some of them Anglo-American; some of them female, some of them mixed sex. She notes that in some of them she is a serious person, while in others she is playful. And it is this, the personal characteristic of being playful or not, which is at the centre of her analysis:

> My problem is not one of lack of ease. I am suggesting that I can understand my confusion about whether I am or am not playful by saying that I am both and that I am different persons in different worlds and can remember myself in both as I am in the other. I am a plurality of selves.
>
> (1989: 286)

Self and social justice: schools

The general distinctions that were made above relate to the boundaries of the self – in particular, the personal and public, where the personal is taken to be internal to the self; a further, related distinction is between the private and public. We can come down from this high ground and see how these distinctions look when we are back down among the everyday world full of particular fields, hedges, footpaths and patches of bog. This is the region where people live, make a living, love, fight, and rub along together as best they can. From down here life appears more complex than it appears from the high ground.

The simple demarcations of boundaries of the self – private, personal and public – begin to shift or disintegrate in a real classroom. You know that you are in a particular classroom by recognising the teacher and the thirty-plus children, each with their distinctive faces and voices, by the smell and feel of the place, and by the atmosphere of buzz or boredom. A real classroom is not full of genderless 'selves' or persons; and there are no severed heads here, either.

Plato thought you had to escape the cave of everyday life to discover philosophical truths. Socrates, his teacher, spent his time chatting, joking, arguing and debating among the crowds in the city centre. His example shows us that there *are* starting places for philosophy in the lowlands, among the bogs and the fogs. Further, since Socrates is one of the best regarded philosophers the world has known, it is clear that very good and useful map-making can result from a determined resolve to get somewhere (rather than only draw better maps).

This is where many practitioners start. Teachers find themselves struggling to be fair to everybody, as they help their pupils grow into successful individuals and responsible citizens. And all this among the everyday complexities of deciding what to do about a case of bullying or the best things to do during a Friday afternoon after a wet playtime. The peaks, if you look up to them, are liable to be covered with clouds. The distinction between the private person and the public issues of social justice that looked so sharp from on high, looks blurred from down here, especially when it is examined in the light of someone considering their own professional practice. But, as Carol Davies, my long-time collaborator, expresses it, it seems pretty foggy down here too (Griffiths and Davies 1995). Teachers cannot avoid the fact that they have to deal with individual children in all their human complexity and also the social issues of justice. This is difficult to see clearly.

This is well demonstrated by some stories related to me by teachers and educational advisers – all of them are, or have been, teachers themselves. They told me about memories of their lives which seemed to them to be of continuing significance in how they conduct their professional lives. The people talking are black, working class and/or gay. These extracts show how the issues of being a private person interact with issues of justice for them. Their personal lives are marked by the prevailing injustices of society, just as their understanding of how to get justice is changed by their personal responses.

> I had the right kind of attitude that allowed me to get through. I looked and observed what people were doing and gradually made decisions as to how I thought people were and whether I could trust them. I think you have to be a certain kind of person, unfortunately, to get through. You have to be, you need to be very careful about every step you take. And not fall into traps. It's easy to get angry about things and act in a certain way. We can all do that. It's harder to control yourself.

> I could feel when I first came to the school that there was a little group of people just didn't know how to handle me [because I was different from them], didn't know where I was coming from. They were very, very, very careful of me. So I sat in the staff room, eating my sandwiches. I always made a point of coming into the staff room and having them.

> I received a Teacher's pack [on the subject] from the NUT. In this pack were autobiographical accounts from young people and from teachers. . . . [One of the pieces] brought tears to my eyes because I'm thinking, 'Well, this is his story. This is my story as well.' I suppose it was the dawning of a realisation that – I think what I did was that I challenged my own myth, that is that I had to keep quiet about this issue. Behind that were all kinds of sub-texts, like I'm not an OK person. It felt like a turning point.

These stories show how difficult it can be to draw the distinctions made by philosophers. The boundaries between personal/private and the political/ public which seemed clear on the peaks are not so easy to draw on the ground. The stories also show how important such ideas are in each person's own professional understanding: being black, working class or lesbian is both a private and a public affair for a teacher. The injustice of being deemed outsiders (others, deviants, different) has affected how these individuals related to school as pupils and, later, as teachers. The effect is probably just as strong for insiders, but it is harder for them to see how incidents such as these help change the way the ground has been covered.

Cooperation and co-construction: philosophy and teachers

A model of cooperation and co-construction

I want to juxtapose the stories, taken from the thick of the fogs and the bogs, with some of the philosophical maps I mentioned earlier. I do so to draw attention to the way that questions of social justice in education and questions of boundaries around the self, private and public, can be brought together, to the benefit of people journeying in both the high and the low ground. Bringing them together is something which has to contend with a long history of separation.

There have always been demarcation disputes and invasions of territory. Trouble between the highlands and the lowlands punctuates the history of the British Isles. This is captured in the famous verse by Thomas Love Peacock:

> The mountain sheep are sweeter,
>   But the valley sheep are fatter;
> We therefore deemed it meeter
>   To carry off the latter.

Similarly, trouble between the highlands of 'theory' and the lowlands of 'practice' punctuates the history of educational research in Britain – and elsewhere in the English-speaking world. I have deliberately not used the terms 'theory' and 'practice' in this chapter. I find them ambiguous and misleading, permeated as they are by Western prejudice about 'knowledge that' and 'knowledge how to' and its relation to minds and bodies (as I argued in Griffiths 1987). However, the terms have some use here, as the theory/practice divide is so recognisable as a trouble spot. A special case of this is the question of philosophy as useful to practising teachers.

Typically, philosophers are more interested in making maps, while teachers are more interested in getting somewhere. But of course, you make better maps if you try to use them, and you find a journey easier with a good map. In other words, there is no 'pure' philosophy or teaching to be found. It is not possible to live on the mountain tops. Philosophers also depend on the fertility of the boggy lowlands, even though they often forget this. Similarly, in the long term, teachers have to try and understand their bit of the world and its relation to other parts, which may only be able to be seen from the top of the mountain – even if it is sometimes easier just to dig one's own garden and forget its connection to the rest of the world. So it should not be surprising to find teachers who are also philosophers and philosophers who are also teachers. However, in the current UK context, as pressures build up both in schools (where most teachers are to be found) and in universities (where there are more philosophers), it gets harder to do both. It gets harder even to meet and talk. This is detrimental to both sides.

This section is a response to this situation. I try to tell a story about the way *both* philosophy and *also* practical understanding of everyday experience are helpful to each other – as long as neither philosophers nor teachers remain in their own defended area only going out of them to make raids. If all sides are prepared to travel and see the world from the other point of view both will go back to their own ground understanding it better. That is, one may be going up (to re-draw the philosophical perspectives on the self). Or one may be going down (to decide what to do in a particular school or classroom). Either way, each party ends up with a better understanding of the terrain and the paths that go through it. Both parties draw better maps (insofar as they want to) and both parties can journey on more easily (insofar as they want to). Even better would be to have people travelling regularly between the two, taking both perspectives. This is what I think philosophers of education should be doing.

However, many philosophers of education see it differently. The standard description of the connection between philosophy and education is, to my way of seeing, a description of raiding parties. The raiding party might be one composed of philosophers using education as one more example where their laws and insights can be applied. (The fat sheep of the lowlands are there to feed the hungry lot up above.) Alternatively, the raiding party might be composed of educationists. They raid philosophical theories for what can be quickly extracted and put to use. (They get one or two sweet mountain sheep from the uplands to add in to their own flock without really changing its composition.)

Surely a better way than raiding each other's goods is to trade or to exchange gifts, or to find some other way of mutual enrichment. The model I propose is of communication in a project where both parties have overlapping interests with the other, and where some of each party regularly visits the domain of the other. It is a conversation from which both parties can go away having learned something to help them on their different projects. Indeed, as a result of the exchange they may now see their projects differently. To return to the metaphor I began with, instead of taking sheep from each other, they can each offer to give the other party one or two from their own flock – or perhaps offer to share some of their pasture. If the givers are alert to the pitfalls of gift giving and receiving, each party will be more likely to be sure they get just the kind of animal they want. Gift giving is difficult, of course: it requires thought, sensitivity and honesty on the part of both giver and receiver. It is also liable to change something significant in the life of both the giver and the receiver.

Notice that none of the parties need agree with each other at the end of the conversation. But they do need to talk. For this they will need to develop a common way of talking. They do not need to insist that the other party speaks in their own particular dialect. Nor do they need to abandon their own dialect, which serves its purpose so well in the context in which it was developed.[4]

An example of cooperation and co-construction

What kinds of goods might be exchanged, which will benefit all parties? To give an example of this, I return to the concern with boundaries of the self. How do the stories that my colleagues told me fit into the frameworks provided by philosophers? I have already pointed out some of the ways in which there is blurring or uncertainty in the boundaries around the self. Now I look in a little more detail at the particular philosophers I mentioned.

To me the search for a single unified self is less helpful than the concept of world travelling, used by Lugones. The concept of a 'world' adds the dimension of history and culture to Descartes' formulation. Her concept allows for a certain kind of unity, a sense to be made of a life, without requiring an impossible distance from the context in which a person finds themself. I asked one of my black colleagues (quoted above) what she does in relation to the black children she teaches. She explained in some detail how she advises them to adjust their behaviour to the context, but without compromising their principles, and without yielding their rights to take part in all that society has to offer. This means behaving differently inside and outside school, including in ways that feel expressive of themselves (how to walk, what to laugh at, in which style to do their hair, and so on).

However, the down-to-earth realities of classrooms also show up the limitations of Lugones' idea of a 'world'. Cultures are far more fluid, changing and overlapping than her idea of a 'world' would indicate, and this is particularly so for children who are necessarily in the forefront of change. My British-born black colleagues forged their own culture, different from that of their parents, and different from that of the predominantly white host culture at the time. Moreover, as any teacher can tell you, the culture in which adolescents find their identity is, at least partially, a culture of resistance. The problem for black, working-class or gay/lesbian people is that, first, their cultures are often (wrongly) seen as resistance cultures, and second, their actual resistance cultures are treated as far more threatening than the equivalent mainstream ones.

The analysis I have just given of the way that my colleagues in schools can understand what is going on is indebted to these (and other) thinkers. Deciding what to do next can be helped by focused and sharpened thinking. At the same time, the reality of a particular classroom sharpens and focuses philosophical thinking. To return to the metaphor, yet again, both travelling and map making are different as a result of the meeting.

New metaphors and new aims

It is time that I drew attention to the fact that my guiding metaphor of landscape and journeys is becoming horribly strained. In fact, it is beginning to give under the pressure. It was altered as I went along: sheep appeared on the way. I introduced them in order to talk about raiding parties, but as a result it has become unclear whether people only visit the summit or whether they live there. I think the problem with the picture is that it is a model of a simpler world than the one we live in now.[5] This image of landscape is one which would have been recognisable hundreds of years ago. It depends on face-to-face interactions in small communities. It exhibits what Lyotard calls 'the nostalgia for the lost narrative' (1984: 41); a haunting 'by the paradisic representation of a lost "organic" society' (p.15). Like Lyotard, I think this nostalgia is misplaced.

In the image I was using, 'high' and 'low' are presented as a dichotomy; but power and authority are no longer understood so simply. This terminology fits the image of power as 'power over', 'the power that says no'. This is the kind of power analysed by Lukes in both liberal and Marxist terms, or by Arendt in her discussion of totalitarianism. However, there is an increasing understanding that there is also the kind of power of the kind conceptualised by Foucault which is more diffuse, and which can be mobilised in shifting formations through discourses and reverse discourses. This is much more diffuse. In our complex, late-twentieth-century world of fragmentation and migration, in which identity is always at issue, the simplicities of a dichotomous 'high' and 'low' positioning no longer describe anything recognisable.

Moreover, at least in the UK, both schools and philosophy are much more complex than the simple, organic image allows. Schools have become more diverse, partly as a result of government policies. Similarly there is a surprising range of departments in which philosophy is done (Griffiths and Whitford 1996). Thus it would be a difficult matter to describe either the constraints on schools and motivations of teachers or the constraints and motivations of philosophers in any unified way. The journeys and maps made by teachers and philosophers are influenced by constraints and motivations which vary from place to place, and within one place. Indeed, the spaces in which people meet and decide about maps and journeys are many and various, depending on computer technology and cyberspace as much as on face-to-face conversations. There are new ways for people in different physical spaces to influence each other.

As a result of this sharply changing context, we need to dream more deeply what is possible in philosophy and educational research. Moreover, I think it is important to do our dreaming with the conditions and symbols of current life – our postmodern condition, as Lyotard describes it. In doing so we need to recognise that we live in a world which has become more fragmented and more differentiated, with shifting dispensations of powers and counter-powers. Different spheres of life, with their associated discourses, are less separate, more discursive, than even Lyotard thinks, in his metaphor of islands.[6] Many of us are hybrids and migrants, at home in cyberspace as in physical space (even if this language is still strange to the very people it describes). Some of these dreams will be virtual reality castles in the air – which may yet become hard copy. Some of them will play with new metaphors and associations to imagine new possibilities: Haraway's (1991) influential paper on cyborgs is an example of the kind of things that can be thought. Some of these dreams will be modest proposals for new ways of doing things, bringing together discourses in new discursive arrangements, creating experimental hybrids.

In summary, it is argued that new metaphors and new pictures, on the one hand, and new projects, on the other, are beginning to clarify and subvert current understandings of the relationship between philosophy and teaching. This is a dream of the future in which there is an understanding of the context of modernity/postmodernity, together with a tolerance of diversity between people and of plurality within persons, in the ways they think and act – as teachers, as philosophers, as teachers who are also philosophers; or as philosophers who are also teachers. There would be a welcoming (rather than mere tolerance) of such diversity and hybridity, because of what it could contribute to the development of aims of education useful for everybody. This is a dream in which just aims of education are developed through just means, as part of an evolving understanding of both justice and education.

References

Cavarero, Adriana (1995) *In Spite of Plato: A Feminist Rewriting of Ancient Philosophy*, Cambridge: Polity Press.

Daly, Mary (1984) *Pure Lust: Elemental Feminist Philosophy*, London: The Women's Press.

Descartes, René (1701, 1911, 1972) 'Rules for the direction of the mind', in *The Philosophical Works of Descartes*, trans. Elizabeth Haldane and G. R. T. Ross, Cambridge: Cambridge University Press.

Griffiths, Morwenna (1987) 'Teaching skills and the skills of teaching', *Journal of Philosophy of Education*, 21(2).

——(1995) *Feminisms and the Self: The Web of Identity*, London: Routledge

Griffiths, Morwenna and Davies, Carol (1995) *In Fairness to Children: Working for Social Justice in the Primary School*, London: David Fulton.

Griffiths, Morwenna and Whitford, Margaret (1996) *Women's Philosophy Review*, Nottingham: University of Nottingham.

Haraway, Donna (1991) *Simians, Cyborgs and Women: the Reinvention of Nature*, London: Free Association Books.

Hutchings, Kimberly (1995) *Kant, Critique and Politics*, London: Routledge.

Lugones, Mar'a (1989) 'Playfulness, "world"-traveling and loving perception' in Ann Garry and Marilyn Pearsall (eds) *Women, Knowledge and Reality: Explorations in Feminist Philosophy*, Boston: Unwin Hyman.

Lukes, Steven (1974) *Power: A Radical View*, Basingstoke: Macmillan.

Lyotard, Jean-François (1984) *The Postmodern Condition: A Report on Knowledge,* trans. G. Bennington and B. Massumi, Manchester: Manchester University Press.

Rorty, Richard (1991) *Objectivity, Relativism and Truth,* Cambridge: Cambridge University Press.

Walzer, Michael (1967) 'On the role of symbolism in political thought', *Political Science Quarterly* LXXXI (June): 191–204.

Notes

1 The chapter is based on work carried out on an ESRC senior research fellowship, 1995–6.
2 I do not distinguish sharply between 'justice', 'social justice' and 'fairness' in this chapter.
3 See my brief discussion in Griffiths (1995: pp. 171–2); also Michael Walzer (1967).
4 I have no space here to develop this theme of multilingualism. I say more about it in my book *Feminisms and the Self.*
5 See Walzer (1967).
6 For a discussion of this metaphor, see Rorty (1991).

14

NEGLECTED EDUCATIONAL AIMS

Moral seriousness and social commitment

Richard Pring

Rarely has there been such a lively concern for the teaching of values in schools. The inspectorate wrote a report, *Spiritual, Moral, Social and Cultural Development* (1994), attempting to define the 'curriculum area'; the School Curriculum and Assessment Authority (SCAA) produced in 1996 a discussion paper, *Education for Adult Life: The Spiritual and Moral Development of Young People*; and the National Forum for Values in Education and the Community disseminated its concerns through a consultation document on *Values in Education and the Community* (1996). The result of that consultation was a rather weighty document from SCAA, *The Promotion of Pupils' Spiritual, Moral, Social and Cultural Development* (1997), which sets out in massive detail what teachers need to do for their children to grow up as good human beings.

The reasons for this rush of interest in the teaching of moral values are no doubt many. Some were captured in the paper given by Dr Tate, Chief Executive of SCAA, in which he denounced the relativism which, in his view, permeated society – and schools in so far as they reflected society. Somehow we must assert once again the abiding moral truths, and the values which should be promoted in education.

I welcome this public deliberation, although I hasten to say that I have never yet met a real relativist. But I believe that much of it misses the mark. First, it separates the teaching of values from the context in which those values are taught – as if the values which insidiously permeate so much of the political concern for 'school effectiveness' were irrelevant to the classroom job of helping children to be better people. Second, the central educational aims of 'moral seriousness' and 'social commitment' have little place in these accounts; there is moral education without a respect for the moral seriousness of those to be educated and without a connection to the wider social and political responsibility of those who are 'morally serious'.

In pursuing this, I make the following major points. First, I briefly outline the context within which the discussion of values ought to take place – but which has been sadly neglected. Second, I return to the aims of education, for only within a consideration of those aims can we correctly place the teaching of values. Third, I emphasise the importance in education of 'personal significance' – of encouraging the *serious* deliberation of that which makes life worth living. Fourth, I relate this personal significance to the wider sense of community, of which the learner is necessarily a part.

Context

We have seen in the last few years an unprecedented governmental involvement in what is learned in schools and how it is taught – unprecedented because now the involvement has become detailed and bureaucratised as never before. It is as though there are at the centre of our political system those with the special wisdom – Plato's guardian class headed by a philosopher king – who can with confidence say what everyone should know and how all teachers should teach. The arrogance of such a position is hard to describe, for, when public uncertainties about the nature of knowledge or about the sort of life worth pursuing permeate the lives of academia and of the community at large, by contrast politicians, and their civil servants and advisers, have no such doubts in determining what exactly should be learned by several million children.

Such central responsibility for the 'what' and the 'how' of learning derives, not from any long and public deliberation over values, purposes or the nature of knowledge, but from the hurried drafts of those who happen to be in the service of the National Curriculum Council, or the School Curriculum and Assessment Authority that were, or the Qualification and Curriculum Assessment Council that is. The result is a national curriculum which, in terms of its content and overall shape, provides its own implicit blueprint of the educated person.

Furthermore, the national curriculum is a peg upon which to hang a system of assessment which can say exactly how that knowledge and understanding should manifest themselves and which thereby provides the evidence for classifying and ordering educational success child by child, school by school. The whole educational enterprise comes to be dominated by the pursuit of 'effectiveness' in achieving these detailed and specific learning goals – identified, as I said, by a new breed of guardians.

There are several points I want to develop here which affect how one might understand and develop moral education. First, among all the changes of the last few years, including the reform of the national curriculum by the Dearing Report (1994), the aim of education – what counts as an educated person in the present social and economic circumstances – is rarely explored to any significant extent. Of course, no document is published without reference to 'moral, spiritual, personal and social development', but this appears as a form of words to counterbalance what otherwise is the pursuit of economic and social utility as the driving force behind educational reform. Indeed, the attack in recent years on the teaching of philosophy in the training of teachers, particularly the attack in the popular press on that great American philosopher John Dewey, is but part of the suspicion of any close examination of and deliberation about the aims of education – the values which do and should direct our educational efforts.

Second, the control of education by government of what children should know and how they should learn, sustained by an all-pervasive system of assessment, leaves little room within the schools for that deliberation of what is worthwhile and for that forming of a moral perspective which is essentially unpredictable, not to be captured in a detailed assessment profile. Possibly the most important *educational* task is that of helping young people to find value in what they do and to decide – in the light of evidence, the experience of others, critical discussion – what sort of life is worth living, and what skills, qualities, dispositions and understandings need to be acquired in order to live that life. The grave danger is that, in making schools more 'effective' in reaching the goals laid down by government and its agencies, this central moral goal of education finds no place.

Third, this increased accountability of schools, exercised mainly through a detailed system of assessment, requires a common language – and a language which integrates curriculum activity and the 'audit' of that activity. Therefore, in the last few years there has been the creation of a new language of education borrowed in the main from the language of management. The importance of this is rarely acknowledged, even by those who are most concerned about the moral purposes of education. And yet how we see the world depends so much upon the language we use. The concepts embedded within a language structure our experience and determine what and how we perceive. That applies as much to the moral world and to the world of personal relations as it does to the physical and social worlds. To perceive the learner as a client or a customer is to see that person – and it is to structure the relationship between teacher and learner – in different ways. Indeed, as I shall indicate, the metaphorical language, through which is described and evaluated the complex relations between teacher, learner and the wider traditions of one's culture and one's community, shapes and transforms the moral nature of the activity. Therefore, we need to question whether, in the pursuit of greater standardisation of educational output, the language of management and control, whereby efficiency can be gauged, is adequate to the moral purposes of education. We need, in consequence, to question how far the rather recent and frenetic concern for moral values as an explicit curriculum aim arises from the poverty of the language now adopted to describe education and to control its outcomes.

This is not so recent. An HMI (1991) report on higher education referred to the 'public interest in management efficiency and institutional effectiveness' and the consequent 'need to use performance indicators to monitor the . . . system. . . . Some concrete information on the extent to which the benefits expected from educational expenditure are actually secured . . . an approach finding most favour is the classification of performance indicators within an input, output, process model.' And the language of *inputs* and *outputs*, of *performance indicators* and *audits*, of teachers as *deliverers of 'a curriculum'* (devised by someone else) and of learners as *clients*, of education as a *commodity* which has a *market value*, and of quality spelt out in terms of lists (often very long lists) of *competences*, of measurable improvement as *'value addedness'* and of cuts in resources as *'efficiency gains'* – such a language serves well the new managerial class, but it arises not from any analysis of what it means to be an educated person or of how we might make sense of that transaction which takes place between the teacher, as he or she mediates the 'best that has been thought and said', and the learner who is trying bit by bit to make sense of these more abiding values.

What should be at the heart of the *educational process* can receive no recognition in the language of management. The language of efficiency is not that of moral struggle, moral deliberation, the searching for what is valuable, the gradual and often faltering introduction to traditions of thought and feeling. Indeed, such a moral language challenges the very managerialism and control with which the pursuit of effectiveness is associated.

This is not an argument against there being performance criteria, but these need to be recognised for what they are: namely, broad criteria which many different practices need to meet if public money can be seen to be not misspent; they should not be confused with specific objectives to be focused upon – a distinction which, despite its importance, has escaped the curriculum planners. The result is a language of 'ends' and objectives established outside the process of being educated – the endless lists of competences, the 'can dos' which can be objectively measured leaving nothing to the flawed 'judgement' of the teacher. 'Education', then, becomes the means to achieve these ends, and is judged essentially by its effectiveness. If it is not effective, then it should adopt other 'means', based on the kind of research which relates means to ends, on what the teacher does to what the learner can do as a result. 'Means' are logically 'separated' from the 'ends', and the quality of the 'input' is measured simply by reference to success or otherwise of the 'output'. The logical consequence of this lies, of course, in the aspirations of some – for example, Jessup (1991) – to dispense with a curriculum, or a prescribed period of time with a teacher, as essential to education, and to substitute instead 'assessment centres', where one's competence in plumbing, in management and no doubt in philosophy will be ascertained. Such competences are logically disconnected from the educational *context* and the transactions which take place between teacher and students as they endeavour to grasp and make sense of that which is worth understanding.

The mistake is two-fold. First, the quality and depth of thinking, which we would wish to associate with the educated person, cannot be reduced to such a list of competences – the serious engagement with ideas, the struggle to make sense and to understand, the entry into a tradition of thinking and critical examination, the search for meaning and value in what is often mundane, the excitement in intellectual and aesthetic discovery. Second, such achievements cannot be disconnected from the 'means' of achieving them. The engagement between teacher and learner as they endeavour to appreciate a poem or to understand a theorem or to solve a design problem is both the means and the end, as Dewey so effectively argued. For as one reaches the so-called 'end', so this becomes the means to yet further thinking – the pursuit of yet further goals. But, then, that is probably why Dewey for so long has been on the index of forbidden books in teacher training – a different language from that of management and control – see Dewey (1916).

The context, then, in which we need to examine the meaning and the possibility of moral education is one in which the increased standardisation and accountability of education, with all the funding and shaming consequences of this, has required a shift in how we conceive education, of how we conceive the relationship between teacher and learner and of how there might be room for those engagements or transactions through which moral development might take place.

The aims of education

To educate is to get people to learn. Any educational system is a system for promoting learning. Teachers are not, as such, social workers or therapists or community workers or child carers – although they may *de facto* be forced into any one or more of these roles; their expertise lies in being able, through training and experience, to help people, particularly children, to learn.

However, 'learning' has an object. One learns something. And teachers' professional expertise lies in their being able to get people to learn particular kinds of skill or knowledge or understanding. Teaching them how to learn *as such* is a contemporary nonsense which ignores the obvious truth that the psychology of learning must respect the logical structure of that which has to be learned. Learning mathematics, because of the structure and key ideas of that particular discipline, is different from learning history or literary appreciation. And, indeed, the same might be said of moral learning. To enhance that, one needs to attend to the nature of that which one has to learn – the way in which the world and personal relationships are to be viewed differently (the key concepts, if you like), the attitudes and dispositions to be formed, the skills to be acquired.

Furthermore, the teacher as *educator* is interested in only certain kinds of learning; namely, those understandings, knowledge, skills, dispositions which one believes to be worth acquiring. 'Education' may be treated as a descriptive term – the Scottish *educational* system, the *education* of the Incas – but even then it is parasitic upon the evaluative meaning of how that word is so often used. To ask if someone is 'educated' is to ask more than if he or she has learned anything. It is to ask whether he or she has learned those things which are judged worthwhile – and sufficient of them to warrant the title 'an educated person'. Indeed, were that not the case, we would not be able to deny certain claims to someone being educated, or to a school providing a 'sound education', unless there was an implicit disagreement over the value of what has been learned. We oppose 'educated' to 'indoctrinated' or 'conditioned', and we contrast it with 'training' precisely because we want to pick out, as valuable results of learning, certain mental states, certain ways of knowing and experiencing.

What, then, are the sorts of learning which we would wish to pick out and evaluate as worthwhile by the concept of education? They must surely be those kinds of learning – those states of mind – which pertain to the learner living a more distinctively human life. There are many things which one might learn – the number of pebbles, say, on Budleigh Salterton beach – but which would seem to be of only marginal significance to living a worthwhile form of life (unless a further account could be given of how, in counting those pebbles, particular skills and qualities were learned that might be valued – perseverance in a difficult and boring task, an aesthetic appreciation of a pebbly beach, the capacity to organise a complex task). Therefore, what kinds of learning in very general terms might one pick out as worthwhile from a distinctively human point of view?

First, there is that knowledge of the physical world, captured in the various sciences, which enables one to understand and to operate effectively within the material universe. It is always a moot point how much one needs to know if one is not to be a professional scientist, but sufficient to be able to operate intelligently within the world, to have a grasp of the scientific arguments which are shaping one's world, and to have a feel for the way of thinking and proceeding with those activities which have transformed the way in which we live and might help others to live.

Second, there is that knowledge and understanding of the social world – of the world of social, political and economic relationships. Without such knowledge and the awareness that goes with it, then control over and responsibility for one's own life are severely diminished. But, of course, such understanding can be pitched at different levels of understanding, the practical (or 'enactive' to use Bruner's well-known phrase) not to be underestimated. Unless you can exercise control through understanding of that social world, then that world will control you.

Third, there is that understanding and appreciation of the aesthetic world – the world as seen through the sensitivity and understanding of the arts and music. That ability to appreciate and to find aesthetic value in artefacts, and indeed in the real world, is learned and enhanced through the refinement of our perception.

Finally, there is that understanding and awareness of the moral world – of the world of ideals and values that are found to be worth struggling for, of the duties and responsibilities which arise from the human context one finds oneself in, of the habits and virtues which will dispose one to act appropriately, of the sense of wholeness and integrity which provides a balance between competing desires and aspirations. In many respects, the other kinds of knowledge and understanding – those of the physical, social and aesthetic worlds – are subordinate to this, and yet profoundly affect it. There is and must be a constant interaction between these different kinds and areas of knowledge. Moral judgement is not separable from a grasp of the physical world in which one has to survive or the economic world in which one has to live and grow and find one's niche.

These different worlds are structured by the ideas and the traditions which we have inherited, albeit they are constantly evolving through criticism, new discoveries, fresh insights, the articulation of purposes only half realised. For that reason, Oakeshott (1972) provides a different metaphor for education and 'its engagement and its frustrations'. Far from it being a body of knowledge to be acquired or a set of competences to be gained, education is the initiation into 'a conversation between the generations of mankind' – a conversation which is made possible because we inhabit a world of ideas through which the material world is structured, understood and communicated. Education, therefore, lies in that gradual learning to take part in this 'conversation between the generations', and to learn and eventually engage with the voices of poetry, of history, of science, of philosophy.

The metaphor is an interesting one, for most good conversations do not work towards a pre-specified conclusion. The end is not known in advance, although how one gets there is circumscribed by certain general rules of procedure (concerning politeness, say, or respect for the other person's point of view, or the demand for evidence). Furthermore, a good conversation transforms the very purpose as it is being pursued. The process of conversing is inseparable from the outcome – the outcome is that transformation of one's thinking as it has been shaped through the process: the seeing things differently, the old puzzles solved and new ones created, the fresh insights that lead to yet further explorations and new desires to find out further.

Education, so concerned, is a living in a world of ideas through which one is constantly coming to see the physical, social, aesthetic and moral worlds differently as a result of argument, correction, evidence or acquaintance with new ideas. And teaching is that engagement with the learner by one who already inhabits that world of ideas and who is able to make it accessible. Of course, in so doing, teachers themselves are inevitably learning, having to make sense to the learner of those ideas which the learner may not previously have articulated and having to deal with questions not previously faced.

The school where such a transaction takes place would be a very different sort of place from that which is in the minds of the 'effective schoolers' or the 'managers of inputs and outputs' or the 'auditors of competences against performance indicators'. The school, instead, would be essentially a meeting place of those who, steeped in the different traditions of thinking and appreciating, initiate those still outside those traditions into these different worlds of ideas – so that they too may understand. And central to this meeting of ideas will be that attempt to make sense of what it is to be a person, of how one might live a life that is personally fulfilling, of what kind of life is worth living. And there is nothing esoteric in this, for would not this be the justification for introducing all young people to the humanities? To refer to Schools Council Working Paper No. 2, *The Raising of the School-leaving Age*, the humanities was that part of the curriculum where the teacher emphasised their 'common humanity with the pupils and their common uncertainty in the face of significant and personal problems'. Remember that, with the raising of the school-leaving age to 16, there were genuine concerns about the motivation and ability of many young people to continue with education. The temptation was to provide a vocational alternative, to devote the extra year to training the less able and the disaffected those employment-related skills which they (and the economy) were perceived to need. But (and this was the achievement of the Schools Council) it was recognised that such young people also have an understanding (however inadequate, uncritical and impoverished) of the world of personal, social and moral relationships which they inhabit, and that it is in one sense the same world that literature, poetry, history, the social studies are at different levels trying to make sense of. Education, therefore, lies in helping such young people to enter, little by little, into that world of ideas – to acquire, in the light of what others have said and done, a more informed and critical understanding of how they see this world, and in so doing to come to think differently, more critically, more defensibly about the kind of life worth living.

Viewed in this way, education is essentially a moral activity – the introduction of young people into a world of ideas through which they come to see (tentatively, provisionally) what it is to be human, to live a distinctively human life, to aspire to a form of life which they believe to be worth pursuing. Furthermore, such an education has both the public and private aspect. The public aspect lies in those public traditions of thinking and appreciating – expressed in books and artefacts – which are the product of the thinking and arguing and criticism of previous generations and which, of course, are constantly evolving through criticism and questioning. The private aspect is that subjective world of the learner, that personal attempt to make sense of experience in its different forms, the product in part of, but not reducible to, that public world of ideas into which he or she is born. And further learning lies in the interaction between that personal struggle 'to make sense of' and that public world of commonsense, cultural, intellectual traditions which are relevant to the very questions to which the young learner seeks answers.

All this must be incomprehensible to those who are responsible for the lists of competences and outputs, for they are looking at education through different metaphors – through those borrowed from business and management. Such metaphors find little room for the deviant and the personal, or for the notions of struggle and deliberation, or for the uncertainties which even the experts must have about the outcome of the process. With their impoverished metaphors, they necessarily have to promote the trivial, for that alone is measurable, and to ignore that which is most important – the personal response and making sense of the world through an interaction with the public traditions of criticism, understanding and appreciation. As a result, moral education, separate from the main process of education, either does itself get reduced to the trivial (the knowledge that something is the case) or hived off to a separate period, a separate 'subject' reluctantly taught by a teacher who quite understandably feels to be lacking in whatever expertise would be required to teach it.

I wish to illustrate this point through two curriculum developments which sadly have failed to influence the architects of the national curriculum and of the general vocational qualifications which claim not only to be vocational but also educational. The first is Bruner's (1964) 'Man: a course of study', a curriculum within the social studies and the humanities which posed three questions: what is it to be human? how did we become so? how might we become more so? These for Bruner were the central questions in education – not only because of their intrinsic importance but also because they were central to the personal concerns of the young people as they tried to make sense of the world and because they were the central concerns of the various intellectual traditions which schools introduced young people to. To answer these questions, it was important to explore those distinguishing characteristics of what it meant to be human – tentatively put forward as language user, tool maker, prolonged childhood, social forms of life and myth maker. By various means – simulation, careful choice of story, study by contrast with other species and cultural groups –the students practically and intellectually entered into a discourse about what it was to be human, how they evolved so, and how those distinctively human qualities might be enhanced further. Such exploration, in the light of evidence collected from the social sciences, anthropology, biology, linguistics and so on, raised central moral questions, but did so within a social and historical context in which sense needed to be made of what was possible as well as desirable.

The second example is that of the Humanities Curriculum Project, one of the first that the Schools Council sponsored to meet the needs created by the raising of the school-leaving age. For Stenhouse, the Director of the Project, the key question was: how can we address the aspirations of secondary education for *all*, irrespective of age, ability and aptitude? How could literature, the arts, history, science be seen to be relevant to all – even to those not noted for their interest in learning and so often alienated from 'school knowledge'?

The answer lay in recognising the significance of 'human studies' in the attempt to answer the very questions which everyone who reflects seriously about how life should be lived is struggling with. Under the guidance of the teachers the pupils would explore such issues which concern both them and society – poverty, injustice, the use of violence, relations between the sexes, racism, war – but to do so in the light of what others have said through dance, drama, art, literature, poetry, myth, theology, history. And teachers and pupils examined these together – the *objective* grounds for the *intersubjective* exploration leading to *personal* resolution. The humanities – the novels, poetry, dance, media presentations, the arts, historical accounts, theology – were the text, the object, around which the teachers and pupils were able to explore what mattered from a human point of view, and were able to test out their ideas before a critical and informed audience. Consensus was not sought, for consensus did not exist within the wider society. But beliefs would evolve through the examination of evidence and argument, refined through criticism – allowing for the kind of divergence in belief which made predictable outcomes and measurable outputs impossible to reach. The successful humanities graduate might be treated as evidence of an *in*effective school!

The humanities as conceived here might be summarised as involving the exploration of values in the concrete situation of practical living, requiring a shift to dependence on the authority of evidence and argument, promoting procedural values of testing ideas against evidence and attending to reasoning and criticism, respecting the different if sometimes unpopular views which are brought to the discussion, attaching importance to the defence and reflection within a heterogeneous group, cherishing those moral values of personal integrity and seriousness in the search for answers to important human questions.

Given this brief account of the aims of education, and of the central importance to those aims of moral purposes so conceived, I wish to point to two areas where much of the concern for moral education seems lacking.

Making personal

The emphasis of both Stenhouse and Bruner was that of making personally significant those understandings which resided within public traditions. But the 'making personal' is so often neglected – the provision of opportunities whereby the young person can reflect, deliberate, test out ideas, explore different routes. All such deliberation is in the light of evidence, certainly, but would not be expected to reach the certainties and the conclusions which give grounds for demonstrating school effectiveness as that is determined by those external to the transaction between teacher and learner. There is no room for such personal development where syllabuses have to be covered and outputs achieved.

There is a fear that this stress upon the personal renders the idea of moral development too subjective – a respect for whatever subjectively a person feels, irrespective of what those feelings are. And, indeed, that would seem to point to a certain relativism – that is, the assumption that nothing is objectively speaking good or bad, right or wrong, but that what counts as good or right is relative to the personal feelings, honestly held, of each person. That, at least, seems to be the spectre which haunts the Executive of the Qualification and Curriculum Authority. And, indeed, such a position gains a certain plausibility from the clear lack of consensus in society over important moral issues such as abortion, euthanasia, the just war and so on.

However, such a conclusion does not follow. Public disagreement over what is right and wrong, and the retreat to personal decision and significance, do not entail relativism. Relativism is the view that there are no objective grounds for making one decision rather than another over what is right or wrong, good or bad. But such a view is not compatible with what might be referred to as the 'moral seriousness' which is reflected in the deliberations of young people – a concern to work out what kind of life is worth living and should command our allegiance.

I am not talking about anything esoteric. I am talking about young persons who stop to think about how they should live their lives, who commit themselves to certain people or causes, who refuse to treat others as mere pawns in their particular game, who pause before embarking upon a dodgy enterprise, who are genuinely puzzled by challenges to received assumptions and values, who take seriously any criticism of standards in behaviour or work, who find challenging the exploration of what is right or worthwhile in literature or art or science, who care about the environment and other social and political issues, who do not run away from the deeper questions of meaning and value and purpose. Such a moral perspective is not confined to the most able or the most privileged. And it must not be confused with cleverness or interest in argument. It is a matter of *seriousness* in thinking about what is worth living for, what is worth pursuing in the arts or the leisure time, what relationships are worth entering into, what kinds of activities should be avoided, what obligations are to be considered sacred. What is distinctive of being a person is this capacity for being serious about life, a capacity requiring the application of intelligence, of moral judgement, of reflection and of sensitivity, which is often fostered by teachers even when much in the commercial environment militates against it, and even when it finds no place in the literature of the effective school or of the learning society.

Young people – by no means only the most able – have in their various ways that potential for 'moral seriousness'. They would, if opportunities were given, value a deeper understanding of those distinctively human problems – those universal 'areas of practical living' concerning the application of justice, the use of violence to pursue desirable or undesirable ends, the relationships between people (whether to do with power, or avarice, or gender), the existence of evil in its various forms (including poverty and cruelty), the sort of lifestyle worth adopting – which the humanities and the social sciences in particular have addressed. Strom and Parsons, in *Facing History and Ourselves: Holocaust and Human Behaviour*, provided the material whereby young people of all backgrounds and levels of attainment could, through the consideration of a wide range of evidence, explore how people could come to behave in the way they did in the most horrific circumstances. It is not simply a matter of right or wrong: it is also a matter of understanding how some people were seduced into cruelty, how others resisted, how others coped. The book, therefore, provides material (the *objective* and *public* basis of reflection and discussion) wherewith each person might, within the *interpersonal* explorations of the group, come to some *personal* resolution of what it means to be human in all its idealism and strength as well as in all its degradation and scheming. Again, how can we enable young people to confront *intelligently*, in the light of evidence and public understandings, those issues of deep personal concern? How can we enable them, in a world which lacks consensus over moral matters, to examine critically what Charles Taylor in *The Sources of the Self* refers to as the 'horizons of significance', whereby each comes to see and value things in a particular way?

Having such moral horizons, howsoever implicit, is essential to the deliberations and the choices of how to live one's future. Taylor argues:

> Perhaps the best way to see this is to focus on the issue that we usually describe today as the question of identity. We speak of it in these terms because the question is often spontaneously phrased by people in the

form: Who am I? But this can't necessarily be answered by giving name and genealogy. What does answer this question for us is an understanding of what is of crucial importance to us. To know who I am is a species of knowing where I stand. My identity is defined by the commitments and identifications which provide the frame or horizon within which I can try to determine from case to case what is good, or valuable, or what ought to be done, or what I endorse or oppose. In other words, it is the horizon within which I am capable of taking a stand.

(Taylor 1989: 27)

To conclude this section, central to *education* as opposed to mere training are two interconnected aspects. The first is a nurturing of understandings of what it is to be human through a gradual participation in that public world of literature, social studies, the arts and science wherein these understandings are developed. The second is an enabling of the pupils to reach a *personal* resolution of what that means in the serious deliberations about how to live – an issue which, at very many different levels (those of relationships entered into, further vocational training taken up, leisures and hobbies pursued, values taken seriously, ideals followed) is the concern of all young people.

Community

As I have indicated, such *personal* search for meaning (or, as Taylor refers to it, 'identity') has an essentially public context. 'Meaning' is not a private or subjective matter. How one understands something or some situation, from a physical, social, aesthetic or moral point of view, is arrived at through participation in a public form of discourse. And this can take place at many different levels – from the most superficial to the most abstract and theoretical. Such forms of discourse develop and are sustained and enhanced in communities of like minded people, and the rules of discourse and the concepts employed may often be only implicit within those communities. It may take a philosopher (of science or of political theory) to lay bare what those rules and concepts are. Education, then, might be seen as the attempt to introduce young people to these different communities, to the different forms of discourse, through which issues of profound human importance are discussed, understood, argued about.

There are many overlapping communities which embody different values, different rules of behaviour, different purposes and understandings. There are the academic communities, whose intellectual efforts are reflected in the subjects taught in schools. There are the broader educational communities, which are reflected in the schools and colleges, and which should thereby provide the framework for the kind of reflective thinking and deliberation which I have been talking about. There are the civic communities, which provide the range of opportunities, otherwise denied, for people to have the basic requirements of distinctively human forms of life – protection, cultural continuity, safeguards against aggression or unforeseen ills. Each of these different communities in which the young learners participate will have its own distinctive values, but one which remains essential to all these different communities is that of justice. And the way in which young people acquire that sense of justice is through participation in a just community. Kohlberg (1982), whose research was focused upon the gradual development of the concept of justice as fairness, went so far as to argue that the current demand for moral education is a demand that our society becomes more of a just community, and that if one society is to become a more just community, it needs to develop democratic schools – schools where the desires and opinions of all, including those of the students, are taken seriously in decisions which affect their lives, and where there is a shift from dependence on authority to greater dependence upon reason, argument, explaining.

Furthermore, such justice needs to be not simply within the institution but within the system of which that institution is part and which infects the values permeating the relationship between teacher and learner. As Halsey (1978) in his Reith Lecture argued: 'We still have to provide a common experience of citizenship in childhood and old age, in work or play, in sickness and in health. We have still in short to develop a common culture to replace the divided culture of class and state.'

This sense of community, embodying such principles as justice and such virtues as compassion, might be regarded as the 'ethos' of the school. And in the absence of a certain ethos, so it is argued – see Power and Reimer (1978) – that the personal capacity to develop these personal qualities, even the capacity for moral seriousness, is sadly diminished. It is difficult to comprehend how, in pursuit of moral values and higher standards of behaviour, the 'structures' of the institutional framework are ignored, and that important moral virtue, namely, the disposition to change those structures which impinge upon personal capacities for development, gets neglected.

Conclusions

The current interest in values education – in particular, moral education – is to be welcomed. But there are serious omissions from the analysis of moral education. The first is the failure to recognise the moral seriousness which is there in all young people and the need to nurture that through the forms of public understanding reflected in the curriculum. In that sense all good *education* should be centred on this moral purpose, rather than determined by the needs of training or economic preparation. Success at the latter may be important, but by itself it ignores the central purpose of education.

The second omission is the neglect of the community context through which individuals' understandings and dispositions are nurtured, particularly the commitment to a more just and equal society.

What is required is, first, a realisation of the central educational questions concerning what it means to be, and to become more, human; second, the recognition that, in answering such questions, we need to draw upon those traditions within the humanities, the arts, the social sciences where such questions are systematically explored; third, a respect for the voice and deliberations of the learner as he or she seeks personal answers to these questions; fourth, a respect for that transaction between teacher and learner whereby the teacher mediates those public traditions to the personal deliberations of the learner; fifth, the creation of the kind of community in which this distinctively human form of life provides the framework for such personal search for what is worthwhile; sixth, a deep suspicion and scepticism of the 'managerial speak' which is so anti-educational as to threaten the drive to improve the moral development of our pupils.

References

Bruner, J. (1964) 'Man: a course of study', in *Toward a Theory of Instruction*, Cambridge, MA: Harvard University Press.

Dearing Report (1994) *Final Report: The National Curriculum and its Assessment*, London: School Curriculum and Assessment Authority.

Dewey, J. (1916) *Democracy and Education*, New York: The Free Press.

Halsey, A. H. (1978) *Change in British Society*, Oxford: Oxford University Press.

HMI (1991) *Higher Education in the Colleges and Polytechnics*, London: HMSO.

Jessup, G. (1991) *Outcomes: NVQs and the Emerging Model of Education and Training*, London: Falmer Press.

Kohlberg, L. (1982) 'Recent work in moral education', in L. O. Ward, *The Ethical Dimension of the School Curriculum*, Swansea: The Pineridge Press.

NFVEC (1996) *Values in Education and the Community*, National Forum for Values and Education and the Community.

Oakeshott, M. (1972) 'Education: the engagement and its frustration', in T. Fuller (ed.). *Michael Oakeshott and Education*, New Haven, CT: Yale University Press.

OFSTED (1994) *Spiritual, Moral, Social and Cultural Development*, London: OFSTED.

Power, C. and Reimer, J. (1978) 'Moral atmosphere', in W. Damon, *New Direction for Child Development and Moral Development*, San Francisco: Jossey-Bass.

Pring, R. (1995) *Closing the Gap: Liberal Education and Vocational Preparation*, London: Hodder & Stoughton.

SCAA (1996) *Education for Adult Life: The Spiritual and Moral Development of Young People*, London: School Curriculum and Assessment Authority.

——(1997) *The Promotion of Pupils' Spiritual, Moral, Social and Cultural Development*, London: School Curriculum and Assessment Authority.

Schools Council (1967) *The Raising of the School-leaving Age*, London: HMSO.

Strom, M. and Parsons, W. (1982) *Facing History and Ourselves: Holocaust and Human Behaviour*, Watertown, MA: Intentions Education Inc.

Taylor, C. (1989) *The Sources of the Self*, Cambridge: Cambridge University Press.

15

RATIONAL CURRICULUM PLANNING

In pursuit of an illusion

David Carr

The centrally planned curriculum

Adopting a familiar analysis of educational and other practical enterprises in terms of four formal constituent features of aims, methods, content and evaluation or assessment, debates about the curriculum might be regarded as revolving largely or exclusively around questions of *content*. A little thought, however, should be sufficient to show that this is a narrow and superficial conception, and most educational philosophers, theorists and policy makers worth their salt — from the time of Plato onwards — have clearly recognised that any adequate view of the curriculum must take into account not only *what* is to be learned, but also *why* and *how* it is to be learned, and how that learning stands to be evaluated. In short, conceptions of the curriculum are tantamount to attempts to answer the basic question of what it is to be educated *per se*.

It follows from this, however, that it is crucially important to be clear about the precise logical status of any query regarding the nature of education — for, if this question is misconstrued, it can only be expected that any proposed answer to it will be a skewed one. And, indeed, it is the main aim of this chapter to suggest that currently prevailing official conceptions of the school curriculum and its role in the promotion of individual and societal prosperity, of the kind that have recently developed in the United Kingdom (on either side of its politically most significant national border) and elsewhere, are — despite their best intentions — deeply infected by a certain common misconstrual of what is really at issue in any inquiry concerning the nature of education.

The overall shape and thrust of the curricular conceptions in question are doubtless familiar enough and I shall engage in no detailed enumeration or exposition of them here. By way of near-to-hand examples, however, one might mention the National Curriculum of England and Wales developed in the wake of official policy documentation and central legislation of the late 1980s, the Scottish Standard Grade courses developed for the last two years of secondary education on the basis of late 1970s policy proposals and the elaborate Scottish 5–14 programme, consequent on late 1980s proposals, which is still in the throes of current development. All these initiatives have the character of centrally prescribed curricula – though they may vary significantly in their precise statutory or mandatory status and concerning the extent to which their development was implicated in wider democratic consultation with relevant professional bodies or the wider public – and all involve considerable specification of curriculum content for all state school pupils in the context of formal provision for assessment and certification (national testing) of a fairly product-orientated nature.

All the same, my present aim is not to argue that any of this prescribed curriculum content or these assessment proposals are actually mistaken as such – though, as I shall proceed to indicate, I do believe them to be often potentially distortive of our understanding of what it is to acquire knowledge and understanding of a variety of areas of human inquiry in particular, as well as of a satisfactory overall conception of what it is to be educated in general – but rather to suggest that there is something deeply suspect about the rational bases upon which ideas of centrally planned curricula are by and large constructed. I shall argue in the next two sections, then, that the notion of rational curriculum planning, from which such central prescription is liable to derive a good deal of its support, follows from two basically problematic ideas about the nature of knowledge and knowledge acquisition in human affairs. In a subsequent section, however, I shall suggest that these ideas follow in their turn from a misreading of the deep logical grammar of familiar discourse about education, learning and understanding.

Towards a science of curriculum

It would appear, then, that attempts to construct a common curriculum for all pupils undergoing compulsory state schooling in a given national or social context are largely indebted to two underlying ideas concerning the nature of knowledge and the character of human learning. Very generally, what unites these two ideas is a common concern to identify objective foundations for, as well as to provide rational analyses of, the epistemological, psychological and pedagogical aspects of human experience, of a kind which might aspire to meet the rigorous standards of natural scientific inquiry. Moreover, though these ideas are unlikely to be unfamiliar to anyone operating in professional contexts of education, a brief characterisation of them is none the less to the point here.

First, there can be little doubt that modern-day educational theory and practice – in Britain and elsewhere – emerged very much in the wake of a particular conception of the theory of knowledge arising from the sceptical philosophy of Descartes but influenced more precisely by a tradition of empiricism extending at least from such Enlightenment philosophers as Locke, Berkeley and Hume to twentieth-century logical analysts and positivists of the likes of Bertrand Russell, Rudolf Carnap and A. J. Ayer. The first main aim of this tradition – deriving directly from Descartes – is to establish firm foundations upon which to build the edifice of human knowledge and inquiry – and to this end, of course, the foundations in question are meant to consist only of judgements which are as far as possible beyond any reasonable shadow of doubt. For Descartes and the rationalists this meant first and foremost the analytically self-evident propositions of logic and mathematics but for the empiricists this was primarily a matter of judgements based on the deliverances of sense experience.

Indeed, for many empiricists from Hume to Ayer, unless the claims of this or that realm of human inquiry are in principle verifiable either by a priori rational demonstration (reduction to tautology by definition) or by reference to immediate empirical experience, it hardly merits consideration as a genuine source of knowledge; furthermore, such views would very much seem to lie at the heart of the Gradgrindian conception of education – as a matter of the inculcation of facts and definitions – so savagely satirised by Charles Dickens in *Hard Times*. And, of course, an epistemological conception of this nature is also profoundly reductionist and atomistic; the aim is essentially to analyse the entire enterprise of human inquiry into its basic constituent components – here conceived as discrete propositions concerned either to report the deliverances of direct sense experience or to explicate conventions of linguistic convention or usage.

It would be less than fair, of course, in any fuller treatment of the development of modern educational epistemology, to place exclusive emphasis on the continuity of the new analytical philosophy of education of around thirty years ago with this much older tradition of British empiricism. For one thing, having learned wisely from such important modern critics of empiricism as Ludwig Wittgenstein – particularly from Wittgenstein's ideas concerning the relative autonomy of different forms of human discourse or 'language games' – the new analytical educational epistemology was certainly very much less inclined to reductionism in the sense lately indicated. However, on the recent admission of Paul Hirst – the leading light of that early analytical educational epistemology – the prevailing conception of 'forms of knowledge' remained deeply foundational and atomist. Essentially, then, it aspired to identify certain fundamental categories of rationally grounded human knowledge or inquiry – allegedly justifiable in terms of their access to this or that type of propositionally conceived constituent truth – which might then be employed by educational theorists as a basis for objective rational curriculum construction.

It is also hard to overestimate the extent of influence that the so-called 'forms of knowledge' thesis of Hirst came to exercise – on both the pioneering attempts of other educational philosophers such as John White to provide a rational justification for an egalitarian common curriculum for comprehensive schooling, and on the architects of national curricula in England, Scotland and elsewhere – some of whose policy productions clearly borrow quite liberally from Hirst. And, though it should be said in fairness that much of this post-Hirstian curriculum policy documentation also badly misinterpreted the notion of 'forms of knowledge' – particularly by giving a highly un-Hirstian instrumental twist to them – most of it nevertheless swallowed the ultimately foundationalist and educationally technicist assumptions and aspirations of that notion hook, line and sinker.

What now, then, of the second conceptual support for the idea of rational curriculum planning? Well, it might appear logical to suppose – once one has done the epistemology required to identify the necessary content of any rational curriculum – that what is next needed is a rational technology of pedagogy apt for the efficient and effective transmission of that curriculum content from teacher to pupil. With regard to this, moreover, educational theorists of the mid- and post-war years were widely led to believe that such a technology might be available as a result of developments of empirical psychology in the wake of pioneering work by Pavlov, Watson and others in the early part of this century – work which was, indeed, popularly known as 'learning theory'. A good deal of this experimental psychology, which reached its high point in the theories of Skinner, Hull and Guthrie, was also rightly characterised as 'behaviourist', and in its systematic and uncompromising construal of intelligent behaviour in terms of conditioned responses to environmental stimuli it owed much to those atomistic associative views about knowledge acquisition of early and late empiricism. For those rightly sceptical of behaviourism, however, scientific conceptions of learning and knowledge acquisition seemed otherwise to be available via the new cognitive psychology of Piaget, Bruner, Ausubel and others – especially as connections came in due course to be made between cognitive psychology and even more scientifically respectable neurophysiological research into so-called information processing.

Empirical psychology in various forms, then, exercised widespread influence over those with aspirations to transform education into a precise science or technology. Behaviourists such as Skinner, for example, tried to give direct technological expression to their work through the development of 'teaching machines' – though this idea had relatively restricted application and limited appeal. However, the idea of construing and constructing the school curriculum in accordance with so-called 'behavioural objectives' has come to enjoy considerably greater currency among educationists – so much so that in many quarters it is seen as the only rational approach to the theory and practice of pedagogy. Moreover, since the idea is suitable for the use of those who aspire to construe human understanding *either* in terms of behavioural responses to stimuli *or* in terms of cognitive processing skills, it is appealing in virtue of both its simplicity and attractiveness to a broad psychological church. And basically, of course, the idea is simply that by compositional analysis a form of knowledge or skill is susceptible of reduction to its constituent parts – its component propositions or actions – with a view to their systematic sequencing for purposes of effective instruction; if learning Geography is tantamount to acquiring a set of propositions, and learning Woodwork is mastering a set of skills, then these skills and propositions can be identified and ordered in such a way as to facilitate optimum learning of the subjects in question.

The foundations of the rational curriculum: some problems

Generally speaking, then, those notions of rational curriculum design which have informed the latter-day curriculum planning of educational policy makers in very many parts of the contemporary world – especially with respect to the construction of compulsory common or national curricula – are more or less a joint product of foundationalist assumptions about the nature and function of epistemology and para-scientific ideas about knowledge acquisition derived from so-called learning theory. The only significant addition to these ideas is the customary invocation of a number of formal principles of curriculum design requiring that the rational curriculum conform to certain basic criteria of balance, coherence, continuity and progression – but, while these also often appear to be paraded as quasi-technical notions of scientific curriculum design, I shall in due course argue that they are nothing of the kind. The main purpose of this section, however, is to show that the lately identified epistemological and pedagogical supports for the idea of rational curriculum design are deeply suspect anyway.

So first, what is wrong with the idea that epistemology – the philosophical analysis of the nature of knowledge – might be utilised for the purpose of establishing the logically unassailable foundations of curriculum content? If the role of epistemology is precisely to place the entire enterprise of human knowledge on firm rational foundations and to establish criteria whereby we might distinguish genuine from bogus human inquiry – as Enlightenment philosophers operating in the wake of the Cartesian project believed – why can it not be employed – as postwar analytical educational philosophers believed – to identify forms of legitimate knowledge apt for curricular inclusion *vis-à-vis* the education of every pupil in any conceivable human circumstances? Is not systematic epistemological inquiry simply a *sine qua non* of effective curriculum planning?

While the utility of epistemological reflection for curriculum studies and even for practical curriculum development should not be dismissed entirely, however, it is clear that the new analytical educational philosophy considerably overestimated its scope and potential in crediting it with a foundational role in curriculum planning. What epistemologists of recent times have generally come to see is that the Cartesian project was actually misconceived precisely to the extent that human inquiry does not progress incrementally by the gradual building of one certainty upon another, that knowledge is inherently provisional, and that therefore – though we cannot entirely dispense with the idea of truth as at least a regulative norm of human inquiry – we are not entitled to regard any of our current theories, explanations and truth claims as beyond the possibility of revision in the light of new evidence of one sort or another. It would follow in educational terms from this view, however, that it is equally mistaken to regard a form of knowledge as focused or constructed upon the recognition of so many indubitable or value-free facts or hypotheses apt for uncontroversial communication to all pupils irrespective of particular interests or circumstances.

There can be little doubt, moreover, that the 'forms of knowledge' theses of analytical educational philosophers were commonly construed or misconstrued as clear ways of mapping the uncontroversial content of school curricula in advance of the development of effective means for delivering such content. However, in assuming that there are fixed truths and final explanations in the various realms of human inquiry, such a conception of curriculum content is extremely static; it appears to suppose not only that categories of knowledge and truth conform to certain unalterable types or categories, but also – even more dubiously – that there might be truth claims in different realms which are quite immune to any sort of revision or criticism. But it is nowadays a major problem of curriculum planning – especially in the light of the so-called information explosion – that traditional knowledge classifications seem now somewhat outmoded; not only do new disciplines compete for space in already overcrowded curricula, but they also compete with traditionally received forms of knowledge whose epistemological credentials and relevance to modern life and circumstances are increasingly called into question. Furthermore, it has been increasingly recognised of late that what were once taught as unexceptionable truths of science, religion, history or geography can no longer be so regarded – not only on the grounds that they have come to be falsified in the light of subsequent inquiry, but also because they have invariably enshrined views of the world which are racist, sexist, homophobic or otherwise *ethically* objectionable. Thus, not only is the ship of human knowledge unavailable for complete rational reconstruction at sea, it is also sailing in uncharted waters and is liable for repair at any given moment due to damage from reefs unseen. Hence, the foundationalist epistemology of the Enlightenment gives way to a contemporary or 'postmodern' epistemology of discourse in which nothing is fixed and final and all questions of epistemological value are, in principle, open.

What, then, of the other sustaining principle of rational curriculum theorising – the idea of a technology of knowledge transmission based on a scientific theory of learning? In short, what is wrong with the notion that we might systematically and rationally plan for the effective communication of curriculum content via the clear identification and specification of so-called curriculum objectives? At one level, of course, it should be said that there is nothing at all wrong with an orderly and systematic approach to the teaching of a subject; such an approach is indeed one mark of a good teacher, and – insofar as thinking in terms of behavioural objectives may help to introduce some system and order – it may be of real assistance for good teaching. Where ideas of behavioural objectives are inclined to lead our educational thinking astray is insofar as they are construed as essentially dependent upon some sort of para-scientific behavioural or information-processing view of human learning. In short, what seems questionable is the idea that if we are to think rationally about human learning, then we should really be thinking scientifically, reductively and atomistically.

There is by now, however, a powerful and well-entrenched case in both psychological and philosophical circles against behaviourist and other psychological approaches to human learning of any degree of scientific sophistication – mainly on the grounds that it seems well-nigh impossible to explain the educationally pivotal notion of *understanding* in terms of either the conditioning processes of reflex psychology or the information-handling processes of cognitive psychology. Indeed, it is an interesting irony that, though it is almost *de rigueur* in contemporary professional educational circles to speak of learning and understanding as matters of 'process' more than product, Ludwig Wittgenstein – perhaps the greatest of modern philosophers – went to extraordinary lengths to argue that understanding is *not* a mental process; in much the same vein, moreover, other major contemporary philosophers have equally sought to prove that ideas of information processing can at best account for the syntactical, but not the crucially important *semantic*, aspects of human understanding.

Indeed, I have tried on other occasions to apply such insights to education and to warn of the potential dangers of construing the transmission of meaning and understanding, with respect to any school subject, exclusively in terms of behavioural objectives. Consider – as just one example of what might go wrong here – the behavioural analysis for instructional purposes of a folk-dance into a sequence of steps or movements; for it is clear that however well the pupils managed to master the steps by clear directive teaching, they could not be said to have understood its *meaning* only via such instruction; but consequently, however, no matter how well they actually performed the dance, they could scarcely be said to be really *dancing* – no more, indeed, than a troop of well-trained baboons could be said to be really dancing. The problem of the behavioural objectives view of learning, then, is broadly converse to that of a foundational view of curriculum epistemology. The trouble with curriculum foundationalism is that it follows in the wake of a largely educational philosophical misunderstanding of the role and remit of epistemology; while epistemology has a role, it is not the ambitious one that educational philosophers have lately entertained for it. The trouble with a behavioural objectives approach, on the other hand, is not that there *are not* any such learning objectives which can occasionally be pursued to legitimate educational effect; it is rather that such pursuit is often linked – in pursuit of a spurious educational scientism – with a conception of human learning which is false and potentially distortive of the educational enterprise.

The grammar and semantics of curriculum discourse

It would appear, then, that the two main ideas which underpin rational curriculum planning are both liable – in their rather different ways – to lead curriculum planners up the garden path of educational technicism. First, a modern philosophical mistake about the nature and scope of epistemology has led to its widespread educational assignment to a kind of under-labourer role as regards the business of knowledge transmission; it has been largely allotted the task of excavating the logical foundations of objective and certain knowledge so that curriculum construction and teaching might then proceed in full confidence that they are concerned only with the transmission of reliable truth. Second, however, a reasonable aspiration to orderly and systematic pedagogy has tempted educationists in the direction of pseudo-scientific conceptions of learning and teaching which are potentially deeply distortive of our perfectly proper pre-theoretical intuitions concerning what is involved in the acquisition of human understanding; in particular, construing learning as a kind of (causal) process focused on the largely incremental acquisition of atomistically conceived task components inclines to the neglect of the all important semantic aspects of understanding a topic or activity.

However, we have also noticed that there are strong and nowadays widely endorsed suspicions of both these ideas on the part of educational philosophers and theorists. While, then, epistemology may yet be a valuable aid to curriculum reflection from the perspective of exploring different ways of conceiving and packaging knowledge for educational purposes, or for evaluating or criticising received conceptions of such packaging, it cannot live up to the foundational or under-labourer role assigned to it by Descartes and his heirs. And, on the other hand, though there is nothing in the least wrong in principle with aspiring to a certain degree of system, rigour and efficiency of pedagogical practice, it also seems that any wholesale efficiency of this kind may be guaranteed by would-be scientific models of knowledge acquisition only at the high price of considerable distortion of the educational enterprise. Moreover, I think that it is possible to explain what has generally gone awry with the overall idea of what I have generally referred to as rational curriculum planning – if we are precisely prepared to disabuse ourselves of the widespread presupposition that designing a curriculum is or should be a scientific or technical matter.

To see this, we might first ask some simple but revealing questions concerning the overall logical form and functioning of ordinary curriculum discourse *vis-à-vis* scientific and technical inquiry. For example, it is a reasonably fundamental point about the discourse of scientific inquiry that it is concerned with the construction of theories about the world which should in principle qualify for evaluation as true or false (leaving aside for now questions about how truth ought to be construed). It should also be clear enough, however, that a school curriculum is *not* obviously apt for evaluation in such terms, and that one would indeed be hard put to say what might be meant by a 'true' curriculum. The reason for this, of course – none the worse for being obvious – is that a curriculum is not a theory of how the world *is* but a proposal to effect certain practical changes or developments in the world; it is not a matter of theoretical explanation but of practical policy.

But, surely, this is no great news and it hardly exactly refutes the view that curriculum planning is a practical *technological* affair that derives its authority and inspiration from various forms of scientific research into (say) the nature of teaching and learning – indeed, the observation that a curriculum is a practical rather than a theoretical matter might be held to support it. There are, however, two reasons for doubting the idea that curriculum planning is a kind of applied science or technology either. The first rests, as we have already noticed, on the observation that there is not really much in the way of *legitimate* scientific theory on which to ground a technology of pedagogy. The second reason, however, is yet more telling – though a little harder to see – and it is that just as we do not evaluate a curriculum as we would a scientific or other theory, neither do we primarily evaluate it in terms appropriate to a technology. For, despite the fact that curriculum planning is as much a practical matter as the technology of aeroplane design, it is a serious mistake – as Aristotle warned millennia ago and others have cautioned since – to assume that *all* practical matters are technological or require to be informed by theory.

For, of course, while we should readily evaluate a product of technology – such as a specimen of engineering – in terms of the extent to which it efficiently or effectively expresses or realises a given set of theoretical principles, we hardly ever think of the success or failure of a curriculum in such terms. Consider, for example, the controversies raised by those curriculum theorists who have been generally inclined to justify offering different sorts of educational provision – so-called alternative curricula – to (usually intellectually) different categories of children. Although it may appear on the face of it that the arguments characteristic of such disputes are addressed to questions of educational efficiency and effectiveness – to issues concerning the proper utilisation of national resources of ability and so on – it readily emerges on closer inspection that the issue between those who support alternative curricula and those who oppose them turns primarily on the quite different consideration of whether greater injustice is done by the unequal educational treatment of equals (in terms of the common humanity of children) or the equal treatment of unequal (in terms of their differences of intelligence, culture, gender and so forth). In sum, curriculum policies and proposals are not primarily apt for evaluation in terms of their truth or their efficiency and effectiveness, but rather in terms of their justice or fairness and the extent to which they do or do not violate such fundamental principles of human association as liberty, equality and respect for persons.

The moral basis of curriculum reflection

In short, although debates about the quality and character of the school curriculum are practical in nature, they are not technological but *moral* disputes; they are closer in logical character to controversies about capital punishment or abortion than to questions about how to build a bridge or repair a faulty carburettor. Of course, this is not to say that there are *no* technological (or at least technical) questions about curriculum design – such as how to ensure that this or that form of curricular packaging leaves adequate pathways for pupil choice, just as, rather more darkly, there may be technical questions, concerning, for example, 'civilised' or humane techniques for terminating life, about capital punishment. But just as it would be shallow and frivolous to conduct a debate about the appropriateness or otherwise of capital punishment exclusively in terms of the effectiveness or otherwise of execution techniques, so it would be equally shallow to try to deal with serious questions about curriculum design and development at the level of what might or might not constitute efficient timetabling.

Moreover, it is quite important to see this if one is to come to a proper appreciation of the role in curriculum planning of those oft-cited basic curriculum principles of balance, coherence, continuity and progression mentioned earlier. For, indeed, it is fairly common to find such curriculum principles – concerned as they are with the formal dimensions of school study programmes – introduced in official policy documentation as though they fulfilled a straightforward metric function *vis-à-vis* curriculum design. In short, it seems widely assumed that attempts to ensure that the curriculum is not unbalanced, incoherent, discontinuous and lacking in progression will be wellnigh sufficient to keep our planning on the right track – indeed, that there is a right track actually embodying precisely *correct* notions of balance, coherence, progression and so on, to be found, presumably, in some Platonic realm of conceptual absolutes.

But this, of course, blithely ignores the reality that there are numerous diverse ways of understanding the application of notions of balance, coherence, progression and the like to the problem of curricular provision. Indeed, as I have argued on another occasion, it is not only that such notions are likely to be interpreted differently in the light of different ethical conceptions of the operations of justice, equality and freedom in human affairs, it is also that it may not be in fact logistically *possible* to design a curriculum which can satisfactorily reconcile familiar conceptions of curriculum coherence with other, fairly widely endorsed ideas about adequate balance. If, for example, one aspires via the notion of curriculum integration to a certain educational ideal of cross-curricular coherence, then this may well require the procrustean exclusion of certain educational elements which are not readily susceptible of such linkage – and, conversely, if one aspires to the ideal of a broad-ranging curriculum one may have to give up on certain possibilities of curricular coherence or integrity.

In short, hard choices may well have to be made in the rough and tumble of curriculum construction – and the choices in question are ultimately consequent upon *evaluative* deliberation about what ought properly to count as ethically defensible aims for a school curriculum conceived as a important agency of human flourishing. And, so we have also argued, the questions to which such deliberation is addressed are not generally susceptible of easy resolution in terms of *either* scientific inquiry *or* technical ingenuity – though scientific and technical considerations may not be left entirely out of the account – for a scientific or technically ingenious curriculum may yet be an *unjust* one; hence, they are rather questions for our deepest moral reflections upon the ultimate purpose and destiny of human life.

As we have argued from the outset, then, questions about the nature and constitution of the school curriculum are not narrowly confined to certain limited issues about the content of education. On the contrary, they touch the very heart of the educational enterprise, requiring educationists to address fundamental questions of human destiny and identity concerning what – from the perspective of human flourishing – it is worthwhile for people to know and to value. It is also crucial that educationists should not shy away from such reflection in the mistaken belief that, if educational or curricular reflection is moral rather than scientific or technical, then it can only be subjective. Reflection upon what is morally conducive to human growth and prosperity is not subjective – but it is *difficult* and above all requires an openness to engage with all the honesty, integrity and courage of our convictions with the wide variety – both genuine and spurious – of rival conceptions of flourishing with which young and old alike are faced in circumstances of modernity. For, after all, the only possible alternative is to accept on the word of others that their version of the school curriculum is the only right scientific and rational one, and to swallow the consequences in the event that they have got it inadvertently or – for one ulterior motive or another – wilfully, wrong.

16

IN DEFENCE OF LIBERAL AIMS
IN EDUCATION

John White

I

Many of the essays in this book revolve around liberal values and liberal aims for education. In a world increasingly attracted towards liberal-democratic ideas, at least as a political ideal if not always fully realised in practice, this is to be welcomed. Yet liberal thinking has many variants. Some of these seem to me to be more in harmony with core liberal values than others. In this chapter I would like to explore this last thought, with a view to uncovering a defensible version of liberalism which can serve as a basis for educational planning.

Close to the heart of a defensible liberalism, I would argue, lies an attachment to personal autonomy – to the idea that individuals should be self-directed in the conduct of their lives, deciding on their major goals themselves and not pressurised into accepting goals laid down by custom or authority and so forth. This is to apply to everyone in the community, not just a privileged few: I take it that this last proposition is one thing that differentiates liberalism from various forms of conservative or oligarchic political thinking. As applied to education, this generates the aim of providing students with whatever mental equipment they need to become autonomous individuals, bearing in mind that self-directedness can never be wholly constraint-free. Among these constraints may be moral restrictions: I will come back to this point later.

I am not sure how far all the authors who have appeared earlier in this volume would wish to espouse something like this autonomy aim. Kevin Harris's critical description of the paternalist educational policies of the Queensland government in the late 1970s gives indications of being based in part on some such value, but it is hard to be sure. His paper is not in the tradition of philosophical writing about educational aims that propounds a view of what such aims should be. In his view, educational thinkers have either come out with unsupported, subjective views of aims they think important; or, like R. S. Peters, they have backed up their preferences by allegedly objective analysis of the concept of education. On Harris's view, 'philosophy of education might have more to do with the aims of education than make "aristocratic pronouncements" or subject such pronouncements to an "analytic guillotine" (p.2). He sees the discipline as 'theorising the role of the state, and especially its relation to power and knowledge': in this way, it can help us to understand whose aims get translated into educational practice and why (p.12).

My difficulty with his chapter is that he has not made it clear just what job there is for philosophers of education to do in the empirical enterprise just mentioned. He talks of philosophy complementing policy sociology, but needs to spell out more fully what its role should be and how it is to be distinguished from empirical studies. What, after all, is 'theorising the empirical'?

Although he does not think that making aristocratic pronouncements about aims or seeking to reveal them by conceptual analysis of 'education' are the best way forward, Harris adds in a note, 'I am not advocating that either practice be abandoned. Both have considerable value' (n. 10). What this value is he does not say. For my part, I was persuaded by his arguments against the two positions in the body of his paper!

Problems arise with all three ways of philosophising about aims that Harris discusses and, indeed, approves. There is a fourth. It has affinities with the 'aristocratic pronouncement' view, in that it explicitly puts forward recommendations about which aims should be adopted; but it differs from it in arguing a philosophical case for these derived from more deeply lying values. In this it is a form of applied normative ethics. Several of the other essays in this collection are in this mode, the present one included.

Robin Barrow's approach to aims belongs to the 'analytical' tradition about which Harris ends up so surprisingly ambivalent. He is in some ways close to Peters in claiming (1) that the aims of education have to do with the pursuit of various forms of theoretical activity for intrinsic reasons, and (2) that these aims are implicit in the concept of education dominant in the Western tradition since Plato. Attempts to derive aims by analysing the concept of education have been criticised since the 1960s. Kevin Harris's and Peter Gilroy's critiques in this volume reiterate these objections and carry them further. At least Barrow's position is not open to the charge that he is assuming a fixed, essential meaning for 'education': he makes it plain that he is dealing with a specific, Western version of the concept. As such, he would seem not to fall foul of Gilroy's critique of essentialist analysis but rather to be providing what the latter approvingly calls a 'functionalist' account of aims since he ties the meaning of 'education' to a specific social context.

This does not get him out of the wood, however. It would still have to be shown that the Western tradition that Barrow picks out is one which we should continue to follow. From a liberal point of view, his position presents a familiar difficulty. If education inducts students into an understanding of science, art, mathematics, history and so on for their own sake, then privileging an understanding of *these* intrinsic goals over that of less academic pursuits like socialising, sports or gardening seems to conflict with the promotion of personal autonomy. It looks like the paternalistic imposition of *one* view of the good life on other people. Of course, Barrow can always hold his own by replying that insofar as we are talking about education (in the Western sense) at all, we *must* be concerned with academic activities – whereupon the liberal is likely to reject this conception of education altogether in favour of one that lays fewer restrictions on the kinds of understanding of possible intrinsic goals from which the autonomous person may choose his or her options. (The fact that Barrow says that his conception of education 'carries with it a commitment to the ideal of autonomy' does not bring him within the liberal camp, since 'autonomy' here is plainly the intellectual autonomy implicit in a mastery of (for instance) science or history, and not the personal autonomy which has to do with a more global self-directedness in living one's life.)

What is Paul Standish's stance towards the liberal aim of self-directedness? In the title of his paper and often in his text, he seems to suggest it would be odd to see education as having aims at all – just as it would be odd to ask about the aims of a town. But perhaps his stabler position is that education has aims, but they are ineffable. Not totally so, maybe: education brings pupils closer to the Good in something like a Platonic sense, but the Good itself is uncharacterisable.

Standish rightly recoils against over-prescriptive specification of objectives but his positive alternative is too under-described either to act as a guide for educators or to enable us to see its compatibility or otherwise with liberalism's autonomy aims. His own discussion of autonomy aims ends up with no clear picture of how far he is in favour of them. He has doubts over whether they are applicable to all pupils, especially the less intelligent of them. One strand in his thought appears to be that, insofar as they are acceptable, they are insufficient, since they require a more substantive filling – to be provided by the notion of a spiritual ascent towards the Good. I would not wish to rule in or rule out such a thought, but if we are to entertain it, it must be given more shape. For how otherwise could such an aim be safely brought into the educational world? Left ineffable, it leaves too much room for Platonic mystics, Christian theologians, deep ecologists and adherents of all kinds of exotic cosmologies to move into no man's land – with all the risks of illiberal imposition that this brings with it.

Kenneth Strike's paper is explicitly within the liberal tradition, or, to be more precise, close to that variant of it found in Rawls's *Political Liberalism*. Personal autonomy does not have such a central place in either Rawls's or Strike's theory as it has in the 'ethical liberalism' which Rawls espoused in *Theory of Justice*. That is because that kind of liberalism, premissed on the ideal of personal autonomy for everyone, is only one kind of 'comprehensive doctrine' about how one should lead one's life; since in a pluralist society there will be many comprehensive doctrines of religious and other kinds, room must be found for all of them to flourish without privileging ones based on autonomy. Aims of education deriving from particular comprehensive doctrines have a legitimate place in a liberal society and are not to be trumped by civic aims – to do with promoting autonomy and democratic character – arising from ethical liberalism.

How liberal is Strike's version of 'political liberalism'? On one reading of it, it seems to allow the possibility of children being indoctrinated into the religious beliefs of their parents. This would normally be taken to be an illiberal treatment of them, given that we are writing into indoctrinating something like fixing beliefs so that they become hard to shift. Presumably it is seen as illiberal because it is at odds with preparing children to lead an autonomous life.

But why should they be so prepared? This is a requirement of ethical liberalism, not political liberalism. If Strike's argument does indeed allow indoctrination, it may be no less liberal for that. This is an odd conclusion for a liberal like myself who sees liberalism as first and foremost a political theory about how *individuals* should live and be treated. Strike's – and perhaps Rawls's – political liberalism appears to put the interests of communities, or members of communities, above those of individuals. If Jehovah's Witness parents bring their children up as Jehovah's Witnesses, there is nothing, it seems, liberally problematic about that.

But is this really Strike's position? His focal concern *does* seem to be the individual. He says, for instance, that *children* have an interest in being initiated into some comprehensive doctrine (p.54). He also adds that 'liberal societies have an interest in diminishing the educational capacity of illiberal comprehensive doctrines' (ibid.); and that there must be some room in a child's upbringing for their comprehensive doctrine to be challenged (ibid.).

All this would seem to allay fears of indoctrination. But how far? Would the doctrine of a Jehovah's Witness be liberal or illiberal? Strike does not give general criteria. If illiberality were defined in terms of what imperilled autonomy, Strike's position would collapse, after all, into ethical liberalism. Given that he does not want this, how else would he define 'illiberal'?

The point about challenges to comprehensive doctrines seems to be contra-indoctrinatory. If this is what Strike has in mind, then once again it is hard to make sense of this except in terms of the child's interest in becoming autonomous. On the other hand, he elsewhere claims that 'criticism is important to the integrity of *traditions*' (p.58, my emphasis). The rationale does not, in other words, begin from the interests of the individual. How deep can the criticism that he mentions go? One can see how totally destructive external criticism might help the individuals of ethical liberalism to free themselves from the shackles of, say, an intellectually unsustainable religious faith, but it is harder to see how it could help a tradition to flourish or survive. Many religious and political systems encourage criticism, but it is often merely internal criticism, which does not favour adherents radically questioning their faith in a no-holds-barred manner. It is not clear whether Strike would only allow internal criticism of this sort. If he did, then from the standpoint of ethical liberalism he would be in danger of condoning the sacrifice of individuals' interests to the interests of religious and other communities; if he did not, he might be more of an ethical liberal than he claims. This seems to me to be his dilemma.

Strike's paper has affinities with Jan Steutel and Ben Spiecker's. They ask whether liberalism brings with it support for critical thinking as an aim of education. They reply, among other things, that (1) it supports encouraging critical thinking about political policy. They do not take a stand on whether (2) it supports critical thinking about the intrinsic value of different conceptions of the good life, restricting themselves to laying out the positions of liberal philosophers on both sides of this argument.

I have problems with both these points, as they spell them out. On (1), *how many* citizens does a liberal democracy need who 'participate in public discussions on political policy'? Granted their point that without such participation liberal institutions like opposition parties or freedom of the press would wither and perhaps perish, could it not be enough if some, perhaps most, citizens participated? Is this a strong enough reason for educators to aim at disposing *all* students to participate? Some people may, as autonomous persons, have better things to do with their lives. Suppose a young woman wants to spend all her time on music. If she were allowed to, she would become a great composer. Instead, she is brought up to believe she really ought to read the political news, follow debates and so on, and as a result her commitment to music begins to seem an indulgence and starts to atrophy. How far should a liberal democratic education go in providing everyone with a political education aimed at active participation?

On (2),we come back to the issues raised over Strike's piece. Steutel and Spiecker point out that personal autonomy, one aspect of which is critical reflection about different accounts of the good life, is a controversial, not a neutral, value, and that some liberals like Larmore, the later Rawls and Macedo would not want a liberal society to privilege it. As in my comments on Strike, if one possible consequence of this were that parents belonging to some fundamentalist sect were to be allowed to bring up their children as committed members of their faith without any exposure to other ideas, I would consider this a sacrifice of the children's interests and hence quite at odds with liberalism. Of course, liberalism must leave autonomous adults the freedom to adopt whatever religion they want, given the usual provisos about avoiding harm to others. In doing this, it must also allow them to adopt a non-autonomous form of life if they so choose. But, equally, it must protect children, until they are old enough to make up their own minds, from those, even – or especially – their parents, who take steps to close them. My only puzzlement about Steutel and Spiecker's position on all this is why they in the end don't take a position in the debate over (2). As I see it, there's only one side that a liberal could be on.

Christopher Winch's main argument revolves around a distinction between 'weak' and 'strong' autonomy. The former has to do with making choices from a variety of socially approved and tolerated ends; the latter, with making choices where no ends have been socially prescribed. Winch argues that a public education system could and should encourage weak autonomy in its students, but that 'it is logically incoherent to suppose that a public education system could promote strong autonomy because to do so would undermine the assumptions and procedures on which that system is based' (p.81). Private education is another matter. If parents wish schools to aim at strong autonomy for their children, there are circumstances in which they should be allowed to do so.

I am not sure what to make of Winch's arguments, partly because I don't know how its terms are to be cashed out. If strong autonomy implied that *any* ends would do, just so long as an agent chose them, then it would be all right if he chose wife-beating or mass murder. No school system would tolerate that, public or private. The circumstances in which, according to Winch, private schools could legitimately promote strong autonomy would be where the latter, although allowing choices 'inimical to the values and assumptions on which the society is itself based' (p.81), disallowed those which violate the rights of fellow citizens. But what would be examples of choices which were both inimical and non-violatory in these ways? Taking drugs? Entering into a homosexual marriage? Gambling? Can what is inimical to society's values or – to go back to an earlier statement – to what society approves or tolerates be laid down in any non-controversial way? Is there a danger of paternalism in suggesting that state schools should restrict the range of ends not harmful to others to which autonomous agents in the making should be introduced as possible options? Again, why should only private schools be allowed to broaden the range?

As Winch says, the term 'strong autonomy' is taken from earlier writings (see White 1990: 102–3; Norman 1994: 30ff.). There it implies being *criti-*

cally reflective about basic social values and assumptions. Of course, one can be critically reflective about something without wishing to undermine it: think of a harmless political philosopher testing the credentials of liberal democracy. There seems no reason why any education system – public or private – should not encourage strong autonomy in this sense.

This sense of 'strong autonomy' seems different from the first we encountered. Yet Winch may be running them together – as in his suggestion that a public education system would not tolerate a form of autonomy (namely, strong autonomy) 'that encouraged people actively to question or undermine' democratic institutions (p.82). Actively questioning and undermining are surely vastly different things.

A number of other writers in this collection – a surprising number, indeed – discuss personal autonomy as an educational aim. I will briefly indicate where I have particular problems with their views.

William Hare's essay on critical thinking discusses, among other things, why its promotion is an important educational aim (and thus treads the same ground as Steutel and Spiecker). His first, 'ethical', justification (p.94), that human beings have a potentiality, unique to their species, to develop into adults capable of a self-determined existence, seems to me to be open to the familiar objection to such naturalism that the ethical conclusion does not follow from the empirical claim.

Penny Enslin rejects the teaching of national identity on the grounds that it is at odds with the development of autonomy. What she shows, it seems to me, is that national*ism* is at odds with it. This comes out clearly, for instance, in her statement that nationalists typically hold that every member of the nation must surrender their 'individual uniqueness in order to have an identity as a member of an organic whole' (p.106). But one can see a value in national identity without being a nationalist: many Scots, for example, are proud to be so yet equally jealous of their individuality. There is an influential – and in my view well-founded – strain of liberal thinking, associated particularly with Isaiah Berlin, that would go so far as to make personal self-directedness conceptually dependent on being brought up and living within a specific culture – which in modern conditions very often takes the form of a national community (see Gray 1995: ch. 4). For a fuller account of difficulties I have with Enslin's views on the nation, see White (1997).

I find myself sympathetic to many of James Walker's – partially communitarian – views on self-determination as an aim of education. I don't quite see, however, why it should be held to be '*the* fundamental educational aim' (p.112, Walker's italics, see also Winch's paper, p.74). Walker also claims that 'the conditions for the development of self-determination are the same as the conditions for its exercise. In education this means the creation of free associations of people in learning communities' (p.113). The first of these statements is not unqualifiedly true. *Some* of the conditions may well be the same in both cases, but I doubt if all could be. If children are to grow into self-directed adults, no doubt they at some point need some experience of making their own decisions about major orientations in their lives. Perhaps this is especially something one would expect to find in older children. It makes much less sense for a child of 3. Another condition of the development of autonomy is that the child must spend a fair part of its time acquiring the necessary learning – of its native language and other things – for him or her to become self-directed. This is surely *not* a condition of the exercise of autonomy. If his thesis about the congruence of conditions fails, Walker's conclusion that education must take the form of free associations of students in learning communities cannot soundly be built on it. At least in the early stages of learning, and not only then, children are very far from autonomous persons and have to be inducted into language and ways of feeling and behaving by people giving them a very firm steer indeed. This is a condition of their becoming autonomous that will not be a necessity for them once they have become autonomous.

Paul Hirst rejects a view of the development of autonomy as an educational aim that posits a distinct self that operates independently of the rest of the person ('autonomy of the self'), as well as one which asserts that 'we exist as individual persons prior to and independently of our social relations' ('autonomy of the individual'). I would follow him in this – although I cannot think of any modern philosopher of education who has held either view. Does his new account of education as the promotion of good lives via initiation into various social practices contain within it any commitment to the liberal value of personal autonomy? It 'necessitates critically reflective response to those practices both internally and in their wider relationships' (p.130). In addition, some practices are optional in one's life rather than necessary; given this, 'wide opportunity for exploration and engagement among diverse practices is . . . clearly essential' (p.131). These points have a distinctly liberal flavour, even though Hirst does not talk about 'autonomy' in this connection. They appear to show that his new emphasis on induction into social practices has ultimately an individualist rationale, in that they subserve the interests of the (autonomous) individual: he says 'the overall aim of education is to be understood as an initiation into those social practices in which a good life can be developed', where a 'good life' is a critically reflective one. (Whether this last point is unqualifiedly true is doubtful: cannot there be good lives in heteronomous as well as autonomous societies?) It would be helpful if Hirst could now relate his new theory more explicitly to liberal theory and its variants. How close is it, for instance, to Rawls's 'political liberalism'? Or to Raz's or Berlin's ideas? Once we knew this, we would be in a better position to locate Hirst's new philosophy of education in relation to that of other major liberal theorists in our field like Eamonn Callan and Kenneth Strike.

Personal autonomy is a central liberal value. It rests on an even more fundamental value in human life – personal well-being. Autonomous well-being is only one variant of the more general concept, given that people can flourish or not flourish in non-liberal – for example, traditional-tribal – as well as liberal societies. Roger Marples' essay deals with this more fundamental concept. Much of his argument is a critique of my own views about well-being as expressed in White (1982 and 1990). The overwhelming number of his shafts are directed towards the earlier of these books and a lot of these strike home. But because I wrote White (1990) precisely to rectify my inadequate account of personal well-being in White (1982), I will leave aside his treatment of blemishes in the latter text, restricting myself to his comments on my more recent position and to problems I see in his own account.

Marples rightly sees me as a kind of subjectivist. This term can have many meanings. In this context it refers to someone who holds that ethical values, including personal well-being, are not locatable in a reality outside human beings' desire-structures. The main difference between Marples and myself is that he is not a subjectivist in this sense, and I am. Marples states that 'subjectivism accepts that values are self-chosen and ultimately a matter of individual preference' (p.134). But this is in a different sense of subjectivism. I don't hold that values are self-chosen: children acquire their values from the communities and practices in which they are brought up. If they are to become autonomous persons, they may – or may not – choose to reject or de-emphasise some of these values, and faced with value-conflict people will differ in their weightings. These last considerations introduce an element of individual variability, if not preference, and I guess Marples would go along with this. But neither of us wants to say that, these points apart, individuals choose rather than discover their basic values.

The main issue is: what sort of discovery is this? For a subjectivist like me, the reality wherein children locate their values is social. This world is still, importantly, constituted by people's desires – their shared desires for things like living without fear of being killed or attacked, for instance. For a non-subjectivist like Marples, lying behind any such social desires must be an independent world of values.

What are his arguments in favour of personal well-being as a value belonging to such an independent order? In his own terms, he sees our 'real interests' as residing in our common human nature. There are, he says, certain things which are 'fundamental prerequisites of normal functioning' (p.142). He lists a paragraph full of these, beginning with 'We are able to envisage alternatives to the *status quo* . . .'. If, like most of the other items, this one is intended as an account of how human beings normally *do* function, it is unlikely to be true. What alternative *modi operandi* did stone-age dwellers envisage? Like some of Marples' other items – taking delight in art and work, formulating ambitions, or experiencing events as comical, tragic or absurd – this one seems to go with a fairly sophisticated level of civilisation. None of these resides in human nature as such. True, as human beings, and unlike trees or boulders, we all, no doubt even the stone-agers, have the innate capability of acquiring such desires, but then we equally all have the innate ability to do all sorts of monstrous or trivial things from self-mutilation to thumb-twiddling that no one, least of all Marples, would wish to claim as elements of personal well-being or components of our real interests.

Our common human nature is central also to Richard Pring's account of 'moral seriousness' as a central educational aim. For him, 'education is essentially a moral activity – the introduction of young people into a world of ideas through which they come to see (tentatively, provisionally) what it is to be human, to live a distinctively human life, to aspire to a form of life which they believe to be worth pursuing' (p.164). How close is Pring's view to the liberal's advocacy of personal autonomy? His emphasis on individuals' working out for themselves what kind of life is worth living is surely akin to it. For me, it picks out an element in the autonomy ideal which is sometimes overlooked – the reflective concern of self-directing individuals with the options which confront them and the need to choose among them. Autonomous choice is not a whim-based, supermarket opting for this or for that, but possesses something of the seriousness of purpose that comes out so strongly in Pring's chapter.

There are two problems I have with Pring's account. First, I agree that as an antidote to current preoccupations with 'effectiveness' and with narrow vocational ends schools would do well to initiate pupils more wholeheart-edly into a study of human nature. But, as foreshadowed in the last but one paragraph, I have some doubts about how far the notion of a 'distinctively human life' could be an ethical foundation for living a worthwhile life, if this is indeed what Pring is suggesting: the perpetrators of Auschwitz did something, after all, of which only a human animal could be capable. Second, while I would wish to build into a concept of personal autonomy of use to educators an altruistic dimension (White 1990: ch. 4), Pring's 'moral seriousness' seems to put rather too much weight on other-directed concerns. As it stands, it seems also to tilt the balance too much towards reflectiveness. The issue here, from a liberal perspective, is whether Pring is urging on us an ethical ideal which steers the pupil towards a particular vision of how life should be lived which leaves out too many other accept-able possibilities. Pring's ideal educands are serious-minded folk concerned among other things with the environment, justice, the use of violence and the existence of evil. I do not wish to denigrate these; but an education on these lines, if not counterbalanced by something like a Millian emphasis on individuality, might discourage inclinations towards more spontaneous, Bohemian, or idleness-loving lifestyles. It might make some would-be artists too morally earnest for their own good. Would Mozart have done what he did for the world if he had taken the ideal of moral seriousness really to heart? (The underlying point is close to one made in critique of Steutel and Spiecker's paper, above p.173).

II

As should be plain from the essays in this book, as well as from other writings, there is as yet no consensus about what liberalism is or what educational aims would be in line with it. One of the main divides is between a liberalism based on a core value of autonomy for everyone in the community, and a liberalism which does not privilege this core value as it recognises that members of subcultures within the community may live in non-autonomous ways and are entitled to equal consideration with others. Rawls, as Strike's chapter reminds us, discusses this conflict as between 'ethical' and 'political' liberalism.

On this issue, my own sympathies are with the former (though without commitment to the whole structure of Rawls's argument in *Theory of Justice*). In other words, personal autonomy is an ideal applicable to all adult members of the wider political community. (I follow Raz in not making it applicable to all human beings; for example, members of traditional tribal societies.) Being personally autonomous includes choosing as an option to adopt a non-autonomous form of life. So, provided that members of non-autonomy-supporting subcultures – such as fundamentalist religious sects – have freely chosen to enter them, they should not be discriminated against as compared with others. A liberal society will welcome and encourage the existence of all sorts of sub-groups and subcultures, whether opposed to, indifferent to or well-disposed to autonomy as a value. One of the reasons for this is the desire that people have – as a feature of their self-identity, for instance – to live with others with whom they share a culture, religion or common interests.

Things become more complicated where children come into the picture. Children have an interest in being brought up in their early years within a coherent and relatively unchallenged view of the world. Children are born to members of subcultures that do not prize autonomy, who wish to bring up their sons and daughters in their own beliefs. But doing so, where this excludes other viewpoints, is often likely to make it harder for these children to become autonomous adults. I agree with Joseph Raz (1994: ch. 8) that 'the opportunity to exit from a group is a vital protection for those members of a group who are oppressed by its culture' (p.187), and that although 'the young of all cultural groups should be educated, if their parents so desire, in the culture of their groups', nevertheless 'all of them should also be educated to be familiar with the history and traditions of all the cultures in the country, and an attitude of respect for them should be cultivated' (p.189). If, knowing of alternatives, the children as they grow up prefer to stay attached to their local culture and its beliefs, this simply reflects their position as autonomous persons. This underlines the point that in a liberal society everyone should be treated as autonomous.

This still leaves a problem. I have claimed that personal autonomy is an ideal applicable to every adult in the community. So far I have tried to show its applicability to those people living a non-autonomous life who freely choose to live thus: these include adults who as children were brought up as just indicated, as well, presumably, as adults brought up outside a non-autonomous community who opt for non-autonomy. But what about adults who were brought up strictly to follow the way of life of a non-autonomous community and who have never considered abandoning it? They have not freely chosen it, so how can the autonomy ideal apply to them? The answer is that a liberal society treats them as if they were autonomous. It does not draw a line between them and other people, disallowing them liberties or other civic rights which people need to exercise autonomy.

A second dividing line between types of liberalism became clear to me on reading John Gray's recent book on Isaiah Berlin (Gray 1995). Gray draws a distinction between Berlin's liberalism and Raz's. For Raz, personal autonomy is the central liberal concept. As I have hinted in this chapter more than once, in Raz's scheme not all forms of personal well-being are founded on autonomy: one can live a life of well-being in a tribal society where all one's major goals are laid down for one. In what Raz calls an 'autonomy-supporting' culture like our own, where major institutions to do with government, employment, marriage, the market and others are premissed on people's making autonomous choices, being autonomous is a condition of achieving a life of well-being. Its justification lies in this relationship. A further feature of Raz's position is that personal well-being – and therewith its autonomous variant – is a function of one's success in achieving one's major goals, given that these goals are *valuable*. 'A life is not a good life for being spent in petty vindictive pursuits, or in self-debasing ones etc,' (Raz 1994: ch.1: 4). In his earlier book (Raz 1986: 298), he rules out a life devoted to gambling, for instance.

Gray holds that Berlin's liberalism is rooted elsewhere – in the notion of (negative) liberty from others' constraints. For Raz, negative liberty is valuable as a condition of personal autonomy and thereby of autonomous well-being, defined in terms of the satisfaction of valuable desires. But for Berlin it is valuable, 'primarily as a condition of self-creation through choice-making' (Gray 1995: 31). These may seem very similar moves; but the difference is that Berlin holds self-creation to be of value *in itself*: it is not, like Raz's personal autonomy, valuable as a condition of something else, that is, personal well-being (in certain cultural circumstances). Self-creation is, moreover, intrinsically valuable whatever form it takes: the goals it embraces do not have to be valuable goals as in Raz's conditions on well-being. 'Such choice may be capricious or whimsical, perverse or unreasonable, quixotic or self-destructive: it remains choice, and, as such, the source of the value of negative freedom' (Gray 1995: 29).

Which version of liberalism should be adopted? The question has obvious significance for a discussion of the aims of education, although it also has more general relevance. I find difficulties with both positions. Of Berlin's, one naturally asks: *why* is self-creation to be preferred to Razian autonomy? One reason that Gray gives is that one form it may take is the choice of a life that is 'not especially autonomous, and which liberal societies can shelter: the life of the nun, of the professional soldier, or the artist passionately devoted to his work' (1995: 32). Perhaps we should exclude the artist from this list: although we talk metaphorically of the creative artist's being in thrall to his daemon, he has not chosen to put himself wholly under others' direction like the nun or the soldier. The latter have indeed chosen a non-autonomous form of life. But why cannot this be in conformity with Raz's theory – as long as they have autonomously chosen this? If so, Berlin's theory does not seem preferable to Raz's in this respect.

To turn to Raz's account of personal well-being, and hence of autonomous well-being: this rules out goals which are not valuable. But what counts as valuable? Sometimes what are ruled out are, in anyone's book, immoral pursuits, as in his above example of petty vindictiveness. Raz sees personal well-being as embracing moral behaviour, so this move is understandable. But another way of conceiving of this relationship is to see morality as setting limits to desirable forms of well-being and often in conflict with the latter. On this view, personal well-being becomes a value on its own, separable from morality.

On immoral goals, there may be no substantive difference, in one way, between Raz and Berlin. If someone self-directingly chooses vindictive ends, presumably both would deplore this – Raz, because it is at odds with his autonomous well-being; Berlin, because, although self-creation allows it, other values debar it. So the issue may turn on whether personal well-being can be shown to have a necessary moral component. I have already cast doubt on this claim and also on Raz's arguments in support of it (White 1990: 57–61, 173–5). This being so, I am inclined to think Berlin's concept of self-creation more trouble-free on this than Raz's notion of personal autonomy.

Given Raz's position on the inseparability of morality and personal well-being, could there be any non-valuable goals, on his view, which were personal rather than moral? Perhaps not completely. But his examples of self-debasing goals and gambling, at least where others' interests are minimally affected, are what some other philosophers, if not Raz himself, would call personal rather than morally significant goals. Insofar as we see them in this way, there is a danger of paternalism if they are to be ruled out as non-valuable. Suppose someone freely chooses a life centring on the roulette table. If this is, on mature reflection, how they prefer to live, why should we not be prepared to say that their life manifests autonomy? If they succeed in getting out of gambling what they want to – their hunches often come off, but more than this they get the buzz that they crave whether they win or not – why should we not say that all this contributes to their having lived a life of autonomous well-being? On Raz's theory, this would be ruled out, but there seems no good reason for this. Once again, Raz's concept seems too restrictive by comparison with Berlin's.

Why, in any case, does Raz rule out gambling as a possible major goal of personal well-being? Perhaps he is assuming, what may well be the case, that although the chances of coming out on the winning side overall are very remote, millions of people go in for it either ignorant of the odds against them or irrationally convinced that they will win a fortune, and so on.

Put like this, the goal does not seem at all worthwhile. It is based on false beliefs, on superstition. On the other hand, suppose our roulette-player is not self-deceived and understands the statistics admirably, but attaches very great importance to risk and excitement. Let us assume, too, that they are quite rich and do not mind descending into poverty as long as for a part of their life they have enjoyed these kicks. If they succeed in their plans, why – once again – should we deny an autonomous flourishing?

All this reinforces Berlin's claim, above Raz's, to be the true torchbearer of liberalism. Self-creation, not Razian autonomy, appears to be its central value. But why is self-creation valuable? If, as Berlin believes, it is valuable in itself – and not, as with Razian autonomy, as a condition of well-being in certain cultural circumstances – then how can this be shown?

Raz's justification of autonomy requires further exploration. It is that in modern conditions (that is, in an autonomy-supporting society where institution after institution assumes autonomous agents), one cannot – not logically, but as a matter of fact – lead a flourishing life without being autonomous. One difficulty with this is that, although in a modern society one must make choices between options in different spheres, one could still attain well-being in Raz's sense of achieving one's major goals even if one's choices were massively under the influence of public opinion, fashion and so on. In other words, one doesn't have to be more than minimally self-directed in order to flourish.

A second problem with the argument is that why an autonomy-supporting society has come into being is left largely unexplained. True, Raz hints at economic forces as one factor; for example, firms' demands for mobility of labour (Raz 1986: 369–70). But surely, ineliminable from any adequate explanation is something like the traditional liberal interest in freeing people from shackles of all sorts so that they can lead their own life. In other words, Raz's framework, within which he sets his justification of autonomy, already assumes that the self-directed life is desirable. There is thus no need for a further justification of it as an empirical condition of something else: namely, personal well-being. As we have seen, that justification is problematic anyway. But the central point is that self-directedness is taken to be independently desirable.

This still leaves the question: why is it desirable? At this point we seem to come round to something like Berlin's position, as interpreted by Gray. Self-directedness, or in Berlin's term – which we have seen reason to adopt – 'self-creation', is something whose intrinsic desirability cannot be shown by adducing further grounds for it. It stands by itself. It is not an empirical condition of well-being, but rather a logical condition of the liberal conception of it.

This cannot be the end of the story, one is inclined to reply. After all, we don't have to accept the liberal framework. Could we not decide to jettison it?

What could we put in its place? We are not talking here, as we talked earlier, of individuals choosing to give up their autonomy by becoming nuns or soldiers, as this would still be within a liberal framework. Our present thought is more radical – of a society no longer liberal at all, in which no one leads a self-determined life. Although we could think this thought in a speculative way, could we *advocate* such a society? It is hard to see what could motivate us to do so. We would have to be happy with leaving everyone dominated by others – either as custodians of custom or more arbitrary wielders of power. How could we countenance this?

Discussions about the rational basis – or otherwise – of morality lead one in the end to values and attitudes that cannot be defended in terms of anything deeper. 'Why should one care for other people?' If the questioner has no altruistic commitment, *reasons* cannot help them. What they are lacking is a basic emotional attachment to others' concerns. I suspect that this Humean insight is relevant to supporting our attachment to liberalism: if we care for other people, how could we wish to leave them to others' direction? We are at the limits of our moral universe. In the past this universe was smaller: if people could not accept that killing or stealing were unacceptable, they dwelt outside it; but they were still inside it if they were happy enough to agree that people in general should follow custom or religious authority. These days – these liberal days – we have gone one stage further, embracing self-creation as well as non-maleficence as an inalienable ingredient of our ethical form of life. If this is so – if in the end we are driven to Berlin's position on the intrinsic desirability of self-creation rather than Raz's extrinsic justification of autonomy – what relevance might there be to educational policy?

One implication is that we avoid Raz's difficulty of determining what counts as a *valuable* option. If we knew what counted, we could in principle present only valuable options to children, excluding the valueless from the start. Berlin's alternative points to presenting an unrestricted range of possible options from which to choose.

But doesn't this still include clearly immoral options like vindictiveness, as well as ones like gambling? Not necessarily, for these could be winnowed out either (1) by the sieve of a moral framework, or (2) by educators shaping the notion of personal well-being in which they were bringing up their charges to include within it moral goodness (White 1986, 1990).

Berlin's position is also relevant to matters of motivation and attitude. It points towards emotional commitment to the ideal of self-directedness, rather than to justifiability in terms of something deeper, as in Raz. If there are no reasons provided, there are no reasons which could prove – as perhaps Raz's do – logically faulty. Pupils will not be brought up – those who can frame this thought, that is – to accept that there are such-and-such reasons for their being autonomous, only to risk having these reasons blown to smithereens by some later discussant and being left rudderless. Berlinian pupils will be habituated, on Aristotelian lines, into self-creation, just as they are habituated into caring for others.

Growing up positively attuned to these values should give pupils a greater confidence in them than many citizens and future citizens, I suspect, repose in them today. For various reasons, including the confusing welter of different moral positions we encounter, many of us are too beset by doubts to live out our ethical values wholeheartedly. We need to throw ourselves into our own self-creation as full-bloodedly as into creating the conditions for other people to throw themselves into theirs. Somehow, as parents, teachers and citizens, we have to help provide children with the ethical adrenalin to do just this.

References

Gray, J. (1995) *Berlin*, London: Fontana.

Norman, R. (1994) 'I did it my way: some thoughts on autonomy', *Journal of Philosophy of Education* 28(1).

Rawls, J. (1972) *A Theory of Justice*, Oxford: Oxford University Press.

——(1993) *Political Liberalism*, New York: Columbia University Press.

Raz, J. (1986) *The Morality of Freedom*, Oxford: Clarendon Press.

——(1994) *Ethics in the Public Domain*, Oxford: Clarendon Press.

White, J. (1982) *The Aims of Education Restated*, London: Routledge & Kegan Paul.

——(1986) 'The problem of self-interest: the educator's perspective', *Journal of Philosophy of Education* 20(2).

——(1990) *Education and the Good Life: Beyond the National Curriculum*, London: Kogan Page.

——(1997) 'National myths, democracy and education', in D. Bridges (ed.), *Education, Autonomy and Democratic Citizenship in a Changing World*, London: Routledge.

BIBLIOGRAPHY

Anderson, B. (1983) *Imagined Communities*, London: Verso.

Anderson, R. (1942) *Teaching Critical Thinking in the Social Studies*, Washington, DC: National Council for the Social Studies.

Anscombe, E. and Geach, P. T. (eds) (1969) *Descartes: Philosophical Writings*, London: Nelson.

Argyris, C. and Schön, D. S. (1996) *Organizational Learning II: Theory, Method and Practice*, Boston: Addison-Wesley.

Aristotle, (1925) *The Nichomachean Ethics*, Oxford: Oxford University Press.

Arrington, R. L. (1989) *Rationalism, Realism and Relativism: Perspectives in Contemporary Moral Epistemology*, Ithaca, NY: Cornell University Press.

Aschner, M. J. (1956) 'Teaching the anatomy of criticism', *School Review* 64(7): 317–22.

Aviram, A. (1995) 'Autonomy and commitment: compatible ideals', *Journal of Philosophy of Education* 29(1): 61–73.

Ayer, A. J. (1967) *Language, Truth and Logic*, London: Gollancz.

Bailim, S. (1987) 'Critical and creative thinking', *Informal Logic* 9(1): 23–30.

Bantock, G. H. (1973) 'Towards a theory of popular education', in R. Hooper, *The Curriculum: Context, Design and Development*, Edinburgh: Oliver & Boyd.

Barrow, R. (1984) *Giving Teaching Back to Teachers*, Brighton, Sussex: Wheatsheaf.

——(1990) *Critical Dictionary of Educational Concepts*, 2nd edn, London: Harvester, Wheatsheaf.

Barzun, J. (1946) *Teachers in America*, Boston: Little, Brown & Company.

Benn, S. I. and Peters, R. S. (1959) *Social Principles and the Democratic State*, London: Allen & Unwin.

Berlin, I. (1969) 'Two concepts of liberty', in *Four Essays on Liberty*, London: Oxford University Press.

Black, M. (1946) *Critical Thinking*, New York: Prentice-Hall.

Blenkin, G. and Kelly, A. V. (1986) *The Primary Curriculum*, London: Harper & Row.

Boden, M. A. (1990) *The Philosophy of Artificial Intelligence*, Oxford: Oxford University Press.

Bowe, R. and Ball, S. with Gold, A. (1992) *Reforming Education and Changing Schools*, London: Routledge.

Bozzoli, B. (1983) 'Marxism, feminism and South Africa studies', *Journal of Southern African Studies* 9(2): 139–71.

Brandt, R. A. (1979) *Theory of the Good and the Right*, Oxford: Clarendon Press.

Brink, E. (1990) 'Man-made women: gender, class and the ideology of the Volksmoeder', in C. Walker (ed.), *Women and Gender in South Africa to 1945*, Cape Town: David Phillip.

Brookfield, S. D. (1988) *Developing Crucial Skills*, San Francisco: Jossey-Bass.

Brown, L. M. (1970) *Aims of Education*, New York: Teachers College Press.

Bruer, J. T. (1993) *Schools of Thought: A Science of Learning for the Classroom*, Cambridge, MA: MIT Press.

Bruner, J. (1964) 'Man, a course of study', in *Toward a Theory of Instruction*, Cambridge, MA: Harvard University Press.

Callan, E. (1988) *Autonomy and Schooling*, Kingston, Ont: McGill Queen's University.

—— (1994) 'Autonomy and alienation', *Journal of Philosophy of Education* 28(1): 35–53.

Carr, D. (1988) 'Knowledge and curriculum: four dogmas of child-centred education', *Journal of Philosophy of Education* 22(2): 151–62.

—— (1992) 'Education, learning and understanding: the process and the product', *Journal of Philosophy of Education* 26(2): 215–25.

—— (1994) '5–14: a philosophical critique', in G. Kirk and R. Glaister, *5–14: Scotland's National Curriculum*, dinburgh: Scottish Academic Press.

—— (1994) 'Educational enquiry and professional knowledge', *Educational Studies* 20(1): 33–52.

Cavarero, A. (1995) *In Spite of Plato: A. Feminist Rewriting of Ancient Philosophy*, Cambridge: Polity Press.

Cloete, E. (1992) 'Afrikaner identity: culture, tradition and gender', *Agenda* 13: 42–56.

Cock, J. (1993) 'The place of gender in demilitarisation agenda', *Agenda* 16: 49–55.

Codd, J. (1988) 'The construction and deconstruction of educational policy documents', *Journal of Educational Policy* 3(3): 235–48.

Cooper, D. E. (1983) *Authenticity and Learning*, London: Routledge & Kegan Paul.

Cooper, N. (1994) 'The intellectual virtues', *Philosophy* 69: 459–69.

Coward, H. and Foshay, T. (1992) *Derrida and Negative Theology*, Albany, NY: State University of New York Press.

Crooks, S. (1995) 'Developing the critical attitude', *Teaching Philosophy* 18(4): 313–25.

Cuypers, S. E. (1992) 'Is personal autonomy the first principle of education?' *Journal of Philosophy of Education* 26: 5–17.

Dale, R. (1992) 'Whither the state and educational policy: recent work in Australia and New Zealand', *British Journal of Sociology of Education* 13(3): 387–95.

Daly, M. (1984) *Pure Lust: Elemental and Feminist Philosophy*, London: The Women's Press.

Dearden, R. F. (1972) 'Autonomy and education', in R. F. Dearden, P. H. Hirst and R. S. Peters (eds) *Education and the Development of Reason*, London: Routledge & Kegan Paul.

Dearing Report (1994) *Final Report: The National Curriculum and its Assessment*, London: SCAA.

Descartes, R. (1701, 1911, 1972) 'Rules for the direction of the mind', in *The Philosophical Works of Descartes* (trans. E. Haldane and G. R. T. Ross), Cambridge: Cambridge University Press.

Dewey, J. (1916) *Democracy and Education*, New York: The Free Press.

—— (1930) *Construction and Criticism*, New York: Columbia University Press.

—— (1971) 'Why study philosophy?' in H. A. Boydston (ed.), *John Dewey, The Early Works* 1882–98, vol. 4, Carbondale, IL: Southern Illinois University Press.

Earwaker, J. (1973) 'R S. Peters – the concept of education', *Proceedings of the Philosophy of Education Society of Great Britain* 4: 21–44.

Eisenberg, A. (1992) 'Women and discourse on science', *Scientific American* (July).

Ennis, R. H. (1962) 'A concept of critical thinking', *Harvard Educational Review* 32(1): 81–111.

Enslin, P. (1993/94) 'Education for nation-building: a feminist critique', *Perspectives in Education* 15(1): 13–25.

——(1994) 'Should nation-building be an aim of education?' *Journal of Education*, University of Natal 19(1): 23–36.

——(1994) 'Identity, democracy and education', Fourth Biennial Conference of the International Network of Philosophers of Education, Leuven (August).

Flanaghan, O. (1984) *The Science of the Mind*, 2nd edn, Cambridge, MA: MIT Press.

Freeland, J. (1979) 'Class struggle in schooling: MACOS and SEMP in Queensland', *Intervention* 12: 29–62.

——(1979) 'STOP! CARE to COME and PROBE the right-wing PIE', *Radical Education Dossier* 8: 4–7.

Frege, G. (1892) 'Sense and reference', *Vierteljahrschrift für wissenschaftliche Philosophie* 41 (reprinted in *The Philosophical Review* 62(3) (May) 1948: 207–30, trans. M. Black.

Friedman, M. (1989) 'Feminism and modern friendship: dislocating the community', *Ethics* 99: 275–90.

Gallie, W. B. (1956) 'Essentially contested concepts', *Proceedings of the Aristotelian Society* 61: 167–98.

Geach, P. (1966) 'Plato's *Euthyphro*', *The Monist* 50(3): 369–82.

Gellner, E. (1983) *Nations and Nationalism*, Oxford: Blackwell.

Gilroy, D. P. (1982) 'The revolutions in English philosophy and philosophy of education', *Educational Analysis* 4(1): 75–91.

——(1996) *Meaning without Words: Philosophy and Non-verbal Communication*, Aldershot: Avebury.

Goodlad, J. I. and Richter, M. N. (1966) *The Development of a Conceptual System for Dealing with Problems of Curriculum and Instruction*, Los Angeles: Institute for Development of Educational Activities, University of California.

Gray, J. (1995) *Berlin*, London: Fontana.

Greenfeld, I. (1992) *Nationalism: Five Roads to Modernity*, Cambridge, MA: Harvard University Press.

Griffin, J. (1986) *Well-Being: Its Meaning, Measurement and Moral Importance*, Oxford: Clarendon Press.

Griffiths, M. (1987) 'Teaching skills and the skills of teaching', *Journal of Philosophy of Education* 21(2).

——(1995) *Feminisms and the Self: The Web of Identity*, London: Routledge.

Griffiths, M. and Davies, C. (1995) *In Fairness to Children: Working for Social Justice in the Primary School*, London: David Fulton.

Guntrip, H. (1973) *Psychoanalytical Theory, Therapy and the Self: A Basic Guide to the Human Personality*, New York: Basic Books.

Haack, S. (1993) 'Knowledge and propaganda: reflections of an old feminist', *Partisan Review* 60(4): 556–64.

Hager, P. (1991) 'Review of Robin Barrow, *Understanding Skills*', *Educational Philosophy and Theory* 23(2): 108–13.

Haldane, J. (1989) 'Metaphysics in the philosophy of education', *Journal of Philosophy of Education* 23(2): 171–83.

Halsey, A. H. (1978) *Change in British Society*, Oxford: Oxford University Press.

Hare, W. (1979) *Open-mindedness and Education*, Montreal: McGill-Queen's.

——(1982) Review of *Critical Thinking and Education*, *Canadian Journal of Education* 7(4): 107–10.

——(1985) *In Defence of Open-mindedness*, Montreal: McGill-Queen's.

——(1985) 'Open-mindedness in the classroom', *Journal of Philosophy of Education* 19(2): 251–9.

——(1993) *What Makes a Good Teacher?*, London, Ont: Althorse Press.

——(1995) 'Content and criticism: the aims of schooling', *Journal of Philosophy of Education* 29(1): 47–60.

——(1995) *Teaching and the Socratic Virtues*, St John's, Newfoundland: Memorial University.

——(1997) 'Reason in teaching: Sheffler's philosophy of education', *Studies in Philosophy and Education* 16(1–2): 89–101.

Hare, W. and McLaughlin, T. H. (1994) 'Open-mindedness, commitment and Peter Gardner', *Journal of Philosophy of Education* 28(2): 239–44.

Harris, K. (1995) 'Education for citizenship', in W. Kohli (ed.), *Critical Conversations in Philosophy of Education*, New York: Routledge.

Hatcher, R. and Troyna, B. (1994) 'The "policy cycle": a ball by ball account', *Journal of Educational Policy* 9(2): 155–70.

Held, D. (1992) 'The development of the modern state', in S. Hall and B. Gieben (eds), *Formations of Modernity*, Cambridge: Cambridge University Press.

Hirst, P. H. (1965) 'Liberal education and the nature of knowledge', in R. D. Archambault (ed.), *Philosophical Analysis and Education*, London: Routledge & Kegan Paul.

——(1974) 'Curriculum objectives', in P. Hirst, *Knowledge and the Curriculum*, London: Routledge & Kegan Paul.

——(1974) 'Liberal education and the nature of knowledge', in P. Hirst, *Knowledge and the Curriculum*, London: Routledge & Kegan Paul.

——(1993) 'Education, knowledge and practice', in R. Barrow and P. White, *Beyond Liberal Education: Essays in Honour of Paul H. Hirst*, London: Routledge.

Hirst, P. H. and Peters, R. S. (1970) *The Logic of Education*, London: Routledge.

HMI (1991) *Higher Education in the Colleges and Polytechnics*, London: HMSO.

Hobsbawm, E. (1990) *Nations and Nationalism since 1780*, Cambridge: Cambridge University Press.

Hollis, M. (1977) *Models of Man: Philosophical Thoughts on Social Action*, Cambridge: Cambridge University Press.

Hume, D. A. (1959) *Treatise of Human Nature*, London: Dent.

Hutchings, K. (1995) *Kant, Critique and Politics*, London: Routledge.

Jessup, G. (1991) *Outcomes: NVQs and the Emerging Model of Education and Training*, London: Falmer Press.

Kant, I. (1956) *Groundwork of the Metaphysics of Morals*, trans. H. J. Paton as *The Moral Law*, 3rd edn, London: Hutchinson.

Kaplan, L. D. (1991) 'Teaching intellectual autonomy: the failure of the critical thinking movement', *Educational Theory* 41(4): 361–70.

Kazepides, T. (1989) 'On educational aims, curriculum objectives and the preparation of teachers', *Journal of Philosophy of Education* 23(1): 51–5.

Kekes, J. (1984) 'Moral sensitivity', *Philosophy* 59: 3–19.

Kelly, A. V. (1989) *The Curriculum: Theory and Practice*, London: Chapman.

Kennick, W. (1991) 'Teaching Philosophy', in *Teaching What We Do*, Amherst, MA: Amherst College Press.

Koertge, N. (1995) 'How feminism is now alienating from science', *Skeptical Inquirer* 19(2): 42–3.

Kohlberg, L. (1982) 'Recent work in moral education', in L. O. Ward, *The Ethical Dimension of the School Curriculum*, Swansea: The Pineridge Press.

Kohut, H. (1971) *The Analysis of the Self,* New York: International Universities Press.

Kuhn, D. (1991) *The Skills of Argument*, Cambridge: Cambridge University Press.

Lindsey, R. (1986) *Autonomy,* Houndmills: Macmillan.

Lipman, M. (1991) *Thinking in Education*, Cambridge: Cambridge University Press.

Lugones, M. (1989) 'Playfulness, world traveling and loving perception', in A. Garry and M. Pearsall (eds) *Women, Knowledge and Reality: Explorations in Feminist Philosophy*, Boston: Unwin Hyman.

Lukes, S. (1974) *Power: A Radical View*, Houndsmill, Basingstoke: Macmillan.

Lyotard, J.-F. (1984) *The Postmodern Condition: A Report on Knowledge*, trans. G. Bennington and B. Massumi, Manchester: Manchester University Press.

McClintock, A. (1993) 'Family feuds: gender, nationalism and the family', *Feminist Review* 44 (Summer): 61–80.

McGurk, N. I. (1990) *Speak as a White: Education, Culture, Nation*, Johannesburg: Heinemann.

McPeck, J. (1981) *Critical Thinking and Education*, Oxford: Martin Robertson.

——(1990) *Teaching Critical Thinking: Dialogue and Dialectic*, New York: Routledge.

—— (1991) *Teaching Philosophy* 14(1): 25–34.

Martin, J. R. (1985) 'Becoming educated: A journey of alienation or integration?' *Journal of Education* 167(3): 71–84.

Masterson, J. F. (1988) *The Search for the Real Self: Unmasking the Personality Disorders of our Age*, New York: Free Press/Macmillan.

Mendus, S. (1993) 'Different voices, still lives: problems in the ethics of care', *Journal of Applied Philosophy* 10(1): 17–27.

Mill, J. S. (1954) *On Liberty*, in *Utilitarianism, Liberty and Representative Government*, London: Dent.

Miller, D. (1989) 'The ethical significance of nationality', *Ethics* 98: 647–62.

——(1993) 'In defence of nationality', *Journal of Applied Philosophy* 10(1): 3–16.

Minuchin, S. (1974) *Families and Family Therapy*, Cambridge, MA: Harvard University Press.

Mkwanazi, Z. and Cross, M. (1992) 'The dialectic of unity and diversity in education: its implications for a national curriculum in South Africa', National Education Policy Investigation, mimeographed.

Montefiore, A. (1987) 'Self-reality, self-respect and respect for others', *Midwest Studies in Philosophy* 3: 195–208.

Morgan, J. (1996) 'A defence of autonomy as an educational ideal', *Journal of Philosophy of Education* 30(2): 239–52.

Murdoch, I. (1970) 'The idea of perfection', in *The Sovereignty of Good*, London: Routledge & Kegan Paul.

——(1992) *Metaphysics as a Guide to Morals*, London: Chatto & Windus.

Nagel, T. (1986) *The View from Nowhere,* New York: Oxford University Press.

NFVEC (1996) *Values in Education and the Community*.

Norman, R. (1994) 'On seeing things differently', *Radical Philosophy* 1: 6–12.

——(1994) 'I did it my way; some thoughts on autonomy', *Journal of Philosophy of Education* 28(1).

Norris, S. P. (1995) 'Sustaining and responding to changes of bias in critical thinking', *Educational Theory* 45(2): 199–211.

Norzick, R. (1974) *Anarchy, State and Utopia*, Oxford: Blackwell.

OFSTED (1994) *Spiritual, Moral, Social and Cultural Development*, London: OFSTED.

O'Hear, A. (1991) *Education and Democracy*, London: The Claridge Press.

O'Neill, J. (1994) 'Should communitarians be nationalists?' *Journal of Applied Philosophy* 11 (2): 135–43.

Passmore, J. (1967) 'On teaching to be critical', in R. S. Peters (ed.), *The Concept of Education*, London: Routledge & Kegan Paul.

——(1980) *The Philosophy of Teaching*, London: Duckworth.

——(1985) 'Educating for the 21st century', The Fourth Wallace Worth Memorial Lecture University of New South Wales (22 April).

Perkins, D. (1995) *Outsmarting IQ: The Emerging Science of Learnable Intelligence*, New York: The Free Press.

Peters, R. S. (1958) *The Concept of Motivation*, London: Routledge & Kegan Paul.

——(1963) 'Education as initiation', London: Harrap; reprinted in R. D. Archambault (ed.), *Philosophical Analysis and Education*, London: Routledge & Kegan Paul, 1965, pp 87–111.

——(1968) 'Michael Oakeshott's philosophy of education', in P. King and B. C. Parekh (eds), *Politics and Experience: Essays Presented to Michael Oakeshott*, London: Cambridge University Press.

——(1966) *Ethics and Education*, London: George Allen & Unwin.

——(1966) 'The philosophy of education', in J. W. Tibble (ed.), *The Study of Education*, London: Routledge & Kegan Paul, pp.1–23.

——(1969) 'Motivation, emotion and the conceptual schemes of common-sense', in T. Mischel (ed.), *Human Action*, New York: Academic Press.

——(1973) 'Aims of education – a conceptual enquiry', in R. S. Peters (ed.), *The Philosophy of Education*, London: Oxford University Press.

——(1973) 'Freedom and the development of the free man', in J. F. Doyle (ed.) *Educational Judgements*, London: Routledge & Kegan Paul.

Peters, R. S., Woods, J. and Dray, W. H. (1965) 'Aims of education – a conceptual enquiry', in B. Crittenden (ed.), *Philosophy and Education*, pp.1–32; reprinted in R. S. Peters (ed.), *The Philosophy of Education*, Oxford: Oxford University Press, 1973, pp.11–29.

Pitcher, G. (1964) *The Philosophy of Wittgenstein*, Englewood Cliffs, NJ: Prentice-Hall.

Plato (1951) *The Symposium*, London: Penguin.

——(1961) *The Republic*, in E. Hamilton and H. Cairns (eds), *Plato: The Collected Dialogues*, Princeton, NJ: Princeton University Press.

Platts, M. (1979) *Ways of Meaning*, London: Routledge & Kegan Paul.

Poole, R. (1991) 'The illusory community: the nation', in *Morality and Modernity*, London: Routledge.

Polster, S. (1983) 'Ego boundary as process: a systemic contextual approach', *Psychiatry* 46: 247–57.

Portelli, J. (1994) 'The challenge of teaching for critical thinking', *McGill Journal of Education* 29(2): 137–51.

Power, C and Reimer, J. (1978) 'Moral atmosphere', in W. Damon, *New Direction for Child Development and Moral Development*, San Francisco: Jossey-Bass.

Pratt, D. (1980) *Curriculum: Design and Development*, New York: Harcourt Brace Jovanovich.

Pring, R. (1989) *The New Curriculum*, London: Cassell.

——(1989) *Closing the Gap: Liberal Education and Vocational Preparation*, London: Hodder & Stoughton.

Quinton, A. (1978) 'On the ethics of belief', in G. Haydon (ed.), *Education and Values*,

London: Institute of Education.

Rawls, J. (1972) *A Theory of Justice*, Oxford: Oxford University Press.

—— (1993) *Political Liberalism*, New York: Columbia University Press.

Raz, J. (1986) *The Morality of Freedom*, Oxford: Clarendon Press.

—— (1994) *Ethics in the Public Domain*, Oxford: Clarendon Press.

Ree, J. (1992) 'Internationality', *Radical Philosophy* 60: 3–11.

Rorty, R. (1989) 'Education without dogma', *Dissent* 36(2): 198–204.

—— (1991) *Objectivity, Relativism and Truth*, Cambridge: Cambridge University Press.

Rose, B. and Tunmer, R. (1975) *Documents in South African Education*, Johannesburg: Ad. Donker.

Rousseau, J. J. (1969) *Emile*, London: Dent.

Rowntree, D. (1982) *Educational Technology in Curriculum Development*, New York: Harper Row.

Sagan, C. (1987) 'The burden of skepticism', *The Skeptical Inquirer* 12(1): 38–46.

Sandel, M. (1982) *Liberalism and the Limits of Justice*, Cambridge: Cambridge University Press.

SCAA (1996) *Education for Adult Life: The Spiritual and Moral Development of Young People*, London: The School Curriculum and Assessment Authority.

—— (1997) *The Promotion of Pupils' Spiritual, Moral, Social and Cultural Development*, London: The School Curriculum and Assessment Authority.

Scheffler, I. (1960) *The Language of Education*, Springfield, IL: Charles Thomas.

—— (1973) *Reason and Teaching*, Indianapolis, IN: Bobbs-Merrill.

Schools Council (1967) *The Raising of the School-leaving Age*, London: HMSO.

Scottish Education Department (1977) *The Structure of the Curriculum in the Third and Fourth Years of the Secondary School* (The Munn Report), Edinburgh: HMSO.

Scruton, R. (1981) 'The significance of a common creature', *Philosophy* 54: 51–70.

Searle, J. (1989) *Minds, Brains and Science*, Harmondsworth: Pelican Books.

Seddon, T. (1990) 'On education and context', *Australian Journal of Education* 34(2): 131–6.

Senge, P. M. (1992) *The Fifth Discipline: The Art and Practice of Learning Organization*, New York: Random House.

Shulman, L. (1987) 'Knowledge and teaching: foundations of the new reform', *Harvard Educational Review* 57(1): 1–22.

Sidgwick, H. (1922) *The Methods of Ethics*, 7th edn, London: Macmillan.

Siegel, H. (1996) 'The role of reasons in (science) education' in W. Hare and J. P. Portelli (eds), *Philosophy of Education: Introductory Readings*, 2nd edn, Calgary: Detselig, 1989.

Smith, A. (1988) *The Ethnic Origins of Nations*, Oxford: Blackwell.

—— (1991) *National Identity*, London: Penguin.

Smith, R. and Knight, J. (1978) 'MACOS in Queensland: the politics of educational knowledge', *Australian Journal of Education* 22(3): 225–48.

Snook, I. (ed.) (1972) *Concepts of Indoctrination*, London: Routledge & Kegan Paul.

Soccio, J. (1992) *How to Get the Most out of Philosophy*, Belmont, CA: Wadsworth.

Sockett, H. (1972) 'Curriculum aims and objectives: taking a means to an end', *Proceedings of the Philosophy of Education Society of Great Britain* 6(1): 30–61.

Stebbing, S. (1939) *Thinking to Some Purpose*, Harmondsworth: Penguin.

—— (1933) *A Modern Introduction to Logic*, London: Methuen.

Stone, C. (1990) 'Autonomy, emotions and desires: some problems concerning R. F. Dearden's account of autonomy', *Journal of Philosophy of Education* 24(2): 271–83.

Strom, M. and Parsons, W. (1982) *Facing History and Ourselves: Holocaust and Human Behaviour*, Watertown, MA: Intentions Education, Inc.

Stromquist, N. (1995) 'Romancing the state: gender and power in education', *Comparative Education Review* 39(4): 17–27.

Taylor, C. (1964) *The Explanation of Behaviour*, London: Routledge & Kegan Paul.

——(1989) *Sources of the Self*, Cambridge: Cambridge University Press.

Tamir, Y. (1992) 'Democracy, nationalism and education', *Educational Philosophy and Theory* 24(1): 17–27.

——(1993) *Liberal Nationalism*, Princeton, NJ: Princeton University Press.

Tarnas, R. (1993) *The Passion of the Western Mind,* New York: Random House.

Thayer-Bacon, B. (1992) 'Is modern critical thinking sexist?' *Inquiry: Critical Thinking Across the Disciplines* 10(2): 3–7.

Thomson, G. (1990) *Needs,* Oxford: Clarendon Press.

Walker, C. (1990) Review of *Woman – Nation, State, Agenda* 6: 40–8.

Walker, J. C. (1981) 'Two competing theories of personal autonomy: a critique of the liberal rationalist attack on progressivism', *Educational Theory* 31: 3–4; 285–306.

—— (1984) 'The development/exercise dichotomy', in C. W. Evers and J. C. Walker (eds), *Epistemology, Semantics and Educational Theory* (Occasional Paper 16), Sydney: University of Sydney Department of Education.

——(1995) 'Self-determination in teaching and learning: an essay review of W. Louden, *Understanding Teaching*', *Curriculum Inquiry* 25(1): 101–10; 115–16.

——(1996) 'Practical educational knowledge: a naturalist philosophy of education', in D. N. Aspin (ed.), *Logical Empiricism and Post-empiricism in Philosophy of Education,* London: Heinemann.

Walzer, M. (1967) 'On the role of symbolism in political thought', *Political Science Quarterly* LXXXI (June): 191–204.

——(1992) 'The civil society argument', in C. Mouffe (ed.), *Dimensions of Radical Democracy*, London: Verso.

Warnock, M. (1973) 'Towards a definition of quality in education', in R. S. Peters, *The Philosophy of Education*, Oxford: Oxford University Press.

White, J. P. (1973) *Towards a Compulsory Curriculum*, London: Routledge & Kegan Paul.

——(1982) *The Aims of Education Restated*, London: Routledge & Kegan Paul.

——(1986) 'The problem of self-interest: the educator's perspective', *Journal of Philosophy of Education* 20(2).

——(1990) *Education and the Good Life: Beyond the National Curriculum*, London: Kogan Page.

——(1996) 'Education and nationality', *Journal of Philosophy of Education* 30(3).

——(1997) 'National myths, democracy and education', in D. Bridges (ed.), *Education, Autonomy and Democratic Citizenship in a Changing World*, London: Routledge.

Whitehead, A. N. (1932) *The Aims of Education and Other Essays,* London: Benn.

Whitfield, C. (1993) 'Boundaries and relationships', *Knowing, Protecting and Enjoying the Self*, Deerfield Beach, FL: Health Communication.

Winch, C. (1996) 'Constructing worthwhile curricula', *Journal of Philosophy of Education* 30(1): 45–6.

——(1996) 'The aims of education revisited', *Journal of Philosophy of Education* 30(3): 33–44.

Wittgenstein, L. (1921) *Tractacus Logico-Philosophicus*, trans. D. F. Pears and B. F. McGuiness, London: Routledge & Kegan Paul.

——(1933) *The Blue and Brown Books*, Oxford: Blackwell.

——(1949) *On Certainty*, G. E. M. Anscombe and G. H. von Wright (eds), D. Paul and G. E. M. Anscombe, Oxford: Blackwell (trans.) (1974).

——(1953) *Philosophical Investigations*, Oxford: Blackwell, trans. G. E. M. Anscombe.

Wring, C. (1988) *Understanding Educational Aims*, London: Unwin.

INDEX